Depression and
New Deal in
Virginia

THE
ENDURING
DOMINION

Depression and New Deal in Virginia

THE ENDURING DOMINION

RONALD L. HEINEMANN

University Press of Virginia
Charlottesville

THE UNIVERSITY PRESS OF VIRGINIA
Copyright ©1983 by the Rector and Visitors
of the Unversity of Virginia

First published 1983

Library of Congress Cataloging in Publication Data

Heinemann, Ronald L.
  Depression and New Deal in Virginia

  Bibliography: p. 239.
  1. Virginia—Politics and government—1865–
1950. 2. Depressions—1929—United States.
3. Byrd, Harry Flood, 1887–1966. 4. Glass,
Carter, 1858–1946. I. Title II. Title: New
Deal in Virginia.
F231.H43 1982   975.5′04   82-13487
ISBN 0-8139-0946-5

Printed in the United States of America

To
Edward Younger

Contents

Preface

Few decades in American history have been as momentous as the 1930s. In the depression and the New Deal, historians have located the watersheds from which the domestic policies of the United States for the next two generations have emanated. There is hardly a social, political, or economic happening of our present age which does not have a relevant origin in the thirties. However, the impact of these events was not equally strong everywhere; this was particularly true in Virginia where a peculiar set of conditions moderated the influence of both depression and New Deal.

Writing the history of Virginia in the 1930s requires a tolerance for ambiguity. The depression was severe in the state, yet mild when compared to its impact elsewhere. New Deal programs benefited thousands of Virginians at the time, yet their enduring effect was minimal. Old Dominion voters gave Franklin Roosevelt landslide victories, yet returned his most vociferous critics, Harry Byrd and Carter Glass, to the Senate with even greater majorities. These paradoxes may be explained by factors that have continually insulated the state from external forces and maintained the status quo—a spirit of traditionalism, a balanced economy, and political conservatism.

This book examines the impact of the depression and the New Deal in Virginia and the responses of Virginians, both great and small, to these events. While no effort is made to evaluate the effect of the New Deal nationally or summarize its activities in the other states, the conclusions reached reinforce the recent findings of many historians that its influence was modest. As elsewhere, changes in the political and social structure of Virginia were limited by the conservative nature of many of the

Roosevelt programs and by the obstacles those programs confronted at the local level. Unfortunately, in the rush to criticize the New Deal, writers have frequently ignored its accomplishments and public support, a view which has characterized previous discussions of its presence in Virginia. While the resistance of the Old Dominion political hierarchy to the New Deal is well known, the support given President Roosevelt and his programs by the ordinary citizens of the state—farmers, blue-collar workers, and the unemployed—is less well documented. Consideration of both viewpoints is necessary in any assessment of the activity of the New Deal. Similarly, Virginia's conservative political climate cannot be cited as the single cause of New Deal "failure" in the state. Economic considerations, notably the relative mildness of the depression, inhibited the penetration of federal programs as well. Although Virginia's reaction to the crises of the thirties was not necessarily unique (statistical data indicate that neighboring Maryland and North Carolina responded in a similar fashion to the depression), few states seemed to have changed so little during the decade as the Old Dominion.

The book is organized both chronologically and topically. The decade-long story of the depression, begun in chapter 1, is continued through parts of chapters 3, 7, and 8. Utilizing the personal remembrances of Virginians obtained through interviews and questionnaires, chapter 2 focuses on how the depression affected different segments of the population. Chapters 3–6 analyze the impact of New Deal programs in the Old Dominion, notably those for the unemployed and the farmer. Chapter 7 studies the political relationship between the New Deal and the Byrd organization, highlighted by the 1936 election, and chapter 8 describes Virginia's own modest effort at social reform.

I am indebted to many people for their assistance in preparing this manuscript. Hampden-Sydney College has generously supported the research, writing, and publication of this study. Professors Hassell Simpson of Hampden-Sydney College, Robert Saunders of Christopher Newport College, and Joseph Fry of the University of Nevada, Las Vegas, read parts of the manuscript and offered their cogent advice and criticism. A dozen classes of Hampden-Sydney students have distributed questionnaires, interviewed parents and other relatives, and endured my diatribes on "do-nothing" conservatism. Guy Terrell deserves special thanks for his summer of reading newspapers and interviewing "old folks" in Richmond. The staffs of the University of Virginia Library, the National Archives, Washington, D.C., and Eggleston Library at Hampden-Sydney were always helpful and generous with their time. Virginia Johnston, Teresa Sutphin, and Jane Holland typed drafts of the manuscript. Throughout this effort, my wife, Sandra, has been a constant support, from the typing of the dissertation, to proofreading, to the offering of criticism.

Portions of this study appeared in earlier form in "Blue Eagle or Black Buzzard?: The National Recovery Administration in Virginia," *Virginia Magazine of History and Biography* 89, no. 1 (1981): 90–100 and "Workers on Welfare: The WPA in Virginia," *Virginia Social Science Journal* 8, no. 3 (1973): 62–67 and are incorporated here with the permission of the editors.

Finally, my greatest debt is to Edward Younger, to whom this book is dedicated as small compensation for all that he gave me as a teacher, graduate adviser, colleague, and friend. Knowing of my interest in Franklin Roosevelt, he suggested this topic as a master's thesis, supervised its expansion into a dissertation, and encouraged its subsequent refinement into a book. For his direction, his encouragement, and his humanity, I will always be grateful.

RONALD LYNTON HEINEMANN

Hampden-Sydney College

1

The Winds of Change

"Virginia," wrote Arnold Toynbee in the 1940s, "makes the painful impression of a country living under a spell, in which time has stood still." Such is the distinction of traditional, aristocratic societies in modern times. From its beginnings Virginia has been a land of two classes—cavalier and indenture, white and black, planter and farmer, Tuckahoe and Cohee, Randolph and Shifflett, UDC and UMW, organization and "anti." Amazingly, these differences have not produced social chaos; instead, the cultural homogeneity of a population that was largely native born, rural, white, and Protestant created political consensus and social stability. The myth of the cavalier, confirmed by the great wealth and social position of the King Carters and William Byrds, infused in a new Virginia aristocracy a sense of public responsibility to lead the society. Those at the bottom were able to identify with their more highly placed "cousins" and deferentially accepted their direction, "resenting it practically not at all," said Virginia Moore, "because there was practically nothing to resent."[1] As a result, the social hierarchy of the Old Dominion has been firm and unyielding, and although periodically challenged by "revolutionaries" like Nathaniel Bacon, Nat Turner, Billy Mahone, and Henry Howell, the old order has prevailed.

By reason of blood, education, and social standing, the heirs of this tradition of noblesse oblige have determined what is best for the Commonwealth. They have been the caretakers of the status quo and the public treasury, and although frequently conservative to a fault, theirs has been an honest, frugal government. Above all else, civility has epitomized the reign of this long dynasty. The standards set by Washington and revitalized by Lee have been adhered to. Even over the divisive issue of

1

race Virginians have generally conducted themselves in a gentlemanly if not a humane way. There has always been a proper manner in which to do things, a manner which does justice to the past while preserving the order of the present. There has been little political demagoguery and almost no social engineering in the state. Except for the great generation of the Revolution, Virginia's leaders have been content to wait and see, their outstanding characteristic being, in the words of Jean Gottman, a "resistance to change."[2] This social order and public philosophy received a demanding test during the Great Depression of the thirties, an experience which dictated the direction of the state for years to come.

The Roaring Twenties promised much but delivered a depression. As the end of the decade approached, there were signs that economic disaster was imminent, but Americans were too intoxicated by good times and bad gin to believe them. Prosperity, a skyrocketing stock market, and a new president who pledged to mate traditional Americanisms to the new technology all augured well for the future.

Much of Virginia shared this exhilaration. Although the Old Dominion, like all southern states, lagged behind the nation in most indicators of economic progress, it was making promising strides forward in the last half of the Jazz Age. Along with an influx of new and diverse industries into the state, substantial increases in wages and salaries occurred between 1925 and 1929, and the value of industrial output climbed by almost 50 percent. In the number of automobiles, in wholesale and retail trade volumes, and in the percentage of banks avoiding suspension, Virginia ranked in the upper half of the forty-eight states. The Norfolk *Virginian-Pilot* trumpeted: "Onward, Upward Is Outlook As 1929 Dawns, Bringing Its New Avenues For Expansion." Governor Harry F. Byrd—whose policies in the preceding three years had encouraged industrial growth, reformed the state government, and produced a treasury surplus—predicted continued prosperity.[3] For the first nine months of 1929 there was nothing to discourage this optimism. The Old Dominion was intent on making money and electing a new governor.

2

The Virginia Democratic party had suffered ignominious defeat in the presidential election of 1928. Saddled with an objectionable candidate, it had failed to throw its full support behind the campaign of Alfred E. Smith and had been stunned by the Republican victory in a state considered safe for the Democracy. The gubernatorial election in 1929 was to prove how severe the defections to the Republicans had been. The campaign was complicated by the presence of Methodist Bishop James Cannon, who had led many Democrats out of the party in 1928 because of Smith's opposition to Prohibition. Intent on extending his "dry" domination over the state, Cannon once again joined forces with the Republicans to try to defeat the nominee of the Democratic organization, John Garland Pollard. Professor of government at the College of William and Mary and former state attorney general, the rotund, fatherly looking Pollard supported the Byrd reforms and pay-as-you-go economics, but he had a reputation for political independence and was not strongly identified with the organization. Most importantly, the fact that he was a Prohibitionist blunted the major issue of the Cannon-Republican nominee, William Moseley Brown. Pollard's overwhelming victory in November over a disorganized and discredited opposition was considered a total endorsement of the Byrd policies.[4]

During the course of the Virginia election, the stock market took its fateful plunge, triggering a period of business inactivity unparalleled in American history. The Great Depression of the thirties was caused by a combination of economic maladies, including overproduction, unequal distribution of income, excessive speculative investment, and unstable corporate and banking structures. The result was a stagnating industrial machine and a corporate investment pyramid without foundation. Collapse of the stock market in October 1929 exposed these weaknesses and contributed to the depression by destroying confidence in business and absorbing capital that might have been invested more fruitfully elsewhere.[5]

Initially, Virginians viewed the maneuvers on Wall Street indifferently. An editorial in the October 25 *Virginian-Pilot* expressed relief that the market was returning to sounder structure and saner values. Three weeks later, on November 16, the paper called the Crash an "isolated phenomenon" and termed the situation "less threatening" than the unemployment crisis of 1921. One estimate of market losses in the state was as low as $250,000. Said the Newport News *Times-Herald*, "It indicates that Virginians did not allow themselves to become parties to that orgy of speculation on a large scale. It is proverbial that Virginians are conservative within the best meaning of the word."[6] The extent of market losses in Virginia is difficult to estimate exactly. Certainly many Virginia stockholders lost fortunes on "Black Tuesday," but the number of investors in the state was probably far fewer than that in the wealthier states. Individual Virginians derived only 4.4 percent ($41 million) of their income from dividends.[7]

While Virginia businessmen and politicians supported President Herbert Hoover's requests for confidence-restoring conferences and business-stabilizing programs, there was little evidence of anxiety in the state. Outgoing Governor Byrd commented, "The close of the year 1929 sees Virginia facing a bright future. Never, probably, in the long history of the Old Dominion has she faced a destiny more filled with promise." University of Virginia economist James E. Ward, Jr., wrote, "This State is even now entering into an expansion of industrial activities on a scale never before equalled in its history." And in his January inaugural address, Governor Pollard referred only offhandedly to the recent financial reverse and pledged to carry on Governor Byrd's program of road building. Later in the year, on a pleasure cruise to the Eastern Shore, Pollard jestingly consigned effigies of "Old Man Depression," "Old Lady Pessimism," and "Miss Fortune" to a watery grave, "the land of unreality where you belong."[8]

In the summer of 1930 the country experienced a widespread drought which aggravated the industrial crisis. Virginia's rainfall for the year was 60 percent of normal, with July and August especially dry. Virginius Dabney, Virginia correspondent for the New York *Times*, commented, "The usually fertile Shenandoah Valley . . . almost looked . . . as if Sheridan had just finished his devastating ride through it." With grazing land in northern and southwestern Virginia, tobacco in Southside, and truck

4

crops in Tidewater also reported suffering, crop forecasters estimated that Virginia farm production would fall to its lowest level since records were first kept in 1866. Heavy losses were expected in corn, peanuts, and apples. Former Governor Byrd, one of the largest independent apple producers in the country, wrote to his friend William T. ("Billy") Reed: "Unless some relief occurs in the next few days not only will a large part of our crop be destroyed but many trees will die. Nothing like this has ever occurred within the memory of anyone living."[9] Although the drought consumed crop surpluses, causing higher wheat and corn prices, that was small consolation to farmers who had nothing left to sell.

To combat the emergency, Governor Pollard created a Drought Relief Committee, with Harry Byrd as chairman, to coordinate the work of the Red Cross, the railroads, and local relief councils. Having previously called for federal assistance to fight the growing unemployment problem, the governor obtained short-term loans worth $2.4 million to match federal advances on future highway allocations which were offered to the states to put idle farmers to work on roads. Railroads joined the relief effort by reducing rates 50 percent on shipments of hay, feed, and livestock.

After this initial burst of activity, the relief program fizzled. Federal loans were given to farmers to purchase seed and fertilizer for fall crops, but Relief Director Byrd complained that the sum, $200,000, was "an absurdity" in view of the need. He recommended an extension of the time for rate reductions and an expansion of the road program with fewer restrictions on who could participate. He also suggested the formation of a Virginia credit corporation to finance relief if more federal aid was not forthcoming.[10] Even the conservative Lynchburg *News*, reminding Hoover of his previous relief work in Europe, called on the president to support larger relief expenditures: "Payment of fixed sums to the unemployed in normal times is one thing and is called a 'dole,' but . . . lending of money for food for the farmer, his wife and babies, victims of a natural cataclysm, is emergency relief and no more of a dole than an appropriation for relief of starving Europeans." Eventually federal loans became more substantial, and $2 million was loaned to Virginia farmers in 1931, but this was a negligible sum compared to the estimated $100 million in losses they had suffered.[11]

Relief work was carried out at little expense to the state. Existing facilities and personnel were used to administer the relief funds; the short-term loans were merely advances against anticipated revenue for that year. Said the Roanoke *World-News,* "Virginia has not spent a penny for drought relief or for unemployment that it would not have spent anyway." Demonstrating an attitude prominent at the national level, Virginia's leaders were reluctant to institute expensive relief measures, believing that budget balancing would have a more vital impact on business confidence. Validated by treasury surpluses in the twenties, this pay-as-you-go philosophy militated against a proper relief program in the thirties. Before 1936 the only relief money Virginia ever disbursed was through its highway department—money which, although it provided employment for several thousand jobless, served primarily to improve the road system. The pleas of a man from Lunenburg County went unheeded: "Hundreds of people in this county [are] in dire need of clothing and food. Isn't there some way in which the State can render some relief to these people? . . . It does seem we are putting good roads and other state activities ahead of feeding and clothing the people. . . . We have been boasting of our road building program, school expenditures, and surplus in the State treasury, are we now going to neglect the greatest asset of the State, namely, its people?"[12] Although depression soon replaced drought as the primary crisis, the precedent for inaction had been established.

As winter approached, Governor Pollard faced still another difficult situation—a labor strike at the Dan River textile mills in Danville. The postwar years had not been good ones for the mill. Production and profits were down, and there were fears that the North Carolina textile strikes would spread northward. The mill had a reputation for fair wages and good employer-employee relations, but with declining sales, management ended the economy dividend paid to employees and instituted a 10 percent wage cut. Supported by the United Textile Workers of America (which was attempting to organize labor in the southern textile industry), 4,000 workers left their jobs on September 29, 1930, demanding restoration of wages and a reduced workweek. On October 2 Governor Pollard offered his services for mediation. Labor immediately agreed, but the president of the mill, H. R. Fitzgerald, was affronted by this challenge to his system of "industrial democracy" and declared that there was "nothing to mediate." The strike remained peaceful until November 26 when riots broke out over the jailing of forty mill workers charged with unlawful assembly. Within a day the governor, at the request of Pittsylvania County authorities, rushed three companies of the National Guard to the scene, and order was restored. Sporadic outbreaks of violence continued, the most sanguinary of which was the killing of a bootlegger who was shot while running a barricade with sixty gallons of moonshine in his car. Utilizing strikebreakers and evicting strikers from company housing, mill management remained antagonistic, and as union funds dwindled, the resolve of the workers waned. When further attempts at mediation proved unsuccessful, the mill hands voted to end the strike on January 29, 1931. Union officials claimed victory in the fight to end discrimination against workers, but their original demands for restoration of wages and recognition of collective bargaining went unrealized. Moreover, many of the strikers were not rehired because of the deepening business recession. The strike was one of the most serious in Virginia's history, and the ensuing unemployment intensified the effects of the depression in the Danville area, already hard hit by the closing of cotton mills and furniture factories.[13]

Although the last quarter of 1930 offered ample evidence that the depression was more than a temporary disorder, economic conditions in the Old Dominion compared favorably with those in the nation. Unemployment in the state had risen to 50,000 during the year, but the percentage of those out of work was below the national average, and unemployment rates in Old Dominion cities were lower than in other cities of comparable size. Virginia Labor Commissioner John Hopkins Hall claimed the state's diversified industry and acquisition of new plants had mitigated the effects of depression. Manufacturing output dropped from $897 million in 1929 to $814 million in 1930, and the number of industrial employees and the amount of wages and salaries paid declined less than 8 percent. The production value of processed tobacco fell slightly, while that of shipbuilding, fertilizers, and chemicals increased.[14]

The stability of the tobacco industry was not reflected among Virginia tobacco farmers, whose income declined 50 percent, due primarily to the drought. The Danville *Register* called it "the most discouraging tobacco season on the local market within . . . memory," a view confirmed by a farmer from New Canton who reported selling 414 pounds of dark tobacco and clearing $2.60 for himself. Wrote William Reed of Larus and Brother Tobacco Company: "From what I can learn about the tobacco situation in some sections of Virginia, particularly Lunenburg, it looks like the crop . . . is absolutely the worst that ever came out of the ground." These conditions adversely affected business in the Southside tobacco district. Banks in particular were hard hit as farmers withdrew deposits and defaulted on loans. Reported the Lynchburg *News* at the start of 1931: "The depression is with us." Nevertheless, Lynchburg was more fortunate than other cities across the country because its banks were still sound and construction starts had remained steady.[15]

Lynchburg's situation was more typical of the rest of the state. Norfolk, with excellent port facilities and the presence of the U.S. Navy, had not yet experienced the depression. Building activity and payrolls had increased, unemployment was negligible, no breadlines had formed, and none was foreseen. Declines in bank deposits and clearances were minimal, and food prices had been relatively stable throughout the year, falling slightly in the last quarter. Except in the tobacco region, conditions were no worse elsewhere in Virginia, causing the Richmond *Times-Dispatch* to proclaim confidently that the depression existed only in the minds of the people.[16]

If there be such a condition, Virginia was nearly "depression proof," combining a diversified economy and conservative fiscal policies with a widespread poverty that was little influenced by economic fluctuations. Its population in 1930 was 2,421,851 (twentieth nationally), two-thirds of which lived on farms or in towns of 2,500 or less, and 27 percent of which was black. The state was not poor, but many of its citizens were. It ranked nineteenth in total income earned in 1929, but only thirty-sixth in

8

per capita income ($435, 62 percent of the national average). Large segments of the population, especially blacks, mill workers, and subsistence farmers, lived in impoverished conditions, but the depression would have a minimal impact on the living standards of many of these poor. Said one, "There were no great changes; we were used to hard times anyway."[17] Indeed, after years of inadequate state services, the advent of federal relief would improve standards for some.

The state of agriculture in the Commonwealth indicated the extent of this "depression proofing." The nation's farmers had already endured a decade of low prices and income, and Virginians were not excepted. Income for 1929 was only three-fourths of what it had been in 1919, and a poll of farmers taken in 1929 showed considerable dissatisfaction with the situation. Nevertheless, Virginia agriculture was better prepared to resist the effects of the Crash than farming in many other states. The state had a high percentage of subsistence farmers (26 percent) who eked out livings on submarginal land and required little or no cash income to sustain their meager existence. One-tenth of its more than 170,000 farm operators had income over $2,500 in 1929, but two-fifths made less than $600. Although farm tenancy was high in the cotton and tobacco growing areas of the state, only West Virginia and Florida in the South had a lower ratio of tenants to farmers than Virginia.[18] Its percentage of mortgaged owner-operated farms was the second lowest in the nation, and it ranked sixth lowest in the ratio of the mortgage debt to the value of the mortgaged farms. Almost prophetically, Virginia agricultural economist Wilson Gee wrote in 1927, "In the event of times of depression and hardship in the farm industry, it is reassuring to know that a state has a relatively low percentage of its farms under mortgage." This low mortgage rate also contributed to fewer bank failures in Virginia in the twenties and thirties. Furthermore, Virginia's diversity in agriculture provided a more balanced farm income. Tobacco was of great importance to the farm economy (around 15 percent of cash receipts), but apples, peanuts, wheat, and potatoes were also high-value cash crops in the state, and dairy and livestock farming were growing in significance.[19]

Although Virginia was still largely a rural state, its total in-

9

come was well balanced between agriculture, manufacturing, and trade. It was one of only six states in 1929 whose production income was so evenly proportioned that none of the sources of revenue contributed more than 20 percent to the total.[20] Its major industries of tobacco and textiles produced items of high demand and necessity that were less susceptible to economic fluctuations. Proximity to the seat of national government and the presence of an ocean port also helped to balance the Old Dominion's economy. State finances were in good order and not overextended, tax rates were among the lowest in the nation, industry was expanding and not reliant on the manufacturing of durable goods, and agriculture, though suffering, was diverse and subsistent enough in nature to endure continued bad times. In a paradoxical way, "progressive backwardness" was an enviable position in which to face the next few years.

Through the first half of 1931 Virginians hoped they would avoid the worst. "If there is any such thing as depression in Norfolk this spring," commented the *Virginian-Pilot*, "it is not being felt in the Easter shopping which right now is in full blast." From Staunton, former Governor Byrd reassuringly declared that general conditions in the Old Dominion were better than those elsewhere in the nation, attributing Virginia's prosperity to low bonded indebtedness and low taxes. The Fifth District Federal Reserve report for the month of June noted gains in retail trade over June 1930 in the cities of Norfolk, Lynchburg, Richmond, and Washington, D.C. Minimal losses were reported for the first six months of 1931 compared with the corresponding period in 1930, whereas other districts suffered losses for both the month and the six-month period far greater than those in the Fifth District.[21]

These heartening conditions, however, proved ephemeral. The unemployed Danville strikers were on the verge of starvation; soup kitchens were feeding hungry schoolchildren in the mountain regions; school terms were ending early in several counties; and a dispensary was distributing food to 3,000 people in Hopewell where unemployed citizens were petitioning the city council for relief. Said one Prince Edward farmer: "Every single farmer in Prince Edward County needs work. Hundreds

10

of families are living on nothing but fat-back and corn meal—and some are living only from day to day on food-stuffs they get from the county, from their neighbors, and from the Red Cross. . . . They tell us, 'for God's sake give us work to do so we will not live by begging.' We've got to do something."[22] On July 30 Governor Pollard publicized his plans to obtain $1 million in short-term loans to continue the expanded highway program that was providing work for the growing number of unemployed in the state. Pollard also wrote to President Hoover asking for a continuation of the federal road advances. Suggesting a $5 million allocation for Virginia to be repaid over a ten-to-fifteen-year period, the governor emphasized the importance of "giving work rather than dispensing charity."[23]

Avoiding a dole and achieving a balanced budget were given top priority by national leaders as well. President Hoover's brand of rugged individualism precluded significant federal intervention to combat the depression. Although he was more active than any previous president in using the power of the office to meet such an economic crisis, he continued to rely on voluntary local initiatives to satisfy the more pressing needs. Speaking at Fort Monroe in October, Hoover expostulated: "No government action, no economic doctrine, no economic plan or project can replace the God-imposed responsibility of the individual man and woman to their neighbors. It is a vital part of the very soul of the people."[24] Yet Frank Bane, Virginia's commissioner of public welfare, was not convinced. Writing in his department's monthly periodical, he stated: "Government has a responsibility in this matter. We cannot and should not expect these private organizations to handle alone a problem far beyond their capacity because of their limited resources. It is the duty of government to work with them and to carry its portion of the increased load."[25]

In September the governor appointed an Unemployment Relief Committee, headed by Richmond businessman and Byrd adviser William Reed, to survey the situation. Discovering a 6 percent unemployment rate in the state, the committee called on businesses to move to a five-day week and to initiate new building projects. Opposed to expensive work relief programs, it did not recommend creation and funding of a state relief effort. Reed confided to Byrd, "I believe Virginia is in better shape in this respect than any state in the Union."[26]

During the latter part of the year, however, concern grew over the worsening financial situation. Norfolk, which had resisted the advance of the depression better than the rest of the state because of Hampton Roads shipping and an "austerity banking program" adopted in the twenties, was now visibly suffering. Officials estimated unemployment at twice the normal figure and considered instituting a Sunday movie program to provide funds for winter relief; the mayor, contrary to a prior prediction, announced that city employees would receive 10 percent pay cuts. Atlantic University at Virginia Beach, which had been founded the year before with great expectations for the future, went bankrupt. In Richmond the situation had deteriorated earlier. Construction was down by half from 1930; relief expenses had risen substantially over the previous year; and the Social Service Bureau was taking care of almost one thousand families. Many projects involving large investments by the city government had been canceled, and there was little hope for improvement in 1932. Lynchburg, too, "suffered keenly" in 1931; several wholesale houses closed, retail trade was down, and the town fathers were following a strict retrenchment policy.[27]

Farm conditions in Virginia at the end of 1931 continued their dismal showing. Farm prices, which had been relatively stable after the 1920–21 panic, began to slip in 1930 and continued downward in 1931. While crop yields generally exceeded those of the drought year, and in many cases those of 1929, prices declined to the point where cash income was almost half what it had been two years earlier. Tobacco sales were the smallest since 1921, and the average price per hundred pounds, $6.63, was the lowest since 1920. Moreover, the prices paid by a farmer for the goods he needed did not fall as rapidly. "The effect on tobacco farmers," said a Pittsylvania minister, "was catastrophic—formerly affluent farmers were living hand to mouth."[28] Several bank failures in South Boston and Danville further aggravated the poverty created by falling prices. C. D. Bryant, director of a Danville tobacco warehouse, addressed letters to his congressman demanding immediate relief for the farmers: "The farmers are wrought up at a high pitch, a great many declaring vengeance due to the deplorable conditions of their families suffering for want of clothing, medicine and other absolute necessities. Numbers of them are not sending their children to school as they have no means of providing them with clothing or school books. . . . We find men on our warehouse floor actually weeping after they have had to sell their tobacco at prices that will mean nothing less than complete disaster."[29]

Virginia industry experienced the weight of the depression for the first time in 1931. Industrial output fell 17 percent, from $814 million to $679 million; wages and salaries and the number of workers declined; and unemployment was estimated at 50,000 to 60,000. Yet Virginia remained relatively better off than most other states. Virginia's industrial employment was off 14 percent and wages were down 24 percent from 1929 figures; across the nation the declines were 26 and 38 percent respectively. Labor Commissioner Hall attributed this resilience to good administration, diversified industry, and favorable location. He praised employers for retaining workers and called for the adoption of the five-day week by others. He stressed the necessity for cooperation in industry, warning: "It seems likely that one of three things is going to result from this depression. Either capital and labor will mutually agree to work out a solution acceptable to both, or our national and local governments through paternalistic legislation will undertake a solution, or a revolution will result in the overthrow of our capitalistic system."[30]

By early 1932 the reality of the Great Depression had struck Virginia. When the General Assembly convened in January, Governor Pollard believed that its primary task was not providing relief but averting a budget deficit. In the two years since the last session, the general fund surplus of $4 million had been exhausted. His solution for this biennium was orthodox—reduce expenditures. Taking the initial economy step, Pollard reduced his own salary 10 percent and recommended that all state employees' earnings be cut by the same amount for a period of one year. He denied the request of the superintendent of education for $2 million in additional funds and ordered road appropriations reduced so that the state might remain within its income.[31]

13

The governor's retrenchment program was enthusiastically applauded across the Old Dominion. Former Governor Byrd predicted a faster return to prosperity if these policies were followed; in fact, Byrd had personally counseled Pollard to curtail appropriations and avoid raising taxes. The Norfolk *Virginian-Pilot* called it a "sound choice" but questioned the minimal highway cuts as compared to more drastic ones suffered by other departments. As conditions worsened, spending on roads became a volatile issue, entangled in political infighting because of its association with the Byrd tax and road programs. As governor, Byrd had "segregated" taxes, designating gasoline and automobile taxes for the highway fund, while income taxes went into the general fund to support state services such as education, and real estate and personal property taxes were left for local governments to assess. Now, however, delegates from the Norfolk area, where most of the road building had been completed, proposed a $5 million diversion of auto license taxes from roads to schools. The Richmond *Times-Dispatch* agreed: "It is ethical and practical for Virginia to use part of its road revenue for schools to relieve the burden of local taxation in these hard times." But both Pollard and Byrd opposed the measure, the governor for the reason that it would reduce the amount of highway work available for the unemployed, Byrd because he thought it would be injurious to his tax system and road development. With such power arrayed against it, the bill died in committee, causing the *Times-Dispatch* to comment, "our Commonwealth has sunk into a fixation that the policies dictated by authority are not to be disturbed by emergencies, even the emergency of poverty."[32]

Concerned with a potential threat to his leadership, Byrd, who was in the midst of a modest campaign for the presidency, suggested a substitute measure to placate those demanding tax relief. He proposed that the state take over the county feeder-road system, thus saving the counties $3.4 million in road expenditures and adding 36,000 miles to the state system. Rural interests applauded the plan as the best means of easing the tax burden in their areas, but urban representatives objected to it because it provided their constituents no relief at all. The *Virginian-Pilot* caustically editorialized: "Highwayolotry as a

State Religion." Claiming that Byrd had distorted the importance of highways to the state economy, the newspaper asserted that education, hospitals, asylums, and public health in Virginia were being shortchanged. In spite of this opposition, the road bill, slightly amended, passed the rural-dominated Assembly with little difficulty, leaving no doubt about Byrd's enduring strength in state politics. The legislature also gave the governor authority to reduce appropriations if anticipated revenues did not materialize and sanctioned the paring of state employees' salaries by 10 percent.[33]

The Assembly's failure to enact any relief legislation for the unemployed was not contrary to popular sentiment. Even if state leaders had been of a mind to raise taxes to finance reforms and relief, they would have encountered strong opposition from the citizenry. Although among the least taxed people in the country, Virginians were demanding tax reductions from their local governments because the depression was squeezing them so hard.[34] Farmers claimed that the earnings from their crops were hardly enough to pay the taxes on the land. Said a Halifax planter: "Do you know what I got from a plantation a few miles from here? A dollar and twenty cents in cash, a bushel of peas, and four barrels of corn, and I let my tenant keep the bushel of peas because it appeared he needed the food."[35] Farmers formed taxpayers' associations to pressure officials into economies in government. As unrest spread, especially in the tobacco belt and southwest Virginia, county after county began lowering taxes. Meeting at the time, the General Assembly recognized the message and was content to rely on the highway program and local relief agencies to alleviate the discomfort of the needy. It is likely that Byrd proposed his road plan to quell this discontent and avert criticism of his segregated tax system; when the new road bill was enacted, he urged county taxpayers to pressure their supervisors to pass the tax savings directly on to them.[36]

Throughout the year, Virginia cities also pared their budgets to match reductions in revenue caused by declining incomes and more frequent tax delinquencies. Norfolk released many firemen, policemen, and garbage collectors from its staff of employees. In April the city fired several teachers, imposed salary cuts on others, and closed city kindergartens for a savings of $18,505. The Harrisonburg City Council cut its budget by 10 percent, and the proposed Charlottesville budget for 1932–33 was $35,000 less than that for the previous year. Richmond officials estimated losses in revenue for 1932–33 to be $1 million; in Lynchburg the estimate was $100,000. The cities also became more industrious in their efforts to revive the economy and give aid to the needy. Richmond, Petersburg, and Culpeper, in conjunction with their chambers of commerce, undertook drives to stimulate business through new construction, home improvements, and antihoarding campaigns. Lynchburg disbursed public relief money for the first time through various private charity groups, while Richmond, which was spending $4,000 a week for relief, organized a "block-aid" plan designed to promote contributions from the more fortunate to the "have-nots" living in the same block. Public and private expenditures for unemployment relief increased tremendously between 1928 and 1932; in Hopewell they rose from $3,400 to $39,244; in Roanoke, from $7,878 to $29,079; and in Danville, from $15,390 to $32,353.[37]

Even as these steps were taken, conditions further deteriorated, causing the governor to initiate the first 10 percent cut in general fund appropriations. Jobless Richmond veterans were preparing to join former comrades from across the country in a march on Washington to demand early payment of their wartime bonus money. A state Department of Labor survey discovered "acute" unemployment conditions in Richmond (9,000 unemployed), Roanoke (8,000), Petersburg (4,000), and Alleghany County (3,000); it noted that the coal mines of southwest Virginia were operating only two days a week at less than two-thirds of normal employment. A lawyer from Grundy lamented: "We are in the red on all sides in Buchanan County. . . . We have 1150 families on the Red Cross flour and a number of others asking to be put on. We have hundreds of families who cannot put their children in school for the want of clothing. . . . Men [are] begging for anything to do at any price. We must have some relief in some way."[38]

The expansion of the Reconstruction Finance Corporation (RFC) in July 1932, authorizing $300 million in loans to the states and $322 million for public works, provided a much-needed new source of relief funds.[39] Having previously received $2.25 million in federal road advances, Governor Pollard now asked for $4.5 million from the RFC to be allocated to his highway unemployment relief plan. He appointed an Emergency Relief Committee to process the applications for funds, organize local agencies, and plan the road projects. In presenting his plea for funds to the corporation, Pollard pointed out that unemployment was highest in the cities of Richmond and Hopewell and in Wise, Pulaski, Pittsylvania, Brunswick, Lunenburg, and Halifax counties, areas that were either industrialized or tobacco-producing. Another summer drought, although not so severe as the one in 1930, threatened once again to reduce substantially the tobacco crop. In September, with their own resources nearly exhausted, Wise, Pulaski, and Halifax counties received an initial loan of $283,367 from the RFC to be used on road work. Many other counties soon followed their lead, and in a year's time $3.5 million entered the state, providing work for thousands of Virginians. Halifax and Wise counties received over $200,000 each, and Norfolk led the cities with $145,000. One million dollars of this money was designated for construction of U.S. Navy ships and military barracks in Norfolk, Portsmouth, and Quantico. Until the advent of the New Deal, the RFC was the major supplier of relief money in Virginia.[40]

The approach of winter brought no respite. Three thousand schoolchildren in Lee County were reported "undernourished and underclothed." Collections from the Community Chest drives were mixed. Richmond and Harrisonburg were among thirty-one cities in the country to exceed a goal set higher than the previous year, but Norfolk, Charlottesville, and Roanoke collected little more than two-thirds of their objectives. The Richmond Red Cross treasury was so depleted that the chapter was forced to rely on volunteers and government surpluses in providing flour and clothing to 300 families. Salvation Army street collections in Richmond declined from $1,338 in 1929 to $359 in 1933, while the number of people the army was feeding and housing jumped fivefold. Roanoke's relief bill tripled, but funds were inadequate to meet the need. A godsend to the Roanoke area economy was the December reopening of the

4,800-man Viscose Corporation, largest rayon-producing plant in the world, after six months of inactivity. In Norfolk the city council ordered streetlights turned off at night in an effort to save $50,000. Calling for cuts in school appropriations and charity and welfare funds, the city manager suggested that evening and summer school programs be terminated and that the number of city employees be reduced by 400. Charity drive leaders claimed that "there has never been within the memory of those engaged in relief work, conditions such as these that exist in Norfolk today." They estimated that 3,000 families in the city were in need of some relief.[41]

In late November representatives of the National Unemployed Councils, a radical left-wing organization, entered Virginia and set up local committees. Attracting considerable support from blacks, the group on whom the burden of unemployment fell heaviest, the Norfolk council demanded food, free water, freedom from eviction for failure to pay rent, aid for unemployment, and jail releases for those involved in "rent strikes." The Richmond Unemployed Council demanded $750,000 from the city for winter relief. Neither city complied with these requests. Money was not available, and the alleged affiliation of the groups with Communists destroyed community sympathy for them. The Richmond council also organized a "hunger march" on city hall, which attracted a few dissidents and ended with the arrest of the leader for marching without a permit. The motley band was derisively tagged "Joseph Stalin's 'Army of Northern Virginia.'" It was one of the few public demonstrations of dissatisfaction to appear in Virginia throughout the entire depression period.[42]

On December 10 Governor Pollard promulgated his second 10 percent reduction in general fund appropriations, which affected spending in education, welfare, and health but not the segregated highway revenue. The small surplus that had existed at the end of the fiscal year in June had since evaporated. Observing that the depression was creating "unparalleled problems" in the state, the governor declared that he was attempting to keep the budget balanced in accordance with the wishes of the General Assembly. The *Times-Dispatch* commended him for acting "with admirable wisdom."[43]

In the United States the winter of 1932–33 proved to be the nadir of the depression. For millions of Americans, the necessities of life had become luxuries; itinerants, soup kitchens, and "Hoovervilles" were common features on the urban landscape; steel production had fallen to 12 percent of capacity, and industrial construction was less than 8 percent of what it had been in 1929; more than a quarter of the labor force was out of work. In the rural areas of the country, farmers struggled to prevent foreclosures on their farms, declared farm holidays, and destroyed farm produce rather than sell it at ridiculously low prices.[44]

Virginia felt the full effect of the depression in 1932. Crop production, largely because of the drought, was well off 1931 figures, and farm income was down by 20 percent; the tobacco crop was the smallest since 1876, although the average price per hundred pounds rose by $2. Wheat was at its lowest known price in 132 years, prompting one farm expert to remark, "It seems likely that 50 cents a bushel for wheat is the lowest average for Virginia since the settlement of Jamestown in 1607." Commercial failures multiplied, while bank deposits, building permits, and the value of those permits decreased. Tax delinquencies, increasing at an alarming rate, were above 20 percent in some counties. Industrial wages declined 25 percent, and manufacturing output fell over $100 million to $575 million. Coal production reached its lowest level since 1911, dropping 23 percent from 1931. Virginia exports declined by almost half, with the smaller tobacco crop accounting for most of the difference; the tourist trade was off by 20 percent. Unemployment in the state averaged 100,000 workers during 1932, hitting a peak in July of 145,000; many others worked only part time. Although unemployment was not so high as elsewhere and total income had not declined as much, a large number of Virginians were clearly in need of financial and material assistance.[45]

Delayed by the soundness of Virginia's economy, the depression finally struck the state in unrelenting fashion. In spite of their diversity and consumer orientation, Old Dominion agriculture and manufacturing could not indefinitely resist the effects of external upheaval. Insidiously, the depression first snared the marginal, dispensable workers; then, aided by the drought, it swallowed the farmer; and finally, it enveloped the industrial laborer and the white-collar employee. Initially, retrenchment was the only solution Virginians could devise to combat the crisis. Faced with declining revenues, city, county, and state governments reduced salaries, staffs, and, eventually, services. As the depression worsened, voices in state and nation began to demand a reassessment of the conservative fiscal policies of their leaders, but such a review was not forthcoming. The citizens of Virginia would have to wait for the inauguration of a new national administration to obtain satisfaction.

2
The Way
It Was

Most Americans who lived through it have little difficulty remembering the Great Depression. It is one of the benchmarks of their lives. The image, however, unlike the memory of a tragic moment, is not so indelibly etched in the mind that it can be perfectly recreated. Rather, remembrances of the depression are a collage of experiences and incidents in which facts are misplaced, chronology is fuzzy, and events are exaggerated. Nevertheless, the general impression many have of the period is often sharp and accurate, especially if the discomfort was extended and the relief minimal.

The memories of Virginians confirm the conclusion that the thirties was the "best and worst of times." Conditions were bad, but they brought forth human qualities that many persons wish were more prevalent today, such as caring for and sharing with others. Furthermore, most Virginians believed they were better off than other Americans, a fact of some consolation in difficult times. The tone of their collective recall is, for the most part, subdued and nostalgic, lacking the sting of frustration and despair that marks the responses of many other Americans who have been asked about their depression experiences.[1] Their personal reminiscences corroborate the statistics—Virginia avoided the worst aspects of the depression. On the other hand, their comments suggest that, as individuals, Virginians did suffer and that the differences from suffering elsewhere may have been only a matter of degree. This apparent contradiction is reflected in the statement of E. A. Dietrich, a Richmond bookkeeper: "Virginia being then much more agricultural was not in as bad shape as the industrial states—Michigan, etc. However, nearly all of one's acquaintances were in difficulty of one kind or another—loss of business, of property, of job, of savings in bank failures (latter killed father's business). I do not recall serious or militant discontent. People were anxious and often contentious, but not aggressively discontented as were, for example, some mid-west farmers."[2]

In general, people were better off on Virginia farms than in the urban areas of the state. Said Clarence Holt of Albemarle: "As we lived on a farm, the food situation wasn't as bad as it was in the towns and cities. Never saw a bread line or soup kitchen in our community—it being mostly small farms." Times were not easy, but those living in rural areas usually had the necessities for survival—food, clothing, and shelter—and with them, important peace of mind. In fact, the remembrances of some are near-idyllic. Russell Burnette reminisced:

Conditions during the depression years became a way of life. People, generally, accepted this with calm and understanding. Most everyone was affected alike. We did without many essential items, [and] managed to get by on the minimum of bare necessities. Everyone worked together as a family unit, including the children. Children and adults were more industrious than they are today. The families were close, [and] enjoyed good social family life and church activities. I was one of ten children living with my parents and grandmother. We managed to provide much of our food, including grain for making flour, poultry and hogs. We had a good time and those years growing up with our large family were the very best years of my life.

Closeness of family and community helped to sustain rural folk through these years. Although the young continued to leave the farm seeking new opportunities, family ties were frequently strengthened. Jobs were so scarce that these farm "runaways" often returned home—along with many who had departed earlier but lost their city jobs to the depression.[3] As this flow from the cities back to the farms increased, there was considerable doubling up of families under the same roof and a greater sharing of workloads. Wrote a Lynch Station farmer: "We were largely self-sufficient. Our life style was simpler but we were happy as we had a large family and a happy home. We were concerned about our neighbors. We cooperated and helped each other. We traded items or lent items to each other if the need was there." Visiting among families was a common form of recreation which reinforced the community bond. Furthermore, the homogeneity of the rural areas proved a stabilizing feature in depression times. There was less bitterness and more togetherness among people who were all in the same line of work and who endured the same weather and prices. Although they hardly welcomed the depression, stoical Old Dominion farmers tolerated bad times with a minimum of complaint.

Nevertheless, it was a time for rigid economizing. Practically no agricultural machinery was purchased, and deterioration in buildings and equipment was widespread. Clarence Holt remarked: "Money for necessities was scarce—for luxuries nonexistent . . . . Many times variety was obtained by swapping places of the apple butter and jelly dish. Recreation was mostly a game of horseshoes on Sunday afternoon which not only furnished entertainment but furthered our education—we learned to measure in $\frac{1}{32}$ of an inch . . . . 'Sunday clothes' were hard to come by—work clothes bore many patches and not always matched. Dresses were made from chicken feed bags; more under garments carried the trademark of 4X flour than of any department store." Rural folks were remarkable at improvising: "petty coats were made from chicken feed bags, lye soap from meat scraps, and toilet tissue from catalogue paper." Extra money was earned by trapping animals, raising popcorn, and cracking black walnuts, while recreation ranged from "stealing a few chickens" to bootlegging. Gasoline was considered a luxury, and money was not available to repair cars, so many a farmer stripped down the chassis, hitched up the team to it, and went to town in a "Hoover cart." Frank Cox of Prince William County declared, "Farmers referred to themselves as well-fed characters wearing patches on top of patches."

The lack of purchasing power had a considerable effect on rural businesses. A Chantilly store owner claimed that the lack of money led to a semibarter economy; credit was a rarity because too much of it could put a man out of business. In some larger rural centers, economic diversity buffered the depression shock. While South Boston experienced several bank failures due to its reliance on the tobacco crop, Farmville's agriculture, trade, manufacturing, and two colleges contributed to banking stability. J. Barrye Wall, longtime editor of the Farmville *Herald*, recalled going down to Main Street during the banking holiday in 1933 to see if there would be a run on the banks. There was none, but, ironically, a friend of his took money from a Farmville bank to Richmond where he subsequently lost it. Wall borrowed money on occasion to meet his newspaper payroll and claimed he bounced a check or two, but the paper extended short-term credit to subscribers and suffered no decline in circulation.[4] Food was readily available in the towns serving rural areas; there were no breadlines and little hunger. "Life was difficult," said Harrison Day of Staunton, "but we managed . . . through most any kind of honest moonlighting." E. B. Carter, a Newsoms store owner, summed up the dilemma of the small-town merchant: "We all managed to eat, but money was very scarce and jobs hard to get. . . . Times were very difficult for everyone."

Sharecroppers were among the poorest members of rural communities, yet many of their problems were little related to the depression. For them the most noticeable change was in the condition of the owners, who now were often forced to work alongside the croppers and pay them in produce rather than cash. A cropper from Nelson County noticed very little change between 1929 and 1931, "except some [owners] could pay in cash; some couldn't; some that had paid in cash were no longer able to." Farm laborers, in particular, faced difficult times because the depression created a larger pool of workers but reduced the farmer's ability to hire help.

The hardest period for Virginia farmers unquestionably came in 1930–32 when prices dropped to their lowest levels and two droughts depleted production. There was little point in raising a crop if it never matured or if production costs were higher than what it would sell for. It was particularly bad for the producers of cash crops, notably tobacco. Hiram Holmes remembered: "Tobacco [was] so low that it didn't pay the warehouse charges. One man [said] he would have to go home and catch the old rooster and sell it so he could have enough to pay the warehouse charges. Someone present advised him to remove the tobacco from the floor and to take it home and spread it on his fields which meant that he would not have to pay any charges." Holmes also recalled a bank closing in Amelia: "I remember an

24

old man going in to town to remove his savings from the local bank because he had heard that it was about to close. As he approached the door someone came to the door of the bank and pulled the shade down. He stood in the street and cried and when someone asked him why he was crying, he replied that he had often heard of banks 'busting' but this was the first time he had ever had one bust in his face."

Farm foreclosures did occur, but not in record numbers.[5] Reminiscent of what was happening with some frequency in the Middle West, an Amherst County farmer saved his farm by bidding for it at public auction and reclaiming it when no one else would buy. There was some discontent in rural areas, notably among the young, who often left home, but there was no rioting or protesting or significant increase in crime. Agricultural agent John Freeman recollected: "People were in a daze—shock actually. There was not much unrest, per se, but had steps not been taken, as were taken in 1933–34, the situation could have become chaotic, to say the least."

The Virginia Agricultural Extension Service was very helpful in its effort to counter the drought and depression. Primarily an educational unit, the extension service emphasized self-sufficiency on the farm to combat declining incomes. This program was known by several names: "balanced farming," "depression proofing," "live at home," or the "cow, sow, and hen program." The farmer was to grow what he required and supplement this with the income generated by the sale of chickens, pulpwood, and cream. Livestock was retained for meat and dairy products, and canning was encouraged; cash crops were deemphasized since returns on them were minimal. Virginia farmers accommodated nicely to the program, particularly those thousands who were already in or bordering on a condition of subsistence farming. Said Henry Megehee: "The Fluvanna farmers were general farmers and raised large gardens so they didn't buy much food anyway. My father raised tobacco and sorghum molasses to sell as our cash crop. Tobacco prices during the depression were so low that sometimes it didn't bring enough to pay fertilizer and selling bills. We stopped growing tobacco and increased the amount of sorghum we grew. Sorghum molasses would sell any year at a reduced price as people

25

had to eat. Most of the Fluvanna farmers continued farming general crops and livestock, using less fertilizer and growing less tobacco."

The extension service also helped to organize farmers into cooperatives for the purchase of fertilizer at lower rates, arranged for seed and fertilizer loans through local banks and the Federal Land Bank, and worked closely with the Red Cross in the distribution of garden seed to needy families. P. H. DeHart, county agent for Isle of Wight, recalled one substantial farmer who was reduced to a gross income of $300 one year and was ready to give up farming. Working with a local debt adjustment committee, DeHart was able to reduce the farmer's debt by half; then he and the farmer developed a farm management plan similar to the cow, sow, and hen program. Thirty years later the farm was worth $150,000. By helping farmers to help themselves, the extension service assisted many rural people through the depression.[6]

In the cities of the Old Dominion the situation was potentially more explosive than it was on the farms. Experiencing wholesale industrial layoffs and attracting large numbers of unemployed drifters, urban centers could not survive as easily as the more self-supporting rural areas. The necessities were available but not always abundant, and for many the depression became a personal ordeal which not even Virginia's advantages could mitigate. The remembrances are sobering. For Hattie McNamara, whose husband and father were both unemployed, life was precarious; at times, she said, the family was "just about to give up." They did without food and clothing and frequently were behind in their rent. A Petersburg trunk maker tearfully told school principal James Scott, "I have enough clothes for my wife and children to last till June and enough money to buy food but when they get hungry and I have no money I am going down on Sycamore Street, break a store window and get them some food." John Cabell of Lynchburg claimed, "If you didn't stay where the food was you didn't eat, [and] starved to death." He remembered hearing of some suicides where he lived and seeing social workers going from house to house with food baskets.

Many urban families relied on relatives on the farm for food, while a few enterprising Richmond residents bartered clothing for the canned fruits and vegetables of Amelia farmers. The family of a $10,000-a-year-executive who was released from his position with American Radiator Company in Newport News trapped rabbits for food while he searched for employment. In Portsmouth one church was feeding one hundred people a day with leftovers collected from the naval base. Margaret Gearing of Norfolk recalled, "If [you] threw a cigarette on the street, people would pick it up and smoke it." B. B. Albert of Roanoke reflected, "I do not recall many bread lines or soup kitchens. There was little in the way of demonstrations nor was there much evidence of discontent . . . . [But] it was a traumatic experience for many families and I hope never to see it again in our beloved land."

Richmond had its share of unemployment and breadlines, problems that were compounded by some banking instability. Said one lawyer: "It was bad here. Everybody was bewildered at the change. Money was scarce and almost everybody suffered a reduction in standard of living. Economically everything slowed down about half. Nobody wanted anything done. There were business failures, much unemployment. My practice [real estate law] was especially affected." But another Richmond attorney had a slightly different view: "Times were bad but not to the point of desperation even in the worst-hit communities. We tightened belts, hitched up trousers, economized, and resolved to beat the depression. In those days people did not want to be on relief. People found they could get along without many things including luxuries. They adjusted to the situation and life went along. . . . My family had to pull in our belts, eliminate vacation trips, [and] entertainment, . . . alter and repair clothes, and reduce living costs to essentials." Arthur Eure, a highway department employee, claimed the price decreases balanced out his salary cuts and enabled him to maintain his standard of living, but he recalled others "who did not fare so well. We who had jobs were told to . . . count our blessings and hold on for dear life." He remembered passing up two better-paying jobs just to hold on to "something certain," demonstrating an obsession for security which affected many people for the rest of their lives.

A job was the most prized possession of depression times.

Joblessness threatened physical well-being, eroded family cohe-
siveness, and forecast the dreaded trip to the relief agency, an
experience so shameful in the minds of some Americans that
they endured considerable suffering before going. Studies of
Richmond unemployed showed a high rate of illness, debt, and
emotional problems among their families, many of whose members had turned to begging, excessive drinking, and criminal activity, even prostitution. There were demoralized home conditions, with declining respect for the father, increased desertion,
departure of older children, and growing domestic difficulties
between husband and wife. Caseworkers discovered people
fearful of the future, depressed to the point of stealing or considering suicide, humiliated, angry, and feeling unwanted.[7]

Although social workers in Richmond believed conditions
were better there than in other locations across the country,
they readily testified to the "dire circumstances" of Virginians
during the depression. Unemployment, breadlines, soup kitchens, evictions, relief-in-kind, and heavy case loads were daily
experiences that became rooted in their memories. Theirs is
perhaps the most accurate description of the worst impact of the
depression in Virginia cities. In testimony before the Senate
Committee on Unemployment Relief, Mrs. Lenore Miffley of
the Family Service Society, a private relief agency, related several stories of Richmonders affected by the depression,
including this entreaty of an unemployed salesman who had
written to the agency: "We received notice from the real estate
man and are worried sick, especially when you seemed in doubt
as to whether you could get our rent money for us. I hope you
can now for we would hate to be put out of another place. We
have tried so hard to struggle through this depression but it
seems almost hopeless. We are living in a constant state of ap-
prehension."[8]

Blue-collar workers in service occupations and industry were
among the first Virginians to feel the pains of joblessness. The
formerly affluent released maids, railroads and textile mills cut
shifts in half, and sawmills and coal mines shut down, causing
people to take to the road in search of work or, in desperation,
resort to begging or charity. Thousands of transients, many of
them remnants of the Bonus Army expedition of 1932, criss-

crossed Virginia seeking work. John Cabell, whose experience was not unusual, recalled a checkered depression career as waiter, cook, construction worker, laborer for a wholesale grocer, and employee for the Lynchburg Training School; he even did a little begging on the side. Panhandling become such a public nuisance that the Roanoke *World-News* urged its readers to avoid giving the vagabonds anything.[9]

White-collar workers, on the other hand, enjoyed greater job security in the early thirties. Government workers, both state and federal, were among the most protected, although Virginia employees did experience pay cuts. Among professional people, educators suffered most in terms of layoffs and salary reductions, while lawyers, ministers and doctors were less affected. The latter lived more modestly and extended more credit to their patients, but they were still very much in demand. Legal business, too, remained good as the depression created a large number of bankruptcies, foreclosures, and liquidations that had to be litigated. Because of a decrease in contributions, most ministers sustained pay cuts and operated on tight budgets, but many churches expanded their local charitable work. As for the piety of their flocks, the Reverend R. P. Welch of Pamplin declared, "Some moved closer to God and others went the other way." Life insurance and real estate were difficult to sell in the thirties, forcing agents of these commodities to diversify. Insurance premiums were often paid in kind—"four or five chickens, a Smithfield ham, or a bushel of potatoes." The banking business slowed, but bankers were not among the major victims of the catastrophe for which many people blamed them. Their losses were more psychological; once considered the pillars of the community, they now were the objects of much scorn. A Petersburg woman confided that the closing of her father's bank forced her to consider concealing her identity; and Carter Glass was fond of telling the story of the "banker in my state who was nearly lynched because he tried to marry a white woman."[10]

In the retail trade survival was more tenuous, especially among small businessmen whose profit margins were slim and whose collateral was limited. Sales in 1933 were off over 40 percent of those in 1929, with furniture, automobiles, and lumber and hardware particularly hard hit. Car dealers felt the pinch of consumers' decisions to extend the life of the family auto a few more years. Salesmen whose business was slow shifted jobs with some frequency. Facing reduced sales and profits, merchants cut workers' hours and pay and then laid them off. Paydays were skipped and little credit was extended out of fear that the bills would never be paid. Such penny-pinching, however, could prove unprofitable. One Petersburg family refused for years to do business in a store that did not grant credit during the depression. Newspapermen had reasonably secure positions since the level of subscriptions was kept fairly constant by circulation campaigns advertising extended credit and reduced prices for long-term subscriptions.[11]

As on the farms, urban dwellers economized and found new diversions. People who had sent out their laundry in the twenties did their own washing in the thirties. Resorting to foot power, they garaged the family car and allowed automobile licenses to lapse. Magazine subscriptions, vacations, and Christmas gifts were all cut back. For some the depression had more significant implications, such as the deferment of college and marriage. A Portsmouth minister remembered advising a man against matrimony in such uncertain times; his advice was accepted and the license returned for the dollar fee. An occasional movie, the radio, and the Ouija board provided entertainment for many, while a few continued the clandestine pleasures of Jazz Age bootlegging in "neighborhood breweries," organized because no one could afford all the ingredients by himself.

The plight of the urban unemployed was directly related to the impact of the depression on industry. The number of those jobless and on relief was highest in the industrial centers of Richmond, Roanoke, Norfolk, and Hopewell and in the coal-producing counties of southwest Virginia. A declining demand for goods and services forced production cutbacks, which generated salary cuts and layoffs, thus intensifying the effect of the economic crisis. No industry or business could entirely avoid this. Hardest hit in the Old Dominion were lumber, flour milling, furniture, and railroad and automobile shops. However, the products of much Virginia manufacturing were consumables— tobacco, processed food, and clothing—the demand for which was less affected by the depression.[12]

The tobacco industry was considered nearly "depression proof." National production of factory-made cigarettes declined from a high of 119.6 billion in 1930 to 103.6 billion in 1932 and then moved upward. However, since "roll your owns" nearly tripled in estimated sales, the number of cigarettes smoked probably did not decline appreciably. In fact, smoking tobacco was the only tobacco product that did not drop in sales during the depression. The leading cigarette brands—Luckies, Camels, and Chesterfields—experienced significant losses, but lower leaf prices encouraged the marketing of cheaper ten-cent varieties, which became major competitors. In Virginia the dollar value of tobacco production dropped by only 3 percent and recovered quickly. The *Times-Dispatch* remarked: "The greatness of the tobacco industry in Virginia is one of the principal reasons, perhaps, for the State's unusually strong position during the period of the business depression. It was many months before we felt the full shock of the economic debacle. While other communities suffered severely, Richmond and Virginia went on for a year or more as if nothing had happened."[13]

Textile mills were less successful but managed to persevere and were surpassing 1929 production figures by the end of the decade. Hurt by both depression and strike, Dan River Mills had a disastrous year in 1930 and off years in 1931 and 1932, but by 1934 production and sales figures exceeded those of 1929. Growth in the production of synthetics was particularly strong. DuPont operated a rayon plant at Richmond and an acetate plant at Waynesboro, both of which experienced modest expansion in this period. Friedman-Marks, a small clothing company based in Richmond, enjoyed spectacular growth—production quintupled, employment quadrupled, and annual value of output went from $1 million to $10 million.[14]

Other industries were less fortunate. The value of the fishing catch throughout the thirties was less than two-thirds of what it had been in 1929 and 1930. Declining food prices forced many marginal food-processing companies such as the small canneries in the Middle and Northern Necks to shut down, but larger, well-established firms like Gwaltney of Smithfield, while suffering poor profit years, were more likely to survive.[15] Since people were not buying furniture, the sizable Virginia furniture industry was forced to retrench and lay off workers. In Martinsville the fortunate ones were on three-day weeks at $3.90 a week. The new Stanley Furniture Company in Stanleytown, which had embarked upon a plant expansion in 1929, nearly went bankrupt. Only the assistance of a friendly banker and the application of extreme cost-cutting measures allowed the company to continue. The president of the firm, Thomas B. Stanley, a future governor of the Commonwealth, took a 50 percent cut in pay, and his employees agreed to several pay cuts rather than be laid off. The quality of the furniture produced also changed, since simpler, less expensive styles were now more in demand.[16]

Elsewhere, the impact was much the same. A Roanoke lumberyard which was in receivership for two years retained its workers but reduced their hours from sixty to forty per week and docked their wages as well. Recalling these days, owner J. C. Hodges said, "God, I don't want to even think about it; that's when a nickel was a nickel." Similar cuts in pay and hours were experienced at the Covington plant of the West Virginia Pulp and Paper Company. Total employment dipped by several hundred at this plant, which often cut back to a five-day week from the normal seven-day, around-the-clock operation. Total net income of Westvaco, including plants outside Virginia, declined from $4.8 million in 1929 to $79,000 in 1932. Newport News Shipbuilding and Dry Dock Company, one of the largest firms in the Old Dominion, had a peculiar response to the depression. Operating on long-term contracts, the company did not feel the major effects of the collapse until 1933, and it sustained income losses in 1935 and 1936 when most other businesses were recovering.[17]

The depression affected public utilities more modestly. Virginia Electric and Power Company (Vepco), which was participating in the phenomenal gains of the growing electrical industry, continued to increase its number of customers through 1931 but then encountered mild losses in 1932 and 1933. Earnings from sales of electricity were down 5 percent and 1.9 percent in these two years. The company suffered greater losses in the streetcar and bus service it provided citizens of Richmond, Petersburg, Norfolk, and Portsmouth. The number of passengers carried declined from 82 million in 1929 to 60 million in 1933. Vepco enjoyed "moderate but steady improvement" in 1934 with increased earnings and customers in both electricity and transportation. By the end of the decade the utility was adding an average of 10,000 electrical customers per year.[18]

Railroads in Virginia were not so fortunate, experiencing significant declines in freight and passenger operating revenues, net income, and customers. By 1932 six leading roads in the state were carrying almost 8 million fewer paying passengers than they had in 1929. Already in a state of decline due to competition with the automobile and cheaper interstate bus service, passenger service on the railroads received its death blow from the depression. By 1939 the six Virginia railroads had recovered fewer than two-thirds of their 1929 fares. Two of these roads, the Seaboard Airline and the Norfolk Southern, were under receivership for half the decade and, along with the Southern Railroad, frequently operated at a deficit. On the other hand, perhaps reflecting better conditions in the Commonwealth, those railways with major portions of their track within the state fared comparatively well. The Norfolk and Western and the Virginian railroads, both servicing the coalfields of West Virginia and southwest Virginia and less reliant on passenger traffic, had some hard years from 1931 through 1935 due to a 40 percent decline in coal production, but both remained solvent throughout the decade. The roads managed this by cutting salaries and wages, laying off employees, retiring equipment, and reducing service. The wage cuts and layoffs were kept to a minimum, however, which benefited the economy of Roanoke, where half of the Norfolk and Western workers lived. Virginia's other "all-state" road, the Richmond, Fredericksburg and Potomac, likewise enjoyed profits throughout the thirties. Even though it relied on passenger traffic for one-third of its revenue, by economizing, locating new freight customers, and reducing fares to stimulate business, it paid dividends from 1932 through 1939.[19]

The depression cut Virginia's industrial output by almost a third, but in the process the Old Dominion improved its standing among the states. Since national production was down by over half, the value of manufacturing production in Virginia as a percentage of the United States' total increased from 1.06 in 1929 to 1.62 in 1933. Maryland's industrial production was down 53 percent; North Carolina's, 33 percent; Ohio's, 60 percent. Whereas the average annual wage per industrial wage earner in Virginia in 1929 was 75 percent of the national average ($982), over the next four years Virginia narrowed this wage gap by 6 percent. Noting less suffering in Virginia than elsewhere, economist James Ward attributed it to the "proper balance between industry and agriculture" and the diversification of industry.[20]

This balance and diversity did not prevent the depression from delivering a sharp blow to education in Virginia, which was already operating on a shoestring. Depleted state and local revenues were translated immediately into educational budget cuts of 25 percent or more, resulting in construction delays, teacher pay cuts and releases, and shortened school terms. By 1932–33 almost two-thirds of Virginia's counties had terms of less than eight months; Grayson County children were attending for less than four months. Only a supplemental federal appropriation in 1934 kept most of the schools operating through the spring term, and it was not until 1938 that the General Assembly put teeth into a 1930 law requiring a compulsory term of 180 days.[21]

Teachers felt the major brunt of this economizing. Their average salary dropped from $909 in 1930–31 to $692 in 1933–34; black teachers received even less. As counties faced the possibility of closing school doors, many teachers volunteered to serve without pay in order that the school year might be completed. Others accepted delayed paydays to allow collection of additional taxes, a frequent occurrence in rural districts which had to await the harvesting and marketing of crops. Since schools continued to operate at least part of the time, teachers did not face mass unemployment (there was only a slight decline in the number employed), but changes in hiring practices and retention policies did occur. As a means of economizing, school superintendents were authorized to include contract clauses stipulating reductions in salaries if funds ran low. They also preferred to hire local people over outsiders and men and single women over married women, desiring to spread the work among able-bodied heads of households. Many school boards had regulations compelling the resignations of single women who married. One

Richmonder recalled that he and his fiancée, a Nansemond County teacher, put off marriage for five years so she could retain her job and income.[22]

Reflecting the dearth of employment opportunities, students stayed in school or returned, causing enrollments to remain fairly constant throughout the decade and further squeezing the already economically pinched system. Few Virginians missed school because of the depression, but those who did usually remained home because of a lack of clothing or shoes. Exceptions in attendance figures were the private schools, whose enrollments dropped sharply. Staunton Military Academy, for example, saw its student body and staff cut by 60 percent.

Higher education in the state was not so significantly affected by the Crash, although the newly established Atlantic University was forced to close its doors. A college education in the 1930s was a luxury enjoyed largely by exceptional students and the wealthy; very few of the latter put it off or dropped out because of financial exigencies. It was the sons and daughters of middle-class families, whose savings had been taken by the depression, who saw their college dreams vanish. Enrollments remained steady through 1932, even increasing at state-supported institutions; they dropped sharply in 1933 and 1934 and then began rising again. Private colleges, especially black schools and the more expensive women's schools, such as Hollins and Randolph-Macon Woman's College, experienced the sharpest declines in student population, the latter dropping from 825 students in 1929 to 562 in 1934. Hampton Institute discontinued its summer school in 1932 and closed its nursing and library schools several years later. Although college professors at both public and private institutions took salary cuts, very few of them were released.[23]

The experience of Hampden-Sydney, the small private liberal arts college in rural Prince Edward County, was typical. With a small endowment, the college was not hurt badly by the stock market crash, but the ensuing depression did hinder efforts to raise additional money. Professors' salaries were cut 10 percent for six years, but the shortage of funds did not force the departure of any faculty. No wage reductions were imposed on the buildings and grounds staff, who were the recipients of the first checks every month. President Joseph Dupuy Eggleston, former president of Virginia Polytechnic Institute, took a 20 percent reduction and frequently "walked the floor some nights looking for $50 to fill a need." Apparently he succeeded, because few boys left the college due to financial difficulty; Eggleston found them jobs cutting wood, caring for chickens, and maintaining the grounds. In similar fashion colleges across the state continued to operate.[24]

Of considerable assistance to education in Virginia after 1933 were the many new federal programs providing money to keep students in college and high school, construct campus buildings, and maintain adult education and literacy classes. All of this New Deal aid was welcomed, but the failure of education in Virginia to make marked advances suggests that its influence was cosmetic. At the end of the decade Virginia still ranked in the lowest quintile among the states in rate of literacy, teacher salaries, per-pupil costs, and percentage of income spent for education. The state was paying less than a third of the cost of education in Virginia. Just as they had a decade earlier, teacher groups were pressing for higher salaries, more pension money, and free textbooks. The Virginia Education Association pointed out that Virginia had the next-to-lowest taxes in the United States but the highest per capita crime rate: "Ignorance does not pay and . . . in ignorance, we pay for the education that we never get."[25]

If any segment of the Old Dominion's population suffered the full effects of the depression, it was black Virginians. The inferior position already held by this minority is well documented. Although Virginia had a better record in race relations than most southern states, its black population labored under tremendous odds. The infant mortality rate for blacks in Virginia cities was double that for whites; the tuberculosis death rate was four times as high; and that from syphilis, three times as great. Job opportunities were limited, attested to by the significant out-migration of blacks. Housing was generally of slum quality—in Richmond, one-third of blacks had no water in the kitchen; 65 percent had no electricity; 70 percent had no inside bath or toilet; and 75 percent, no gas. Black illiteracy was put at 19.2 percent in 1930; for whites it was 4.8 percent. Responsible in part was the fact that two-thirds of the 1,800 Negro schools in Virginia were one-room, one-teacher schools whose average yearly term was considerably shorter than that for whites. These conditions were accompanied by insidious forms of discrimination that black Virginians confronted throughout the twenties and thirties.[26]

Conditions and discrimination were not alleviated by the Crash, and in many cases they were intensified by economic pressures. Stated a 1933 report of the Danville Community Welfare Association, "Our tobacco factories do not employ as many colored men and women workers as formerly, nor do they work them as long, and after the tobacco selling season is over there is little work for these people to do." [27] Black wages were at the bottom of the wage scale, with maids making as little as fifty cents a day and farm laborers twenty-five cents a day, while black industrial workers had negligible union protection. Negroes were abundant in the lower-paying occupations, such as laundryman, barber, and domestic, which provided services people now found easier to deny themselves. In May 1934 four-fifths of those on relief in Norfolk were black, and 42 percent of those employable were domestics. Citing the large body of "unemployed colored" in Danville, the *Register* called on citizens to stop firing domestics and "find a more humane method of economy." Negro businesses, reliant almost solely on black buying power, were severely squeezed, and many closed, including some of the few black banks in the state. Meanwhile, unemployed whites, enjoying the preferences of white employers, dropped down to take jobs normally reserved for blacks, who were generally the "last hired, first fired." In fact, the Norfolk Housewives League purportedly was instructing unemployed white women in the techniques of domestic service, and other organizations were calling on employers to fire blacks and hire whites. One white farmer commented that he saw no discrimination during the depression except that "a nigger was a nigger and a white man was a white man and the nigger got what he expected."[28]

Not surprisingly—and this was confirmed by many blacks—decades-old discrimination and poverty made the transition to greater deprivation somewhat easier; in fact, some blacks noted very little change, being "used to hard times anyway." Few of them lost money in banks since, in the words of one, they "didn't have any to lose." For them there were only two classes, rich and poor, and they usually belonged to the latter. While more likely to be tenants than owners, blacks who lived on farms were able to get by. Yet even here they held the inferior land, and in smaller units, and they lacked supplies and mechanical equipment. Also, with jobs scarce, tenants and seasonal laborers could no longer find supplemental income as easily as before. In a twelve-county survey taken in 1933, half of the blacks reported difficulty in locating steady work. It was particularly hard in the years of drought because the owners were forced to reduce their labor forces.[29]

In the cities, to which Negroes had been migrating in greater number since the turn of the century, conditions were worse. William Robinson of Norfolk remarked: "People were hungry [and in] a general state of helplessness and shock. [There were] no organized protests or demonstrations. Everyone seemed gripped with feelings of hopelessness." Although few whites ever admitted they were without basic necessities, several blacks like Robinson recalled different circumstances. There were reports of nearly starving Negro children around Suffolk who were not going to school because they had no clothes and who were without medical services. Said Leroy Whaley: "Depression in Richmond was very bad. Many people not only went without food but also clothes—even myself and children. Housing conditions were bad. You couldn't afford a good house." Black employment patterns were often very haphazard; Robert Pressy of Hampton, for example, was a custodian, dishwasher, and cook and caddied in his spare time. He remembered that jobs seemed to be available on an equal basis but that whites got paid more.

Although blacks were among the first to receive charity because of their poverty, such relief was minimal at best and often was dispensed in a discriminatory fashion. In Richmond, Negroes at times were denied work relief by the city, and the mayor reportedly asked private employers to do the same. Jane Guild, writing in *Survey Graphic*, concluded that there was "flagrant discrimination" in Richmond "in the dispensing of relief to

38

Negroes by both public and private agencies." Blacks eventually made up over half of Richmond's relief rolls. The situation was no better in Norfolk when in early 1933 the relief scale for blacks was cut from $2 to $1.25 a day, while whites retained the $2 scale. Officials argued that since blacks made up four-fifths of the relief rolls, it was easier to stretch remaining funds by reducing their portion. It was not surprising that "hungry Negroes" were more likely to listen to or be the targets of propaganda from the left-wing unemployment councils. Commented the *Journal and Guide*, "Norfolk is very fertile soil for communist growth."[30]

However, blacks did not pursue this alternative in great numbers. They were content to press their demands for equal treatment through accepted channels of protest while continuing to rely upon self-help. Both the *Journal and Guide* and the Richmond *Planet* urged "buy black campaigns," and the latter newspaper called on Negro housewives to help black peddlers, transients, and salesmen. Hoping to shock liberal white consciences and boost black morale, the newspapers constantly referred to the discrimination by white employers and white-controlled relief agencies and pressured the dispensers of relief to change their policies.[31]

The growth of public relief was the clearest indication of the magnitude of the depression, reflecting directly the large numbers out of work. Despite the efforts of many dedicated public and private social workers, organized relief efforts in Virginia were overwhelmed by the depression. The inadequacy of public welfare facilities forced private agencies like the Family Service Societies, Travelers Aid, Salvation Army, and religious charities to undertake a greater assistance role, but as the private contributions on which they relied dried up, their efforts, too, proved insufficient to meet the demand. The growth of the relief problem in Richmond exemplified the difficulties faced by relief workers across the state.

Before the Crash the chief relief-dispensing agency in the city was the Family Service Society (FSS), formerly Associated Charities, which received its funds from the Community Chest and other voluntary contributions. It paid rents, bought food and clothing, and occasionally provided cash allowances for the unemployed and families whose heads had died, become ill, or deserted them. Family Service was assisted in its work by the other independent but smaller charitable agencies such as the Bureau of Catholic Charities and the Red Cross. The public side of welfare was handled by the Richmond Social Service Bureau (SSB), which administratively was under the direction of the Virginia Department of Public Welfare but was funded primarily by the city. It dispensed Mothers' Aid—money Virginia appropriated for mothers with dependent children—and distributed fuel and shoes to the needy. Other cities also operated this dual system of public and private relief, which seemed adequate for the care of the destitute during the prosperous twenties. Virginia counties continued to rely on private philanthropy and the public almshouse to take care of the poor.[32]

The depression created an entirely new situation. The need became too great for these agencies to meet, particularly when the state refused to appropriate money. Even though the Community Chest drives often raised more money each year (FSS spent the largest amount ever in 1933—$120,000), they could not match the need. The private groups, which also had to work with those who were ineligible for public assistance—the employed poor and nonresidents who could not be assisted until they had lived in Richmond for a year—had to transfer more and more of their expanding case rolls to the Social Service Bureau. The case load of FSS was so large that the concept of individual casework was nearly abolished. Family Service's allowance for food was $1.10 per person per week, an amount which, although above that of the service bureau, still had to be supplemented with Red Cross surplus food. Although FSS initially adopted a relief-in-kind approach, calling in orders to grocery stores which would be paid by the agency, it eventually gave money directly to the recipient to purchase food. Usually relying on the Red Cross clothing room for clothing demands, FSS occasionally advanced a man some money if he needed clothes or tools to get a job. In providing shelter, the agency stretched its resources by doubling up families under one roof or skipping months in the payment of rents, practices that angered a number of landlords. Medical costs could not be paid, and ill recipients were referred to doctors or clinics. The unemployed were referred to the Richmond Employment Bureau or the Citizens Service Exchange, a self-help organization which facilitated the trading of services for goods.

There was little complaining about the work of FSS. Many preferred private relief to public relief, thinking it superior, or perhaps, more "private." Some protested that they did not get enough money, while others grumbled that money was not made available "unless you sell all your furniture." But there was frustration for the caseworkers as well. One family, living in overcrowded conditions, was given a new bed, but they then threw out their old one because parents and children were used to sleeping together. Most recipients stayed on FSS rolls for a short time, but many returned several times, and a few remained for as long as ten years. Social worker Marguerite Farmer believed that while the depression was responsible for the initial growth of relief rolls, it was the predepression poor who constituted the continuing welfare problem. [33]

The Social Service Bureau, in taking over more of the relief load, saw its expenses skyrocket. City appropriations went from $50,000 in 1931 to $235,000 a year later. The amount of coal and wood it was delivering almost tripled over a three-year period. Assisted with RFC money in 1932 and with New Deal funds thereafter, Richmond saw its relief expenditures rise to $700,000 in 1934. The bureau's case load doubled, and its caseworkers were averaging 645 cases apiece. Following the formation in early 1933 of a Mayor's Emergency Relief Commission, composed of representatives of all the agencies and other local citizens, the bureau became the primary relief dispenser in the city, with the independent private charities performing investigative and referral duties. SSB took over the transient bureau and began to administer the expanding federal programs as well.

Promoting public consciousness of relief needs, the private agencies performed commendably under testing circumstances, but as people became accustomed to large-scale public relief expenditures, the effort of private philanthropy diminished, a victim of the depression or, as some social workers claimed, a willingness to "let Uncle Sam do it." Forced out of its primary role, the Richmond Family Service Society assumed functions then untouched by government—marriage counseling, legal-aid as-

41

sistance, placement of foster children, and homemaker programs for welfare recipients. In Danville and Petersburg the FSS expired altogether, succumbing to high demand and inadequate funds. Its demise was due to no fault of its own.[34]

Although private philanthropy proved unable to meet the demands of the unemployed for relief, Virginians continued to demonstrate a spirit of generosity. Volunteers manned the relief agencies and did all that was physically possible to help their neighbors. The Norfolk and Western Railroad gave away wood from dismantled boxcars, and the Clover Creamery of Roanoke donated thousands of gallons of buttermilk throughout the depression.[35] A mutual self-help ethic seemed to be in operation. Wrote Wilbur Murphy of Bedford: "In my area there was plenty of unemployed people and people going without food. . . . Knowing the generosity of my grandparents, people came from all around begging for work to do just to get food. Grandpa never refused anyone. They didn't forget Grandpa because when he died crowds of people over half of which were white came to the funeral and did what they could to help the family."

The depression, however, was beginning to challenge the traditional ethics of self-help and laissez-faire. There was a growing belief that a basic change had occurred in American life, of which the depression was only the current manifestation. The complexities of modern life were making it difficult for men to be the sole determinants of their destiny. Said E. A. Dietrich of Richmond, "I realized that conditions could exist when competent and willing people could not find work." Faced with this revelation, Americans began to relax their longtime aversion to government involvement. Russell Burnette of Rustburg commented, "People were greatly in need through no fault of their own and I support the theory that the government should help those who cannot help themselves." Hesitantly, most Virginians concurred, but being fearful of the possibility of a social upheaval or the appearance of a "federal octopus," they continued to emphasize "people helping themselves."

Self-help, stoicism, political indifference, and a feeling that Virginians were better off than others all combined to minimize protest in the Old Dominion. There was next to no support for the left; the Communist party polled eighty-six votes in the 1932 election, and although Norman Thomas's Socialists enjoyed a brief "resurgence," they received less than 1 percent of the vote (2,382 votes).[36] The general apathy that affected the nation at large was even stronger in Virginia.[37] The absence of an active union movement in the state limited what little class consciousness existed among workers, and the extent of subsistence or general farming as opposed to market-oriented one-crop agriculture kept rural discontent low. Having insulated the state against the worst of depression, this traditional social order would prove almost impervious to the "revolution" soon to take place in Washington.

3
New Deal
in Town

Frustrated by their inability to cope with the crisis and angered by the platitudes offered by their leaders, Americans looked to the 1932 presidential election, hoping a change in leadership would be the necessary panacea. Since there was little doubt of victory for the Democrats, the contest for their nomination was spirited. Among the candidates was Al Smith, who believed his sacrificial effort in 1928 entitled him to be the party's choice in a year when selection in July was tantamount to success in November. Smith's major opponent and the front-runner was Franklin D. Roosevelt, governor of New York, whose attack on the depression in the Empire State had attracted national attention. His comeback against crippling polio and his effervescent spirit were strong assets for a candidate to have in this year of despair. Some sentiment favored the Old Dominion's Harry Byrd as a compromise candidate. The former governor was widely known for his record as a state executive, and his candidacy was commended not only by his own organization but by other prominent political and business leaders as well. Byrd himself caught the presidential fever and made an aggressive bid for the nomination, but it was apparent that he did not have the national stature of the major candidates—Roosevelt, Smith, John Nance Garner, and Newton Baker. Although Byrd was nominated as a favorite son by the Virginia Democratic convention and presented to the Chicago convention by Carter Glass, the coveted prize went to Roosevelt on the fourth ballot. Byrd's disinclination to join forces with Roosevelt may have cost him a high position in the new administration, possibly even the vice-presidency. Virginians applauded the party platform, especially those planks demanding return to a balanced budget and reduced government spending, but they were less ardent over the prohibition repeal plank.[1]

The result of the election in Virginia was a foregone conclusion, but organization leaders, remembering their "defection" in 1928, worked fervently to prove their new loyalty. Byrd played a particularly strong role in the campaign as head of the executive finance committee of the Democratic party. At Roosevelt's only campaign stop in the Old Dominion, Byrd called him "one of the greatest apostles of Thomas Jefferson who taught that the duty of government was to all of its people and not merely to especially privileged groups." The Virginia press was predictably, but more avidly than usual, in favor of the Democratic candidates. The Lynchburg *News* declared that Virginians "are ready to turn to another party and to new leaders. They are ready for a new deal . . . they know of the Roosevelt record, of the Roosevelt administration of the affairs of a great state."[2]

FDR won a landslide victory over Hoover in November and carried both houses of Congress into the Democratic column with him. Virginia supported him by a better than two-to-one margin and unseated the only remaining Virginia Republican in the House. The Roosevelt triumph augured well for the Old Dominion. The president-elect offered Senator Glass the secretaryship of the Treasury, a post he had held during the second Wilson administration, but after vacillating for weeks, the senator refused the position. He wrote to Roosevelt: "My associates in the Senate and public sentiment in Virginia unite in the judgment that I can better serve you and the country where I am than by a transfer to the Treasury . . . . I shall ever be ready to serve your administration to the full extent of my capabilities."[3] Actually, Glass's weakened state of health (which he had mentioned to Roosevelt) and basic disagreement with the president-elect on the question of inflation, a disagreement soon to be made public, were the underlying reasons for his refusal. Virginia did, however, obtain cabinet representation when Roosevelt named Senator Claude Swanson secretary of the navy. Governor Pollard speedily appointed Harry Byrd to fill the vacated Senate seat.[4]

Upon Roosevelt's inauguration March 4, 1933, in the midst of a serious banking impasse, Virginians rallied to his side. The Portsmouth *Star* depicted the president as a man with "strength of character, strength of purpose, clarity of thought and definiteness of determination to attack the problems of the nation." Newly sworn-in Senator Byrd supported limited debate on the president's program in order not to impede its progress. The *Times-Dispatch* commented: "In short Senator Byrd stands ready to grant the President dictatorial powers during the period of the emergency. And we believe the people of Virginia would back him on that issue . . . . Mr. Roosevelt may be counted on to exercise any extraordinary authority wisely and patriotically." After the president declared a national bank holiday, the editor asserted: "America has discovered her true strength. Her courage is unbounded. A supreme opportunity has been seized and turned to the advantage of his country by a dauntless leader, and America is ready to go places and do things!"[5]

Two days before the nationwide closing of banks, Governor Pollard declared a bank holiday in Virginia, explaining that the state "could have acted without the holiday except for banks in other States tying up Virginia funds." Old Dominion banks were in remarkably good condition. Suspensions and closings were far below the national average, and several banks had declared regular dividends and reported increased earnings in 1932. Norfolk banks even expressed some objection to the holiday. Banks reopened on March 14, and the nation and Virginia prepared to move forward with their new president.[6]

Although increased spending was anathema to their conservative consciences, Virginians greeted the legislation of this congressional session—the Hundred Days—warmly. The president's quick seizure of command and his initial economizing by reducing federal salaries temporarily restored business confidence. Virginia cities reported an upswing in business activity, employment, and food prices. Even such radical departures from traditional governmental practices as the Tennessee Valley Authority (TVA), the Agricultural Adjustment Administration (AAA), and the Civilian Conservation Corps (CCC) drew general support from the state's congressional delegation and the press. The Portsmouth *Star* observed: "It is rather important that we refuse to get excited by the prospect of radical changes. A new deal is, after all, a new deal. It ought to be plain to the blindest man that our old ways of handling all these things no longer work. We need, above all else, to be daring. If we are going to have great changes—well, let's have them, and more power to them." The *Times-Dispatch* was undeterred by the cost of the relief program when it declared: "Work must be provided. Government dollars must go to it just as Government dollars went to the army and the navy in times of war . . . . Mr. Roosevelt is facing the problem squarely. He is economizing elsewhere that he may relieve unemployment."[7]

Only Senator Glass among leading Virginians criticized the measures adopted by the New Dealers. Taking an opposite tack from the Virginia press, he warned: "Roosevelt is driving this country to destruction faster than it has ever moved before. Congress is giving this inexperienced man greater power than that possessed by Mussolini and Stalin, put together."[8] But Glass's votes against most of the important pieces of legislation put him in the minority. Except for the beer bill and an early vote on NRA (he cast an affirmative vote on the final bill), Harry Byrd did not join his colleague in protest of the New Deal. Even Glass's own newspaper, the Lynchburg *News*, in summation of the Hundred Days, refrained from attacking the revolutionary nature of the legislation and credited Roosevelt with "boldness and determination." Reviewing the session, the Portsmouth *Star* concluded: "It proved that the legislative branch of a Democratic government can work efficiently and speedily if the executive branch knows how to demand it. It justified our traditional faith in our representative democracy." The *Times-Dispatch* eulogized, "Franklin Roosevelt will rate with our greatest Presidents."[9]

This confidence in the new leader and his program contributed to the upswing in the nation's economy that continued through the summer months. The June Federal Reserve report for the Fifth District revealed gains in employment and bank deposits and predicted better farm conditions. Several Virginia plants announced wage increases; Dan River Mills returned to full-time operation; and the reopening of the Viscose rayon plant in Roanoke caused the Roanoke *World-News* to rejoice, "The depression is definitely over." However, enough reverses occurred to remind people that such optimism was unwarranted. Strikes materialized at a Martinsville cotton textile plant and at the American Novelty Company in Petersburg; furniture plants in Bassett, Galax, Bristol, and Marion closed temporarily due to higher wage demands; the Blackwood Coal and Coke Company in Wise County went into receivership, as did one of the larger banks in the state, the American Bank and Trust Company of Richmond; and reduced tax collections for 1932 forced cities to make additional cuts in their budgets. At the end of May, Governor Pollard announced another 5 percent salary cut for the state employees and a 30 percent reduction in department appropriations for the second year of the biennium, effective July 1. Although Virginia had begun the fiscal year with a surplus of $560,000 and had cut appropriations by $3 million, the state ended the year with a deficit of $619,000.[10]

Pollard's previous economy measures had produced little complaint, but the announcement of the 30 percent slash brought a vociferous objection from the chairman of the State Corporation Commission, William Fletcher, who blamed such steps for "wrecking the work of State departments and grinding down already underpaid State employees." Education Superintendent Sydney Hall claimed the retrenchment would cause the closing of some county schools in February of the following year and force sixty-two counties to operate less than an eight-month term. He objected to the disregard for public service at the expense of public credit and asked for an additional $700,000 to keep the schools open. Anti-Prohibition forces also attacked the governor, demanding that the state terminate Prohibition and create a new source of revenue in liquor taxes. Requesting a special assembly session, Delegate Vivian Page of Norfolk declared, "Pollard is . . . out of touch with the sentiment of the man on the street and on the farms in Virginia."[11]

The Prohibition preferences of the governor and organization leaders had caused them to reject earlier proposals for a special session, but the pressing demands for rural tax relief and congressional passage of the Twenty-first Amendment repealing Prohibition promoted the movement. As public sentiment grew in favor of repeal (Richmond restaurants were already openly selling beer), Byrd, fearing the issue might influence the upcoming gubernatorial race, shifted course and forced Pollard to capitulate. Over objections that it would be too costly and lead to higher taxes, the governor called a special session to legalize beer, institute repeal machinery, and implement the creation of a federal public works program in Virginia.[12]

The August session of the General Assembly quickly approved this agenda. It permitted the immediate sale of state-taxed beer and improvised a dual referendum striking down national and state Prohibition which Virginians overwhelmingly endorsed in October. Legislation securing the benefits of the National Industrial Recovery Act for Virginia was also passed. The delegates imposed a $500 penalty on violators of National Recovery Administration (NRA) codes and suspended the state antitrust laws for the duration of NRA. In response to the governor's request for approval of the acceptance of a $16 million loan from the federal government for road building, 30 percent of which was to be a grant and 70 percent repayable out of state gasoline taxes, the Assembly assented to the intent of the request without mentioning the amount of money in the act. Finally, in a burst of liberality, it passed an additional appropriation of $150,000 for the public school system to prevent county schools from closing early. Many Virginians believed the loan legislation was unconstitutional, but at that time the recovery program was working its magic on the people and rejection of participation would have been unpopular.[13]

By September, public disavowal of any phase of the Roosevelt program was unthinkable. It seemingly had performed miracles on the economy and on the mood of the people; events in Virginia confirmed this euphoria. Virginia farm prices made remarkable gains, moving up by a third in both June and July, while national farm prices were inching upward less rapidly. H. N. Young of *Virginia Farm Economics* credited the improvement to the April departure from the gold standard. The number of Virginians on some form of relief declined markedly, and a national unemployment census showed Virginia with the second lowest percentage in the country of people on relief. The Virginia Department of Labor noted an increase in employment of 20 to 25 percent since April and estimated unemployment at

60,000 to 70,000. A new deal for the American people had arrived.[14]

The agency primarily responsible for much of this success was the National Recovery Administration. In June 1933, three months after taking office, Roosevelt prodded Congress into enacting the National Industrial Recovery Act, which created a $3.3 billion public works program and launched a complex scheme for economic revitalization. To administer the latter plan, the president established the NRA and appointed General Hugh Johnson as director. Designed to stimulate recovery through industrial self-government, the NRA proposed to reduce unemployment, improve labor standards, and promote cooperation among trade groups and between employers and employees. To accomplish these goals, the NRA permitted business to administer its own affairs, particularly the control of production and prices, with limited government supervision. Suspension of the antitrust laws and the establishment of minimum wage and hour standards and the right of labor to bargain collectively (section 7a) theoretically balanced the interests of management and labor, but the industrialists, primarily through their trade associations, dominated the life of the NRA from the beginning.

The rules by which each industry operated were drawn up into a code agreement negotiated by representatives of government, management, labor, and consumers. Once approved by the president, the code was administered by a code authority, composed of business and labor elements, which created state and local authorities to superintend the code for that industry in their area. Violations of trade and labor practices were reviewed by the authorities, which attempted to obtain compliance with code requirements. Failing that, the NRA endeavored to mediate the dispute, first at the state level and then through regional and national adjustment boards. Final adjudication rested in the courts.[15]

Reflecting a restored sense of confidence generated by Franklin Roosevelt, the agency enjoyed a few months of unparalleled success. The summer of 1933 was the summer of NRA. When code-making negotiations stalled, Hugh Johnson organized a nationwide campaign to get individual employers to sign presidential reemployment agreements signifying their acceptance of the new wage and hour standards. Overnight the country was transformed into a mass parade demonstrating support for the NRA. A blue eagle emblem, displayed to indicate an employer's adoption of the standards, found its way onto the windows of two million businesses. In the face of such public excitement, the major industries began to accept code agreements. The cotton textile code, which had been drawn up before the campaign, set the pattern for the others to follow, reducing the workweek from fifty-five to forty hours and establishing a minimum wage of $12 a week. Robert West, president of Dan River Mills, helped draft this code, which created new jobs as a result of the hour cutback but also boosted the prices of cotton goods.[16]

The intoxicating effect of the NRA spread through the cities of the Old Dominion. Municipalities undertook citywide drives complete with torchlight parades to enlist code participants. Blue eagles appeared on store windows and newspaper mastheads. In Roanoke, "Shanghai Mickey" was tattooing people with blue eagles and the slogan "We Do Our Part" for fifty cents. Chairman of the state drive Mason Manghum estimated that NRA was responsible for reemploying 10,000 Virginians in its first three months. Six months later, John Corson, who eventually became state NRA director, wrote, "Every Virginian . . . is now affected in his daily living by the operations of the National Recovery Administration in this State." Over 31,000 Virginia businesses approved the codes, which supposedly provided better wages and hours for 195,00 workers. In the first months of operation, fewer complaints of code violations were reported in Virginia than in most other states, while local compliance boards across the Commonwealth announced general acceptance of the program by all participants.[17]

These compliance boards began the administration of the NRA in Virginia in September 1933. Informally attempting to adjust disputes between management and labor, they became less important once state machinery went into operation. The state NRA office, which opened in Richmond in January 1934, acted as liaison between Washington, the code authorities, and employers and employees. It reviewed most of the complaints received, passing along a few cases of a technical or more complex nature to the state adjustment board and the rest to Washington. The Adjustment Review Board, in its eight meetings, handled twenty-one cases and made seventeen adjustments, upholding the ruling of the state office each time. The three board members were Colonel Le Roy Hodges, managing director of the Virginia State Chamber of Commerce, the neutral member; B. G. Slaughter, former president of Tubize-Chatillon Rayon Corporation, who represented industry; and R. T. Bowden, former Virginia Federation of Labor (VFL) president, who represented labor. The local boards had similar representation. Through General Assembly action, Virginia was one of twelve states that had complementary legislation making the NRA applicable to firms in intrastate commerce and imposing a $500 fine on violators; however, these provisions were rarely invoked.[18]

By the beginning of 1934 the cries of consumers, labor, and industry about the deficiencies of the NRA were increasing in number and volume. Rising prices, the reluctance of business to recognize labor, and Hugh Johnson's bombastic nature were cited as the agency's prominent liabilities. A National Recovery Review Board, headed by famed lawyer Clarence Darrow, condemned the NRA for its monopolistic features and recommended a return to the antitrust laws. In September, Roosevelt ordered a reorganization and pressured Johnson to resign.[19]

Despite the initial support given the NRA in Virginia, the honeymoon was brief. The editor of the Farmville *Herald,* an ardent advocate of the NRA in the summer of 1933, wrote six months later, "We do not think the blessings of NRA may be found in Farmville." The state director reported that enthusiasm for the various codes waned quickly after the initial glow of success. Among the code authorities in the state, only those of the motor vehicle retailing trade and the lumber and timber industry cooperated fully with the state office, while those of the baking industry, the cleaning and dyeing trade, and the retail drug trade adopted a more unfriendly attitude.[20]

Three months after the Virginia office formally opened, 500 complaints had been received, many of them involving unfair practices by grocery stores, restaurants, lumber and timber firms, and furniture manufacturers. Most protests arose over wage and hour violations. One Norfolk employer told his employees that he had joined "for the record" and that those who complained of no pay raises would be fired; other employers raised wages and then were repaid by employees for "services rendered"; elsewhere, minimum wages became maximum rates. Two unusual entreaties illustrate the insurmountable problems faced by NRA officials. A Richmond restaurant cook objected to a rearrangement of his working hours which prevented his hearing "Amos and Andy" each evening. In another bizarre case a young bride wrote to the Virginia NRA demanding to know why her husband had to work all night long. Upon investigation, it was found the fault did not lie with the codes but with another woman. The failure of industry to recognize labor's right to organize and bargain collectively, a management policy of long standing in the weakly organized South, produced repeated charges from the Virginia Federation of Labor and individual labor unions that section 7a was being violated; in some instances strikes occurred over this.[21]

Industry, too, registered many complaints. Before the NRA was established, southern wage scales had been considerably lower than those in the rest of the country. To avoid financial hardship for southern businesses, NRA officials established wage differentials between the regions that raised wages in the South but left them lower than the northern scales. Even with this concession, however, NRA codes injured small southern businesses, whose owners complained of higher labor costs and the monopolistic practices of their larger competitors. Two Virginia slate companies declared they would have to close unless they could be exempted from the NRA wage scales, and the canning industry in Westmoreland County was sharply curtailed by increased wages and costs of materials. The Union Envelope Company of Richmond, forced to discharge forty people because of the higher standards, asked for an exemption for longer hours to meet its contract commitments, but the request was denied. In addition, some Virginia industries were grouped with their northern counterparts and denied wage differentials. Many of the state's industrialists, including James F. Ryland, president of the Virginia Manufacturers Association (VMA), objected to this discrimination.[22]

The closing of small marginal firms imposed special hardships on their released employees, many of whom were blacks who were particularly hard hit by NRA policies. The low income occupations traditionally available to blacks, such as domestic work, were exempted from wage standards, causing much suffering among these workers as prices rose. In the businesses that remained opened, Negroes holding jobs affected by the codes frequently were replaced by whites when their wages rose to minimum levels. Said the Norfolk *Journal and Guide,* "Recovery cannot be accomplished by bestowing all the benefits of the NRA upon white workers and crucifying Negro workers on an economic cross."[23]

The inadequacies of the codes, which were burdened by a mass of details about pricing procedures, wage and hour provisions, and production controls, were a major problem facing the NRA on the state and national scene. Responsible for the administration of over 500 codes, including the dog-food and horsehair-dressing industries, the NRA was inundated with thousands of reported infractions. The case against Economy Casket Company of Portsmouth, which lost its blue eagle for violating the funeral supply code, was an example of this bureaucratic overkill. Rising prices, which outstripped wage increases and negated additional buying power for the consumer, also contributed to the agency's ineffectiveness in stimulating recovery. Dan River Mills raised wages almost 50 percent, but the reduction of the workweek to forty hours limited the net gain to 11 percent, hardly enough to cover the inflating cost of living. Furthermore, the retail code exempted towns under 2,500 population and businesses employing five or fewer persons, making it effective in only forty-three Virginia communities.[24]

A related shortcoming of the NRA was its lack of enforcement power. State Director Corson wrote, "Moral persuasion plus removal of the Blue Eagle Emblem is the only means of enforcing . . . a Code, and the latter means at this time does not prove very effective." The G & H Clothing plant in Fredericksburg, which had closed and put 500 persons out of work rather than comply with an NRA order to restore $200,000 in back wages and operate under the codes, resumed business under a federal court injunction preventing the NRA from enforcing its ruling. The subsequent loss of their blue eagle did not deter the owners from operating. Nor did it impress Richmond cleaners and dyers, whose trade practices had been outlawed by the NRA. A spokesman concluded: "We are through with codes and eagles. Richmond cleaners and dyers will be able to get along hereafter without any interference from the NRA and we will not apply for the new insignia." Standard Drug Company of Richmond, which also lost its blue eagle for selling items below minimum price, denied it had ever been given one.[25]

Old Dominion political leaders, who had opposed the NRA from its inception, did not lament its difficulties. Fourth District Congressman Patrick Henry Drewry claimed that the establishment of the NRA was an unconstitutional act and apologized for having voted for it because "our jobs are dependent on being 'regular' until the fickle public finds it has been buncoed."[26] The leading opponent of the NRA was Carter Glass. Writing to Representative James Beck of Pennsylvania, the senator bitterly assailed the legislation: "The so-called Recovery Act is not only unconstitutional, but it has been administered with a degree of brutality that has created a reign of terror and put industry, and individual business, in involuntary servitude." The old Jeffersonian objected to using the blue eagle on his Lynchburg newspaper and challenged Johnson to enforce the codes against him. Addressing another Virginia publisher, Glass said: "It is difficult to know how to advise you since you do not indicate whether or not you signed this code. If you did make the mistake of signing it, you should keep your agreement. If you did not sign it, and I were in your place, I would tell them to go to hell." In an even more vitriolic letter to Walter Lippmann, Glass excoriated the NRA as an attempt "to transplant Hitlerism to every corner of this nation." The senator raged:

The government itself has resorted to blackmail, boycott and to a species of threats that will forever mark a black page in the history of the country. I had a personal interview with General Johnson last week, at which I plainly told him that his blue eagle was fast becoming a bird of prey and that he was creating a reign of terror among thousands of struggling small industries which are threatened with bankruptcy by reason of the brutal methods employed. I personally know this to be a fact with respect to my own state and its industries, and I have no reason to think it is different in any other state. Thousands of the very concerns which are publicly exhibiting the blue eagle are privately cursing the symbol as a black buzzard.[27]

A Virginia Manufacturers Association poll of sixty-eight businesses in the state appeared to bear Glass out. Thirteen firms desired continuation of the NRA, twenty-eight favored its dissolution, and fifteen thought it should be continued with modifications. The VMA concluded, "NRA is not entirely satisfactory." However, a survey conducted by the *Times-Dispatch* of six selected industries and businesses presented a more favorable picture of the NRA's acceptance in Virginia. The retail automobile trade was two-to-one in favor of its continuation. Most dealers reported better business along with higher profits, wages, employment, and costs. The retail druggists approved of the NRA by a nine-to-one margin. Sales, profits, employment, costs, and wages were all up 11 to 15 percent. Nevertheless, one recalcitrant owner said, "Repeal the whole damn thing and let us go back to the United States Constitution." The wholesale food and grocery trade was two-to-one in favor of the NRA and reported gains similar to those of the drug trade. On the other hand, dissatisfaction with the NRA was great in the retail lumber business despite higher profits. Both the solid fuel and construction industries disclosed declines in profits and employment and rising costs. While men in these groups desired modifications in the NRA, the construction contractors, when asked for a definite yes or no on the NRA's continuation, responded negatively, three-to-one. Most complaints from all trades listed the greatest deficiencies as noncompliance in the respective industries, a failure to enforce regulations, and high wages. Virginia Electric and Power Company blamed the NRA for higher operating expenses due to increased fuel prices and labor costs.[28]

Like the state's senior senator, the Virginia press quickly lost enthusiasm for the NRA. The Lynchburg *News* believed any reorganization should be based on the "abandonment of the dictatorial methods pursued by the NRA and lessening of the powers of that administrative body." The *News* had put NRA hours and wages into effect but did not subscribe to the code, an act which, the editors thought, "might involve the surrender of rights guaranteed by the Constitution of the United States." The Richmond *Planet* viewed the NRA as a flop and of no help to the Negro; the *Journal and Guide* labeled it the "Negro Removal Act." Virginia editors maintained that the NRA should have confined its efforts to the large industries rather than attempting to regulate every business in the country. The *Times-Dispatch* and Portsmouth *Star*, both of which had strongly supported the NRA in the beginning despite its revolutionary nature, concluded that it had outlived its usefulness, The *Star* acknowledged:

We began with a great fanfare of trumpets, and some of the enthusiastic saw the New Jerusalem, or something like it, coming down out of the clouds. Wages were going to be raised, profits were going to be assured, men were going to be put to work, and chiselers were going to bleed and die, willy-nilly.

So we got started. And little by little the bright colors faded. What looked simple, in the first flush of excitement, began to appear remarkably complex.

Some men were put back to work, but the unemployment problem continued to grow. Some profits increased and others vanished.

Some wages went up and others did not. Chiselers bled and died only sporadically, and not by platoons.

So now we come to a great reorganization, under new leadership, and there is much disillusionment about it all.[29]

On May 27, 1935, the Supreme Court in a unanimous decision declared the NRA unconstitutional, finding the power to fix wages and hours by codes an illegal delegation of congressional power. Following a year of disenchantment, the decision was neither unexpected nor entirely unwelcome. Although the NRA had increased employment and wages, restored confidence in the government's ability to effect improvement, and fostered better working conditions, it had not tapped the spirit of cooperation among government, business, and labor that full recovery required. Price fixing, the avoidance of collective bargaining, and profit making through price increases rather than business expansion all indicated that business was unable or unwilling to consider the needs of the consumer and laborer while advancing its own interests. The experiment in industrial self-government had failed.[30]

In Virginia the Court's decision was hailed in some quarters and resignedly accepted in others as unfortunate but necessary. State Director Corson called it "timely" but hoped new legislation would preserve the best features of the NRA.[31] Ninth District Congressman John Flannagan was more emphatic: "If the Constitution stands in the way of regulating by law ruthless and unfair competition, protecting labor by fixing minimum wages and hours . . . and abolishing child labor and the sweat shop, then it is high time we amend our Constitution."[32] The *Times-Dispatch* was concerned about the effect on the economy of such an immediate liquidation and recommended an NRA replacement, while other newspapers, pointing to the good that had been accomplished, feared an erosion of the standards that NRA codes had set. The Roanoke *World-News*, however, reveled at the defeat of the "unauthorized attempts of brain trusters to make America over." And the Richmond *News-Leader* concluded, "Under the great fear of the depression, the mob-mind of the American people was aroused in support of a well-intentioned but dangerously unlawful exercise of dictatorial power by the president with the consent of Congress." Both Virginia senators were pleased with the Court's decision; Glass tartly remarked, "I have always been opposed to any such exercise of tyranny as was practiced under the act."[33]

Labor Commissioner Hall had a far different view of the value of NRA. While conceding the deficiencies of the program, he attributed recovery in Virginia to the NRA's codes and the public works expenditures. He cited better working conditions, higher wages, and declining unemployment as evidence of the NRA's contribution to the state's revitalized economy. After the Recovery Administration was terminated, Hall noted an increase in child labor and more numerous violations of maximum hour laws. Other labor officials lamented its loss and looked to the newly proposed Wagner Act to maintain collective bargaining rights. Past VFL President R. T. Bowden said, "I can't conceive that the country would be willing to give up the obvious benefits . . . derived from NRA." W. E. Robinson of the

Richmond Trades and Labor Council criticized the Court for being "out of touch with the times."[34]

Fearing a return to unfair practices and cutthroat competition, many merchants indicated that they would voluntarily uphold the NRA wage and hour standards, action that was urged by the governor and the Richmond Chamber of Commerce. The state NRA office said it would accept and publish statements of compliance from businesses that followed this course. Large firms such as Dan River Mills, Virginia Carolina Chemical Corporation, and the American Tobacco Company had no difficulty in continuing NRA standards, but smaller companies were among the first to extend hours and cut wages. Within five months some furniture companies were reported working sixty-hour weeks and paying twenty to thirty cents an hour with no overtime pay. Dry-cleaning plants and the lumber companies were the most frequent violators.[35]

In sixteen months of code administration the state NRA office received 3,916 complaints alleging code violations. Over one thousand were immediately rejected as unfounded and were not investigated. The remaining 2,888 cases, of which 80 percent were wage and hour complaints, involved 190 different codes; they were either adjusted, rejected, or referred to other agencies. Eleven blue eagles were removed for labor violations, while many others, especially among canning firms, were taken away by regional office decisions. The state office remained open until January 1936, staffed by a skeleton force which compiled lists of post-NRA code violators and submitted final reports.[36].

Ill-conceived and too reliant on business and labor to divest themselves of self-interest, the NRA proved not to be the panacea for permanent national recovery. Unemployment did not decline appreciably, and 1920s prosperity did not return. While its impact in Virginia was favorable because the state's workers benefited from the most minimal improvements, even in the Old Dominion its liabilities were apparent: too many codes, too many bureaucrats, too little muscle, and too little trust. Roosevelt had discovered that economic recovery demanded more than fireside chats and blue eagle emblems.

If the NRA could not satisfy the appetite of a depressed

economy, other legislation produced by the Hundred Days was life-sustaining. The New Deal directed its major efforts toward the relief of the unemployed and the farmer. Through the Federal Emergency Relief Administration (FERA), the Works Progress Administration (WPA), and the Agricultural Adjustment Administration (AAA), aid was tendered these elements of society who were hardest hit by the depression. The size of this effort requires separate treatment of the relief and farm programs in subsequent chapters. Less noteworthy, but of considerable importance in relieving depression conditions, were the New Deal public works, conservation, and housing programs.

Among the largest disbursers of relief was the Public Works Administration (PWA), which, under the direction of Harold Ickes, secretary of the interior, managed the $3.3 billion public works program created by the Industrial Recovery Act. Prudently operating under Ickes's scandal-proof guidelines, the PWA funded local projects up to 30 percent of their cost (later increased to 45 percent). The remainder of the cost had to be borne by the sponsor but could be financed with loans from the PWA. Each state had an advisory board which acted as intermediary between the community and Washington. The PWA paid a minimum of forty-five cents an hour for unskilled labor and $1.10 for skilled workers for a maximum thirty-hour week. Although workers were to be drawn from the relief rolls of the community, only 30 percent of total costs had to be spent on labor, suggesting that the PWA was more oriented toward pump priming the economy than assisting the unemployed. Schools, public buildings, bridges, municipal power plants, sewer and water systems, and hospitals all were acceptable projects to the PWA if they could prove themselves economically feasible.[37]

The benefits of this program were not immediately apparent in the Old Dominion. Although the PWA allotted $7.4 million to the Virginia highway department for road construction, and plans were made to have PWA continue the building of several post offices begun by the RFC, localities initially were reluctant to apply for the federal largesse because 70 percent of the cost had to be appropriated from the local treasury or borrowed from the PWA. They were also opposed to paying the minimum wage of forty-five cents an hour, which was above the prevailing wage in some areas. Shenandoah and Frederick counties both turned down loans for schools because of these reasons. Additionally, Virginia officials bellowed at the large proportion of PWA funds spent on federal projects, notably military expenditures, at the expense of state improvements, and they prevented the state from tapping the $16 million loan for roads, fearing its unconstitutionality. The hesitation and objections, however, did not deter the PWA from offering money to the Old Dominion. The agency approved a $3 million hydroelectric plant for Danville, a $2.5 million sewer complex in Arlington County, a $663,000 public housing project in Richmond, and a $600,000 waterworks for Lynchburg. In its first year of operation, the PWA approved $90 million worth of projects in Virginia, $82 million of which were federal.[38]

Electric power plants were among the most beneficial of the PWA projects, providing increased power and reduced electric rates for the community. Private utilities, including Vepco, at one time challenged the right of the PWA to loan money for publicly owned power plants, but the Supreme Court upheld the legality of the PWA's entry into this field; a South Norfolk power project, one of those in contention, was allowed to proceed. Although Culpeper had the first municipal electric facility to be built with PWA funds, the most noteworthy power plant project in Virginia was the Pinnacles unit outside Danville. Rejecting the first PWA offer to finance 30 percent of the $3.4 million project, residents approved in October 1935 a 45 percent grant and the accompanying city bond issue. The power site was in the mountains eighty-five miles from Danville at the headwaters of the Dan River. The PWA eventually paid $1.5 million for the plant, access roads, conservation measures, and a secondary storage dam. The dam was dedicated and operations were begun on a partial basis in June 1938.[39]

Education facilities in Virginia also received PWA money. In its first three years of operation state schools received $11.8 million from the PWA—$6.2 million for secondary education buildings and the rest for higher education; $1.75 million of this went to Negro schools. From 1933 to 1937 the PWA either replaced or improved 175 structures serving 35,000 students. Much of the effort went into consolidating the weak county systems with their widely dispersed, run-down, costly-to-operate schools. Raymond Long, director of school buildings for the state Board of Education, commended the PWA's work in Virginia in a letter to Secretary Ickes: "On behalf of the public schools and institutions of higher learning in Virginia, may we offer our sincere appreciation to the Public Works Administration for the outstanding opportunity it has offered the public schools and educational institutions in Virginia to improve our physical plants under the Public Works Program . . . . may [it] be possible to continue a somewhat similar program that may bring even more far-reaching results." Long acknowledged that without PWA help school-building improvement could not have taken place. He also praised PWA's bond-financing methods as the "most valuable contribution to the field of municipal finance in the last twenty years." A General Assembly act of the special session of 1933 had authorized localities and institutions of higher learning to accept federal loans on self-liquidating projects and issue bonds with which to pay them off. In the case of the colleges, permission of the governor was necessary and the bonds were repayable only with student fees, not with public funds. The PWA often purchased these bonds when banks would not. Several buildings at VPI, William and Mary, and Mary Washington were financed in this manner.[40]

Numerous other structures were included in the list of PWA achievements. The agency built or added to hospitals at Hopewell, the Medical College of Virginia, the University of Virginia, the Eastern State Hospital for the Insane at Williamsburg, and the Veterans Administration Hospital at Roanoke. In addition to financing city public housing and slum clearance programs, the PWA through its own housing division constructed low-cost housing developments across the country. The first one, and the only one in Virginia, was at Altavista where fifty small units were put up at a cost of $100,000. The PWA constructed two libraries in the state—Alderman Library at the University of Virginia and the $1.8 million State Library in Richmond, $800,000 of whose cost was paid for by the federal government. Attentive to the needs of the black community,

PWA channeled funds to Virginia State College, elementary schools, and recreation centers.[41]

After their initial objections, Virginians responded favorably to the PWA. As recovery set in and communities could better afford to finance their share—now reduced to 55 percent—drawing-board projects became realities. Because of their more permanent value and the nature of the construction work involved, PWA projects were preferred over the smaller "makework" projects of the WPA. Furthermore, Ickes's tightfisted administration satisfied the public that the dollars were being spent carefully. Even Carter Glass in a charitable moment wrote Ickes, "I have always been confident . . . that the public funds expended by you had been more prudently and economically handled than the funds expended by any other public official in Washington."[42]

Relations between Ickes and the Virginia senators were not always so cordial. In March 1935 when Ickes threatened to halt work on Skyline Drive for lack of funds, a ploy designed to divert Byrd's attacks on a new multibillion dollar relief bill, the junior senator demanded a probe of PWA to determine how much of the original $3.3 billion was left. When the treasury reported that $1½ billion was still unspent (although most of this had been obligated), Ickes's plot backfired. Further friction arose during the 1938 "purges" when Ickes blasted Glass as "typical of the political hyprocrites that bite the hand that feeds them . . . . no Senator comes oftener and with more insistence for PWA grants than does . . . Senator Glass." Labeling this a "wanton falsehood," Glass called Ickes a "confirmed blackguard" and defended his record of standing on convictions while advancing the interests of his constituents. In spite of these encounters, Virginia continued to receive PWA money.[43]

Economic recovery and new economy measures in 1937 led to a decision to allow no new proposals, but the onset of recession soon forced the president to ask Congress for additional billions for relief. The opening of a new treasure trove provided money for Richmond's deepwater terminal, a Staunton sewer system and sewage treatment plant, Newport News harbor improvements, schools and university buildings, and other Virginia projects totaling $4.8 million, of which the PWA would pay $2.2 million. Mayor Fulmer Bright believed the loans and grants would inaugurate "a new era of marked prosperity for the City of Richmond."[44]

In a six-year period the PWA financed the most colossal building program in the nation's history. It spent over $4 billion on 34,522 projects in every section of the country. Virginia had 350 nonfederal projects costing almost $60 million, of which the PWA granted or loaned $32 million. It paid an additional $85.3 million for 740 federal projects in the Old Dominion, including ships, a wind tunnel, military barracks, the Colonial, Blue Ridge, and Skyline parkways, post offices, and other federal buildings. Hampered by a mountain of paperwork and numerous complaints about wages, the PWA surmounted these obstacles to leave a record of unquestioned value to the nation and to Virginia.[45]

Perhaps the most popular New Deal program in Virginia was the Civilian Conservation Corps (CCC). The concept of a character-building adventure in the nation's forests to alleviate unemployment and beautify the countryside had both a practical and idyllic appeal. Although there were sporadic cries of creeping militarism and some comparisons drawn between the Corps and the Fascist Youth Leagues, the legislation creating and financing the CCC had no difficulty passing Congress. Said the *Times-Dispatch*, "If reforestation has a Fascist tinge, then we must grin and bear it. If it smacks of Sovietism we shall let Moscow make the best of it. This is a grim war, and it must be fought out with the best weapons available. It is not time to stand on fine spun theories." After the CCC had been in existence for two-and-a-half years, Wilbur Hall, chairman of the Virginia Conservation and Development Commission, expressed a desire that it "be made a permanent part of American governmental life."[46]

The CCC selected unmarried, unemployed young men between the ages of eighteen and twenty-five to spend six months in camps doing conservation work. They were paid a $1 a day, most of which was sent to their parents in $25 monthly allotments. Direction, discipline, and some vocational training were provided by military and civilian supervisors. Governor Pollard quickly enlisted Virginia's youth in the program and easily filled the initial quota of 5,000. The first CCC camp, Camp Roosevelt, was set up at Luray in the George Washington National Forest; by 1937 over eighty camps had been established in Virginia, twelve of which were for Negroes, with monthly enrollments ranging from 5,000 to 20,000.[47]

In its nine years of work, the CCC spent $109 million in Virginia, the fifth largest state expenditure in the country. The state ranked fourth in the number of camps and seventeenth in the total number of native enrollees. The CCC employed 107,210 at one time or another in the Old Dominion, 64,762 of whom were Virginia youth and 10,435 of whom were native camp officers and supervisors. Their contribution to the state was monumental: 15.2 million trees planted in reforestation and erosion control, 986 bridges constructed, fire hazards reduced over 152,000 acres, 2,128 miles of new telephone line strung, and 1.3 million fish stocked. The conservationists stressed erosion and flood control, forest landscaping, and improved wildlife conditions, but they also worked on the restoration of historical sites at Jamestown, Williamsburg, Yorktown, Fredericksburg, and Spotsylvania and combated floods along the James and Potomac rivers. The final Virginia report summarized, "In no State did the CCC make a greater or more lasting contribution to the well-being of its citizens than it did in Virginia." John Guthrie of Charlotte Court House, who became general inspector of the CCC, believed its work was a godsend for the army and navy when war came.[48]

The development of a park system was an important gift of the New Deal and the CCC to Virginia, which before 1933 had no state parks. One park had been donated to Virginia in 1932, the Richmond Battlefield Park, but no funds were available to develop it, and it was eventually turned over to the National Park Service. The CCC, providing the labor and materials, created a $5 million system which cost Virginia only $100,000—"the biggest bargain of the New Deal." In June 1936 six state parks— Westmoreland, Cape Henry (Seashore State), Fairystone in Patrick County, Staunton River near Roanoke, Douthat in Bath and Alleghany Counties, and Hungry Mother west of Marion—

were opened. Emerging from the depression at the time, Virginia made funds available through the Conservation and Development Commission to continue operation of the parks. Shenandoah National Park and Skyline Drive also were opened under the auspices of the New Deal, which provided the money to complete the road and its extension, the Blue Ridge Parkway, which ran all the way south to the Great Smokies.[49]

The impact of the Tennessee Valley Authority (TVA) in the Old Dominion was less significant than that of the CCC. Created May 18, 1933, the TVA administered an integrated river valley system designed to stimulate agricultural and industrial development, improve navigational opportunities, control flooding, foster conservation programs, and provide electric power to the people of the region. Virginia was originally included among the seven states participating in this regional development program because the Powell, Holston, and Clinch rivers rising in southwestern Virginia drain into the Tennessee River. However, the area involved was so distant from the major construction efforts along the river that few Virginians were affected by the TVA. It was not until 1945 that a contract was let with the city of Bristol to provide TVA power for about 5,000 customers. A decade later sales to Virginia were expanded through contract with the Powell Valley Electric Cooperative in Jonesville. The TVA made a modest contribution to several thousand Virginia farmers who used its fertilizers and participated in its soil conservation programs.[50]

Another form of "conservation" was the New Deal effort to save homes from foreclosure. At the time of Roosevelt's inauguration, over 1,000 homes a day were being foreclosed. To ease this problem Congress created the Home Owners' Loan Corporation (HOLC), which was authorized to exchange its bonds for the mortgages in difficulty. The agency guaranteed the interest and later the principal of the bonds, thus protecting the interests of the real estate dealers and bankers. Easier payment terms were negotiated with the mortgagee, who was then responsible for paying off the "loan" to the HOLC. With a state office in Richmond and district offices in Norfolk, Roanoke, Danville, Harrisonburg, and Alexandria, Virginians took advantage of this service. Once the guarantees were made clear, Virginia real estate dealers and building and loan associations enthusiastically supported the HOLC program. During its existence, the agency loaned $38 million to 12,031 Old Dominion homeowners. Because the severity of the depression was diminished in Virginia, the ratio of applicants to those eligible was lower in the state than in the rest of the country. Thirty-eight percent of those homeowners eligible in Virginia applied for loans, the fourteenth lowest percentage in the nation. The percentage in Arkansas and Mississippi was over 90 percent; in twenty-five states, it was over 50 percent.[51]

Whereas the HOLC was oriented toward immediate relief, the Federal Housing Administration (FHA), established by the National Housing Act of 1934, aimed at more permanent recovery. Designed to stimulate the construction industry, the FHA insured the loans of private lending agencies to individuals who desired to modernize their homes or build new homes. Title I of the act—home repair and modernization—which provided "guaranteed" loans up to $2,000 at 5 percent interest with up to three years to pay, went into effect almost at once. Within three months, Virginia banks loaned over $500,000 to 1,338 recipients. In January 1935 Title II of the housing act became effective, and the FHA began insuring bank loans for new home construction. In fifteen months 1,313 mortgage loans totaling over $5 million were approved in Virginia. Through the end of 1937, private institutions in the state loaned $7.4 million under Title I and $20.1 million under Title II. Although the FHA also financed a few low-cost housing projects, it was not until the creation of the United States Housing Authority in 1937 that slum clearance programs were begun to provide housing for the nation's one-third ill-housed. By 1941 fifteen such developments were under way in Virginia.[52]

Although public works and housing programs would have their greatest impact over the long term, these and other alphabet agencies also had an immediate effect on the popular mood and on the economy, with the comforting assurances of the president and the early momentum of the NRA having particularly positive results. Martin Hutchinson, a Richmond lawyer and secretary of the Democratic state committee, best described the state of things in Virginia in late 1933 when he wrote, "Business conditions do not seem to improve here in Richmond, but I have the feeling that we are at least in better condition at this time than we were last year at this time." Reviewing conditions in their respective cities, newspapers in Roanoke and Danville corroborated his assessment. Statistics also confirmed that 1933 was a year of improvement for the state. Farmers enjoyed higher crop production and crop values over those of 1932; cash income rose 13 percent to $79 million. Cotton, peanuts, and potatoes all increased in value, but tobacco scored the biggest gains as production almost doubled and the average price rose to $12.60 per hundred pounds. In manufacturing, value of output rose to $616 million, and the number of employed and the amount of wages paid inched upward slowly.[53]

However, the depression was far from totally relieved. The bloom was wearing off the NRA and the country faced another winter of severe unemployment. Congressman Drewry wrote to his son Jack: "Everything OK—except finances—hang on until November 4th. Sorry, old sport, but times are hard. I am scratching . . . vigorously . . . to keep things going." From a friend of his who worked as a freight agent on the Norfolk and Western Railway Drewry heard, "Business since October 1st has steadily declined—It does not look good." Reflecting rural sentiment in the state, Curry Hutchinson, a clerk of the Virginia Senate from Giles County, wrote to his brother Martin, "There is an awful undercurrent of unrest in all agricultural sections . . . our state needs good roads worse than it does silver lined and gold trimmed schoolhouses, or SKYLINE Drives."[54] Although the new president was demonstrating what could be done when boldness replaced indecision, the New Deal had not rolled back the depression but had only begun the long, tedious lifting of its heavy burden.

4
"Bread and Circuses"
FERA

Although agencies such as the CCC and the PWA eventually employed millions of people and pumped billions of dollars into the economy, immediate relief for the jobless was the most pressing need confronting the New Deal. The failure of overextended local and private relief facilities to meet the crisis threatened to reduce many Americans to a pauper's existence. Some state governments and the Hoover administration had made modest efforts to alleviate the misery of the unemployed, but they were restrained from doing more by political factionalism and the prevalent ethic of rugged individualism. Franklin Roosevelt did not face such constraints. While he, too, was a product of the Puritan ethic, his pragmatic nature allowed him to cast aside this self-help philosophy and experiment with a variety of approaches to the problems of depression. Nowhere did Roosevelt break more with traditional concepts about the role of government than in the field of public relief.

The first relief bill, the Emergency Relief Act of May 1933, made available $500 million in grants to the states for relief, half of which was to be distributed on a matching basis, with the other half to be used on a discretionary basis where it was needed the most. The bill created the Federal Emergency Relief Administration (FERA) to supervise the distribution of these funds and define general policy. To oversee this program Roosevelt appointed Harry Hopkins, the innovative and indefatigable social worker from Iowa who had headed his New York relief administration. The FERA proposed to furnish food, clothing, and shelter for the destitute and to provide work relief for employables where possible. State agencies would supervise the program and submit plans for federal approval, while local relief units would direct individual projects. This division of responsibilities limited federal control and led to frequent debates between Washington and state capitals over policy and funding. The conflicts prevented the achievement of uniform minimum standards, but suffering was greatly relieved because the FERA usually followed the more generous policy of giving funds where the needs were greatest, often disregarding the failure of many states to match the grants.[1]

Virginia was one of those states which never authorized funds for direct relief until after the FERA was terminated. From the inception of the federal relief programs, state leaders claimed that money spent providing work for the unemployed on the highways was the equivalent of direct relief appropriations. Relief officials retorted that Virginia was sacrificing not at all since other states were spending for both roads and relief. The argument lasted for the life of the FERA, and although Hopkins threatened to end allotments to Virginia, he never carried out his ultimatum, a decision which allowed the Old Dominion to follow a more independent course of action.

Having inadequate statewide welfare facilities and no experience in direct relief, Virginia initially was ill equipped to handle the large sums of money disbursed by the FERA. During its first half year of existence, the FERA was primarily a dole disburser, and the Old Dominion was not a major recipient. About 80,000 to 100,000 Virginians were on relief during 1933. A Virginia Emergency Relief Administration (VERA) was created in June 1933 to administer the funds, and William A. Smith, a Petersburg engineer with city management experience, was appointed relief administrator. "A good organizer" with "good political contacts," Smith was responsible to the governor, not to Washington, which raised doubts about his independence of the Byrd organization. While he was not an authoritative personality and could never convince his superiors to abandon their highway relief philosophy, Smith's leadership of the VERA and later of the Virginia WPA provided the state with efficient and honest administration of relief monies.[2]

By late 1933 it was obvious to Hopkins that winter would bring an increase in the number of unemployed and more acute demands for food, clothing, shelter, and fuel. To combat this crisis, he convinced Roosevelt to create the Civil Works Administration (CWA) to employ four million Americans on a variety of small work projects devised at the local level but approved and supervised by Washington. Hopkins used the FERA machinery in the states to implement the CWA, often appointing the state FERA administrators to serve as CWA directors; now, however, they would be on his payroll in addition to serving in their state jobs. The federal government contributed 90 percent of the $952 million cost of the CWA, using PWA money, funds from the FERA (which continued a curtailed direct relief program), and an additional emergency relief appropriation. Despite the prevalence of numerous "make-work" projects and the charges of waste, corruption, political favoritism, and inefficiency, the CWA saw the nation through the winter of 1933–34, employing more than the four million originally intended while serving as the forerunner of more extensive work relief programs.[3]

The transformation of Virginia into a relief-conscious area was the most remarkable achievement of the CWA in the state. Over 200,000 unemployed Virginians were registered, two-thirds of whom were from rural areas; the maximum number of workers employed at one time was 82,122 in January 1934. Utilizing local public welfare units, CWA Director Smith appointed civil works committees to submit projects and administer them once they were approved by Washington. In four-and-one-half months the agency expended almost $13 million in Virginia, all but $753,000 of it in federal funds. Seventy-five percent of it went for payrolls on projects whose costs ranged from $50 to $118,000. The money financed school improvements, street and road construction, improved sanitation facilities, public buildings, parks, mosquito control, and airport projects. Matching funds were not required, and Virginia officials were relieved that "the State could get federal money without making large appropriations from its own treasury." Only five states—Georgia, Idaho, Missouri, Nevada, and Tennessee—gave less than the $1,094 contributed by the Old Dominion.[4] The works program enabled thousands of Virginians to survive the winter in far better condition than would have otherwise been the case and gave impetus to relief organization in Virginia. Richmond District head H. H. McCanna commented, "Time and again CWA employees stated that their jobs had been 'lifesavers' to them, and there was no doubt that the statement was the truth. . . . most important was the social uplift to the individual that could be tangibly recognized in instances too numerous to mention."[5] Even the *Times-Dispatch*, which had been critical of the cost and the reported corruption, commended state administrators for their "character, intelligence, and honesty" and concluded that the CWA had been an "influence for good."[6]

Because of the high cost of this initial federal work relief program, Hopkins decided to terminate it and return to the direct relief efforts of the FERA. However, the success of the CWA and his own inclination in favor of work relief prompted him to divert more FERA funds into this kind of assistance. Within a year over two million people were employed on FERA projects similar to those supervised by the CWA. Moreover, funds were channeled into special programs such as rural rehabilitation, college student aid, and emergency education. A new relief program was born out of the achievements of the old.[7]

The resumption of FERA aid in Virginia on a full scale was delayed by the prior weakness of the state program (which required a VERA reorganization), the necessity of reapplication by the needy, and Virginia's own reluctance to provide funds. Once it commenced, most of VERA's effort went into work relief projects on schools, roads, parks, and sewers. The emphasis on work rather than the dole reversed the national tendency, making it easier for Virginia to shift into the subsequent works program (WPA) than other states which had relied so heavily on direct relief. By mid-1935, 40,000 to 50,000 Virginians were at work on over 2,500 projects. Thousands of others received aid from the special programs operated by the FERA for transients, college students, and impoverished rural residents.[8]

Transient camps were established across America to care for the wanderers—people seeking work, adventure, or escape from the dreariness of home or the inadequacy of relief. Immortalized by John Steinbeck, whose powerful novel *The Grapes of Wrath* described the trek of the Joad family from Oklahoma to California, these migrants appeared in all sections of the country. In Virginia, transient bureaus were set up in Richmond, Norfolk, Roanoke, Lynchburg, Bristol, Danville, and Staunton. Camps were established at Blackstone, Montgomery, Seaside, and Tazewell, with a camp for blacks at Chatham, where, said state Director M. S. Burchard, they were to be provided "equal care." The bureaus and camps accommodated persons who had been in the state for less than twelve months, providing them with food, shelter, medical care, and, frequently, transportation home. As a means of paying their upkeep and warding off boredom, transients worked on school and hospital grounds, airports, waterworks, and mosquito control.[9]

Offering adequate facilities, regular employment, and a more stable life, the rural camps were more effective than the urban bureaus, whose turnover rates were much greater. The camp in Montgomery, which sheltered 250 men, had its own woodworking and tin shops, gardens, and cannery. On the other hand, in Richmond, where over 11,000 transients registered in 1933, there was no sense of stability. Quartered in the YMCA, Salvation Army headquarters, or private homes, transients cut wood, served as janitors, and took other odd jobs to earn their three cents an hour—employment that at least curtailed back-door begging and panhandling in the streets. In October 1934 a regional transient camp was established at Fort Eustis which eventually accommodated 3,000 to 4,000 men. Largest in the country, this camp operated separately from the other Virginia camps, becoming a self-sustaining community with its own scrip system, education and recreational programs, and work projects in the Tidewater area.[10]

The usual problems accompanied the creation of these camps. Local residents complained of the drunkenness and lawlessness of their inhabitants (especially at Fort Eustis) and of the competition they provided local relief projects and private employment. Residents of Chatham questioned the placing of a Negro camp in their midst, but they were assured that whites would be in supervisory positions. Camp members everywhere protested inadequate food and harsh and preferential treatment by the supervisors, but for the most part, these were the normal responses of men dissatisfied with their condition who could see no future ahead of them. A tragedy marred the Virginia program when a fire swept the building housing the transients in Lynchburg, killing seventeen and injuring seventy. Not built for occupancy or equipped with fire escapes, the structure had been the only place available to house these itinerants. In spite of these problems, the camps generally served their purpose well, temporarily sustaining the dispossessed, the disgruntled, and the disheartened.[11]

The college student aid program was designed to employ on a part-time basis those students who otherwise could not have continued their studies without some assistance. Begun nationally in December 1933, it reached its zenith during the winter of 1934–35 when 100,000 young people were aided. Its duties were later taken over by the National Youth Administration when the WPA replaced the FERA. The program provided a student with $10 to $20 per month in return for work, which was usually of a research or clerical nature. By autumn 1934 thirty-eight colleges in Virginia were receiving funds that allowed 2,000 students to return to school.[12]

The Emergency Education Division of the FERA began operating in October 1933, utilizing unemployed teachers in adult education, literacy classes, vocational training, and nursery school work. In Virginia in 1933–34, 800 teachers, 80 percent of whom were women and 30 percent of whom were black, taught classes in home economics, agriculture, industrial arts, and business. Maximum employment occurred in April 1935 when 1,547 teachers were instructing 46,000 adults. In another phase of emergency aid to education, FERA funds in 1933–34 kept 5,855 Virginia teachers employed in rural schools, allowing almost 3,000 of these schools to remain open for 200,000 pupils. Due to conflicts between Washington and Richmond, this phase of the program was not repeated in 1934–35.[13]

To compensate for the peculiar ways the depression was affecting women, a Women's Work Division was formed under the VERA in December 1933. Ella Agnew of Richmond, who had been the first home demonstration agent in the nation, was appointed director. An associate of Miss Agnew remembered her as a "remarkable woman," a "Southern lady" with "good connections" in Washington. Mrs. Mary Roberts recalled, "She was really the main force behind the women's work and white collar projects in the State of Virginia. She was a model for all of us, stern and yet compassionate, a good organizer, a clear thinker, and a person who believed in what she was doing."[14]

Concentrating her efforts on obtaining equal job opportunities for women under the relief program, Agnew sent letters to the local relief directors urging them to create jobs for women in libraries, clerical and recreational positions, and sewing rooms. This latter activity soon became one of the biggest and most productive relief efforts in the state with over one hundred sewing centers producing thousands of garments for the needy. Six mattress centers were also in operation. Thwarted in her effort to establish CCC camps for young women, Miss Agnew did convince the FERA to use women in slum clearance work and in creating bird and wild-flower sanctuaries across the country. Striving to create employment for those who had difficulty in getting it, she devised projects for Virginia shut-ins such as mending, soapmaking, and rugmaking. Other pursuits for women included visiting housekeepers with homemaking advice, serving as public health nurses, making safety inspections of FERA work, and rat catching. Designed to reduce the threat of epidemics caused by rats overrunning the Portsmouth and Norfolk wharves, rat catching was assigned as a last resort to the poorest and most unskilled black women who were without work. Armed with dogs, brooms, and sticks, they scoured the docks, earning $8 a week as their bounty.[15]

Among the most active participants in the relief program were the rural people of Virginia. Although less affected by the depression than urbanites, many marginal farm families, who had long endured impoverished conditions, took advantage of the New Deal programs to better their lives. The central piedmont and the mountain counties near the Kentucky and West Virginia borders had the highest percentages of people on relief. In June 1935 the FERA was taking care of 21,936 rural relief cases in Virginia—approximately 127,000 people, about 60 percent of its total relief load. While most of the rural families received direct handouts or work relief assignments, the FERA undertook the actual rehabilitation of others by providing them with loans and small grants to purchase seeds, equipment, fertilizer, and livestock with which to improve their farms; some families were relocated on more fertile lands. This work was taken over and expanded by the new Resettlement Administration in June 1935 when the FERA transferred 3,500 families to it.[16]

In addition to its rehabilitation work, the FERA operated a surplus commodities program which purchased surplus crops and distributed them to the needy, thus putting cash directly into the hands of the farmers ($650,000 worth of potatoes were bought in Virginia) and improving farm prices by removing surpluses from the market. The FERA also brought 15,000 head of cattle to Virginia from the drought-stricken West for fattening by Old Dominion farmers. Both of these activities eventually pushed the FERA into the small manufacturing business; to process the purchased animals and crops, the relief agency opened a meat-processing plant and tomato and vegetable canning plants in the state. Related to this phase of FERA work was the Virginia garden project, which provided seeds and instructions on preserving and canning foods; under its supervision, Virginians planted 29,000 gardens in 1934 that fed 177,000 people.[17]

The FERA also contributed to another project that eventually received nationwide attention—the Citizens Service Exchange of Richmond, a self-help cooperative founded in December 1932 to provide relief other than food (e.g., fuel, clothing, furniture) on a work-exchange basis. The exchange ran its own sewing rooms, cobbler shop, and barbershops, renovated run-down homes, gathered wood, and provided medical and dental services. Hundreds of destitute Richmonders participated in this cooperative. According to Lorena Hickok, an FERA investigator, the exchange lacked a solid market for its products and enough capital to satisfy family needs, but it enjoyed strong local support that enabled it to serve as an employment agency when jobs in the private sector became available. The only opposition came from "politicians" in the Department of Public Welfare who, said Hickok, were "sore because it wasn't turned over to them."[18]

Through this maze of relief programs, which touched the lives of the unemployed, the rural poor, college youth, and transients, the FERA spent $26 million in the Old Dominion; the number of Virginians with whom it had some contact is estimated conservatively at 375,000 to 500,000. Considering the opposition of state officials and the absence of any indigenous statewide relief facilities, its achievements were remarkable.[19]

Despite the success of these programs the perennial problem between Washington and Richmond was Virginia's refusal to contribute money for direct relief. From the very beginning of the FERA, Hopkins had warned that some states were in for a "rude shock" unless they provided funds for the unemployed. "There is nothing sacred," he said, "about some of these State taxes, the gasoline taxes for instance, and no reason why in many cases these revenues should not be applied to feeding the sufferers from unemployment. It is not the intention of the Federal Emergency Relief Administration to carry 100 percent of relief costs where State and local resources can still be tapped." State Welfare Commissioner Arthur James defended Virginia's policy by pointing to measures taken by the state to alleviate the condition of the poor: (1) a reduced state budget, (2) a reduced local tax load attributable to the Byrd road plan, which saved the counties $3.5 million, and (3) use of the highway department as a relief agency to administer RFC money and $1.6 million in state funds, which provided work for the jobless on the highways. Virginia resorted to these arguments in defending its relief posture for the duration of the FERA.[20]

Although these measures were not inconsiderable, other states were appropriating funds for both direct relief and highway construction. Virginia, with its excellent fiscal rating, was sacrificing not at all when it appropriated money for highway work that would have gone to that department regardless of conditions. Said VERA Director Smith, "Virginia will provide some work for the unemployed on its road program but this money can scarcely be classified as being spent for either relief or work relief."[21] Hopkins wrote Governor Pollard that he could not accept the idea that the money being spent on roads was a relief contribution unless it were used specifically for relief purposes. He urged the special session of the General Assembly in August 1933 to provide funds for direct relief, but the legislators ignored his plea, as they continued to do until the federal government ceased direct relief.[22]

Nevertheless, Hopkins persisted. In early 1934 he wrote to his assistant administrator, Aubrey Williams: "I think Virginia should be made to defray a share of the cost of relief. You will recall that the Governor was agreeable to this, but the matter was held up due to the attitude of Senator Byrd." He telegrammed newly inaugurated Governor George Peery that Virginia must "pay its fair share of any future cost of relief of the unemployed."[23] Pressure was brought to bear once more on the General Assembly when FERA field representative Alan Johnstone, probably with Hopkins's consent, demanded that the state put up $2 million for the year's relief expenditures or run the risk of losing federal money and throwing thousands back onto the unemployment rolls. Byrd indignantly labeled this an unauthorized ultimatum, and the Assembly adjourned without making a relief appropriation. A FERA relief statistician concluded that there was "no justification" for Virginia's refusal since the state was financially secure, having reduced its debt and instituted no substantial new tax increases. Its local governments, he said, were also better off than their counterparts in other states. Johnstone believed the Assembly favored relief legislation but was deterred from acting by the opposition of the "machine" and the "able and astute Senator Byrd."[24]

Central to this dispute was the propriety of Virginia's response to the depression. The conflict with Washington was a result of different social and economic philosophies. Hopkins believed that immediate aid to those in need should be the primary objective of the government, no matter what the means or costs. As his later work with the WPA bears out, Hopkins preferred a system of work relief, but he was willing to implement a "dole" if the situation demanded it.[25] The leaders of the organization, although not entirely unsympathetic to the needs of Virginians, were more concerned about the preservation of individual character and the maintenance of fiscal integrity. They believed their highway relief program satisfied these objectives, while federal handouts were deemed guilty of destroying individualism and encroaching on state authority. Furthermore, appropriation of state money at a time when revenues were low would violate the sanctity of a balanced budget. As elected officials they shied away from the higher taxes they believed necessary to finance relief appropriations, despite the fact that Virginia had one of the lowest tax rates in the nation. A Virginia cattle farmer wrote to Governor Peery, "I do not know what the consequences would be if Virginia were cut out of the

Federal relief funds, but I certainly admire your position in resisting burdening the state with unnecessary taxation along this line."[26] The governor received many typed letters from businessmen and lawyers containing similar sentiments, but more numerous were the scrawled-out letters of the poor imploring him to provide relief funds.

Another argument frequently used by Virginia politicians in defending their failure to provide relief funds was that the Old Dominion was not getting back from the federal government anywhere near what it was paying to it in taxes. Virginia ranked seventh in the nation in total taxes paid, the great percentage of which was in taxes paid by the Virginia tobacco manufacturers but passed directly on to tobacco consumers across the country. It was a specious argument but one often resorted to by Glass and Peery when combating the call for more state relief funds.[27]

Devotion to fiscal conservatism may have blinded the leadership to the real situation in the state. Because of reduced funding, many unemployed Virginians were unable to obtain direct assistance, and those on the rolls were receiving less than half the monthly amount expended per case nationally. C. P. Spaeth, president of the Amalgamated Labor League of Norfolk, called on the federal government to take over all relief activities in the state because of "incompetence" and a "callous disregard of human suffering" on the part of Virginia's leaders. At a November 1934 meeting of the Virginia League of Municipalities, Richmond's Mayor Fulmer Bright predicted "revolution" beginning "right here under the dome of the capitol of Virginia" with "people breaking store windows to get food" if adequate relief funds were not provided. Asking for $5 million in state funds, the city leaders claimed that conditions had not improved in the last year and cited a growing number of white-collar workers who, having depleted their savings and their pride, were now joining the relief rolls. The mayors also argued that the highway relief program of Governor Pollard had proved less beneficial to the urban areas.[28]

Although there is little evidence that the citizens of Richmond or those elsewhere in the state were on the verge of "revolution," Mayor Bright did not underestimate the need for additional relief funds in his city. With winter approaching, it was natural that the poor would expect more CWA-type aid. As prices rose and new names were added to the relief lists, the costs of aiding these people increased. The cities were running out of money, and there was fear that federal funds would be terminated. As Mayor W. R. L. Taylor of Norfolk remarked, "The federal government has done its full stint, and now we have come to ask what the State will do to help us."[29]

Earlier, in September, Hopkins had threatened once again to end federal funds. Quoted as saying he was "tired of hearing alibis" and that "the sense of public service in some parts of this country is mighty low," he asked that the fourteen states providing little or no relief money, one of which was Virginia, put up more funds or forfeit direct federal aid. Distressed by this threat, Senator Byrd complained that Virginia was not being credited with holding down expenditures, while "those states that are most extravagant and waste money are the ones that are rewarded by the Federal government."[30] Governor Peery, opposed to calling a special session, supported his highway program as the best means of distributing relief and reiterated the same points Public Welfare Director James had made the year before. Hopkins replied that the amount contributed to relief should rest on the ability of the state to pay, not on how much or how little it was putting into roads. However, on December 14 he relented and told the governor and Senator Byrd that relief funds would not be cut off until Congress set new guidelines. The *Times-Dispatch* bitterly criticized the selfishness of state officials: "Behind all the maneuverings of the Virginia political leaders, the reluctance of those leaders to provide any State funds for the relief of the cities may be clearly discerned. . . . they are determined not to spend any of the State's money for the State's neediest unemployed. They are great advocates of State rights when such advocacy meets their convenience, but when it doesn't, they believe in letting Uncle Sam hold the bag."[31]

Virginia could afford to be more penurious with the resources it applied to the relief effort because its unemployment did not compare with that of other states. The percentage of its population on the relief rolls was usually half that of the national average, and for the peak period of July 1934–June 1935, Virginia ranked behind only Delaware and Vermont as the state with the smallest percentage of population on relief—8.6 percent, an average of 208,626 persons. In comparison, the national average was 15.6 percent; North Carolina's was 10.6 percent; New York's, 15.2 percent; Alabama's, 18.3 percent; and South Dakota's, 36.6 percent, the highest in the country. Better economic conditions, predepression subsistence living in rural areas, and a strong sense of rugged individualism affected the size of Virginia's relief rolls, but the absence of state funds also reduced the number of recipients and the amount of aid they received. Less money meant less relief.[32]

Could Virginia have undertaken a satisfactory relief program? The Virginia League of Municipalities concluded: "It is useless to argue the ability of the State to do so. Her low bonded indebtedness and sound financial condition which are the envy of states throughout the country speak for themselves." In a compelling series of articles on relief in Virginia, Cabell Phillips, *Times-Dispatch* reporter, indirectly affirmed that not only was Virginia financially able to sponsor this work, but had it done so, more relief money would have entered the state. Comparing the unemployment and relief statistics of Maryland, West Virginia, and North Carolina with Virginia's, Phillips suggested that the Old Dominion's relief load was low because the state was more exacting in determining who was to get relief; that is, one had to be poorer in Virginia to get on the rolls. He also concluded that the states that were spending their own money were getting more federal relief money; "credit rating means nothing when repayment is not expected," he wrote. West Virginia and Maryland, in spite of their higher state debts, were maintaining spending in other areas as well. Finally, Virginia's financial position was such that, of all of the states studied, it would have had the easiest time borrowing. Phillips left little doubt that Virginia was neglecting its people.[33] Hopkins and the FERA should have been more sympathetic to the state's claim that highway spending was assisting thousands of unemployed, but this does not excuse the organization for ignoring the human needs staring it in the face.

Between the forces arrayed against each other on both sides of the Potomac was VERA Director Smith, who, despite having to appease Richmond and Washington, continually asked that the level of relief in Virginia be raised. Since Washington would not let people starve, relief monies were never cut off from Virginia, but they were pared, in part because of Old Dominion parsimony, in part because the need was less. With fewer funds and smaller relief rolls, VERA's administrative costs were inordinately high, running about 15 to 18 percent of total expenditures compared with a national average of 10 percent. When Eighth District Representative Howard Smith objected to the high cost of administration in his district, Hopkins replied that administrative costs were higher where relief expenditures were low, hinting that the lack of a state contribution was to blame. The absence of a strong foundation of local relief offices also contributed to higher initial administrative costs.[34]

Like most bureaucratic agencies, the FERA generated much red tape. Numerous letters were written regarding claims for reimbursement for work done, damage to machinery, and disabling injuries. In one case a half-dozen letters were exchanged over a broken pane of window glass. The Lynchburg fire produced many requests from dependents for compensation, which the FERA could not pay because the transients were not employees of the federal government. Routine paperwork such as project inspections, safety surveys, and periodic reports added to the confusion and slowed down the service rendered relief recipients.

Recipients were among those registering complaints about waste, inefficiency, low wages, and discrimination in the selection of relief workers. Labor unions protested vociferously that low relief wages would pull prevailing wages down. They accused the relief administration of defeating a strike and using yellow-dog contracts to discriminate against union members, both of which the VERA vehemently denied. Bitter about the absence of collective bargaining and the arbitrary wage decisions of the FERA, workers overlooked the fact that they were dealing with a relief agency, not a private employer.[35]

Discrimination of another sort was also laid at the FERA's door. In an editorial entitled, "The Raw Edge of the New Deal," the Norfolk *Journal and Guide* condemned the practice of racial prejudice in federal programs. It claimed blacks usually were assigned the inferior work, such as "ditch-digging," and were paid

less than whites for the same jobs; it cited the emergency education program in which black teachers were paid $25 to $75 per
month while whites were paid $90 to $125 per month. Although
the rate of pay was the same, the number of hours blacks could
work was restricted. One official responded, "You don't expect
us to change the system of paying teachers in Virginia because
they are working under the Federal relief system, do you?" The
Richmond *Planet* was also openly critical of the FERA for its discrimination against Negroes who, it pointed out, were not
getting a share of funds comparable to their percentage on relief.
Having leveled a similar barrage against the CWA, these black-
owned newspapers persevered in their censure of New Deal
"Jim Crowism" for most of the decade.[36]

Malingering, boondoggling, and disruption of private employment were other complaints frequently hurled against the
FERA. These accusations had some truth but were often exaggerated. At one point Hopkins relayed to VERA Director Smith
a report that men in Northern Virginia were refusing private
employment at $2 per day in order to go on relief at $13 per
week. Smith replied that the report was mythical; the prevailing
labor rate in that region was $.75 to $1.00 a day, and relief funds
barely reached $13 a month, not $13 a week. When Senator
Byrd expressed displeasure about relief work siphoning off
workers from private labor, Roosevelt was overheard to say: "I
know what's the matter with Harry Byrd. He's afraid you'll force
him to pay more than ten cents an hour for his apple pickers."[37]

In order to prove or disprove the charges of inefficiency, the
Times-Dispatch commissioned Cabell Phillips to investigate the
FERA in the rural areas of the state. The result, a series entitled
"Relief and the Farmer," endorsed the work of the FERA in
Virginia. Phillips determined that the agency had brought about
something of a social welfare reformation in the rural areas, that
relief had not reduced the labor supply for private employers as
charged, that essential tasks which the localities could not undertake had been performed by the FERA, and that the talk
about FERA extravagance and subsidization of the lazy was
unjustified. Phillips found that a majority of the rural population
approved of the relief program; nowhere could he get his
sources to give concrete evidence of a boondoggle, though many
were willing to claim this was the case. He did point out, how-

ever, that the VERA was overzealous in adding people to the relief rolls who were no worse off than they had been for the past ten years without assistance. He concluded that relief had increased the dependence of these subsistence farmers on the government and urged that the rural case load be reduced, especially in spring and summer. Responding to this criticism, Director Smith declared, "We recognize that for many of these families the economic depression has not brought about a financial emergency, and that the condition under which they are living at the time of applying for relief is more or less the standard to which they have been accustomed. However, their need for assistance is obvious, and it is most difficult for the most astute case worker to say in many such cases that their condition is not due at this time to lack of work opportunities."[38]

The FERA in Washington was more critical of the VERA's standard of relief and the absence of state funds than it was of inefficiency. When Welfare Director James made the offhand remark that "it takes people a long time to starve," a Columbia University social worker retorted: "Of course it takes people a long time to starve. But doesn't the state of Virginia give any thought to what people may suffer and feel and be driven to while they are starving?"[39] A study of the VERA conducted in October 1934 called for a more centralized relief organization and a greater effort to develop a sense of responsibility toward the dependent groups. It found that local identification with the FERA program was nonexistent since funds were dumped into the communities without direction. Smith was praised as "constructive" and "honest" but typically southern in his paternalism toward the Negro and the poor white. Virginia officialdom came under fire as well. "There is a definite opposition to relief as such in this state," the reporter declared, "a feeling that it is not needed in rural counties and an unwillingness to admit the extent of its unemployment." In a subsequent report, field representative Alan Johnstone remarked: "The State of Virginia continues to have a smug attitude with reference to relief clients. Its public officials have no particular interest in them and, in spite of rather ample resources and an excellent financial condition, the leaders in the public life of Virginia have no conviction that the State should bestir itself to help them."[40]

In spite of this criticism the FERA continued its work in Virginia. The monthly reports of the VERA to Washington indicate the extent of the distress. In April 1935, one of the peak months of FERA aid, 51,640 cases were dependent on federal funds—close to 250,000 people; 1,022 new work projects were begun during the month which would cost $1.8 million when completed; 46,051 persons were in emergency education classes instructed by over 1,500 unemployed teachers; transients being cared for totaled 10,352 (exclusive of Fort Eustis); and 2,742 families were in the rural rehabilitation program. Expenditures for the month totaled $2 million, almost all of it in federal funds. The average expenditure per case was $16.07; administrative costs were 12.8 percent of the total; and 9.7 percent of the population was on relief, including 14.3 percent of southwest Virginia and 10.2 percent of the southeast region.[41]

April also brought with it a renewed demand by Hopkins for an allocation for relief by Virginia. He again threatened to end federal allotments if state aid were not forthcoming. Foreseeing no possibility of a state outlay, Governor Peery resignedly commented, "Spending has got to stop somewhere, sometime." The press was less indifferent. Exclaimed the *Times-Dispatch*, "[Virginia] can well afford to spend some of its wealth in caring for the economic casualties within its borders." The Richmond *News-Leader*, a newspaper which often aligned itself against the New Deal, believed that Virginia "would have lost less in money than she has lost in self-respect" had adequate funds been appropriated. "There are worse things than deficits, bad though they be," concluded the editor; "we should . . . accept precisely the obligations that the other American states are carrying." The Clifton Forge *Review* summarized: "The newspapers in Virginia appear to be of one mind in the matter of convening the General Assembly in extra session for the purpose of providing relief for the unemployed. . . . Those well off . . . do not appreciate what it means to be without food and shelter, therefore we suggest that they do a bit of investigating and find out for themselves what it means to be actually in need of the necessities of life." On the other hand, the Roanoke *World-News* conjectured that Hopkins's pressure tactics were retaliation for the antirelief attitudes of Virginia's senators. Citing reasons why no special session was necessary, the newspaper declared, "And not the least of these reasons is that Virginia does not want to be ordered about by a bureaucrat from Washington."[42]

This time Hopkins partially carried out his threat. When Superintendent of Education Sidney Hall asked for federal aid to prevent the closing of rural schools, a request that had been complied with a year earlier, Hopkins wrote to Governor Peery, "I think you will agree with me that Virginia is quite able to pay for her schools and that being the case, I am sure you would not expect the Federal Government to do so."[43] A $600,000 grant was withheld on the grounds that federal money could be given only when a state was unable to make an appropriation. However, funds for regular projects were not terminated; nor was their administration taken over by Washington, both of which occurred in other states, often because of reported corruption. The monthly allotments remained high (near $1 million per month) until late in the year when the FERA was being phased out.[44] Although Hopkins once stated that Old Dominion leaders "made out a pretty good case" on behalf of their highway relief program, it is likely that the real reasons he did not cut off all the funds were his desire not to withhold aid from Virginia's needy and his unwillingness to antagonize Glass and Byrd, especially the powerful and caustic elder statesman from Lynchburg.[45]

Conclusion of the FERA was announced early in 1935. The last grant was received in November, and all projects were ended by December except for transient relief. In its two-year, eight-month existence, the FERA spent $3 billion in the United States. Virginia received $26,302,851 of this, ranking thirty-third in the nation. The contribution of the state was $34,452, most of it going for administrative expenses; localities provided $2,248,924. Thus, from 1933 through 1935 the federal government paid over 90 percent of the relief bill in Virginia. The number of people cared for in the Old Dominion rose slowly to a peak of 51,919 cases (approximately 250,000 people) in May 1935 and then quickly diminished. Despite the large number, the percentage of the population on relief always was among the lowest in the nation, reflecting Virginia's lesser need and more parsimonious nature. Virginia usually ranked among the bottom eight states in the average monthly amount of relief given each case, reaching a high of $17.70 in May 1935, when it ranked thirty-fifth.[46]

Southwest Virginia with its unemployed coal miners and poor mountain farms had the highest rural relief rate in the state.

Wise County led the counties with an average number of 9,780 on its relief rolls from July 1934 through June 1935. Lee and Washington counties, also in the southwest, were next highest. In contrast, Arlington County, benefiting from the growing federal bureaucracy across the Potomac River, averaged 26 persons per month on its rolls, and the James-York Peninsula, with its abundance of military establishments, had the lowest area relief rate in the state. Richmond and Norfolk led the cities in the number on relief and in expenditures (both spent almost $2 million), but Bristol and Hopewell had the largest percentage of their people on the dole. Wise also consumed the most money of all the counties—$587,406. No other county spent over $200,000, but eighteen counties, largely in the southwest and Southside, expended over $100,000.

While 60 percent of the relief cases were rural, a greater percentage of the urban population was on relief—one in nine compared to one in thirteen in the farm areas. Blacks composed 36 percent of the relief rolls in Virginia, a percentage twice that of the national average; more blacks were on relief in Old Dominion cities than whites. Among the unemployed workers in Virginia (79,263 in March 1935), most were farm laborers (12,474), domestics (12,086, 75 percent black), unskilled laborers (11,552, 50 percent black), and semiskilled workers in manufacturing and other industries (10,881). A large number of inexperienced youth between the ages of sixteen and twenty-four, farm owners, carpenters, and painters were also on relief, but the depression struck primarily at the less skilled groups in the population. It was these people, especially the poor rural whites and the urban Negroes, whom the FERA aided most.[47]

This initial New Deal relief program led an ambivalent existence in the Old Dominion. Its aid was accepted, but a joint federal-state commitment was rejected by the Januses of the organization. Its projects were successful, but the philosophy behind them was scorned by the traditionalists. Although Virginia was not alone in its failure to support the FERA, its ability to pay was superior to most. Stymied by conservative economic doctrine, the FERA's effectiveness in the Old Dominion was impaired, but not destroyed. Without federal money, the situation in Virginia could have become critical; with the FERA, while relief was still inadequate, survival was possible.

5
"Bread and Circuses"
WPA

During 1934 it became apparent to the New Dealers that the continuing high level of unemployment required more extensive national machinery to deal with it. Believing that the opportunity to make a living should be available to every man, Roosevelt and Hopkins settled on a program of small work projects for the needy employables to be controlled by the federal government. The responsibility for the unemployables (the disabled, the blind, etc.) was left to the states, a decision which put pressure on Virginia to enter the direct relief field. Coupled with social security legislation and the Wagner Labor Act, the Works Progress Administration (WPA) was the beginning of a "second" New Deal directed at a more permanent solution of the social and economic ills affecting American life.[1]

The WPA was a federally directed program, as the CWA had been. Although communities assisted in the selection, planning, and funding of the work, final approval rested with the WPA in Washington, which set the rigid guidelines to be followed. The primary purpose of the WPA was to employ a maximum number of jobless. Therefore, 90 percent of the workers had to come from the relief rolls. Wages were not to be above those paid by private employers so that WPA work would not draw men from this field. An employee was required to work a certain number of hours to earn his "security wage," which in Virginia ranged from $21 to $75 per month, a rate among the lowest in the country. Projects had to be locally sponsored, publicly useful, and performed on public property by the available excess labor supply. Since there was potential for conflict with the PWA because of project similarity, a $25,000 limit was placed on WPA projects, but if the PWA refused the job, the WPA could have it. Continuing his role as New Deal relief director, Harry Hopkins was the heart and soul of the new program. It was his concern and his leadership that vitalized the WPA.[2]

To implement the new relief program, Congress authorized spending $4 billion, the largest peacetime appropriation in United States history to that point. With substantial Democratic majorities in both houses, the bill quickly passed, but not before it was forced to overcome obstacles thrown up by the Virginia delegation. It was approved in the House, 329 to 78, with Representatives Colgate Darden, A. Willis Robertson, and Howard Smith among only ten Democrats in opposition. Congressmen Drewry, Clifton Woodrum, John Flannagan, and Otis Bland voted for the bill. In the Senate, Byrd and Glass led the fight against the large open-ended appropriation that gave the president great discretion in the use of the funds for public works, housing, highways, rural electrification, and education. Glass, surprisingly, endorsed continuation of the dole because it was less expensive. Byrd, likewise, preferred the present dole arrangement of the FERA. With words that would echo through the halls of Congress for thirty years, he called for an end to the "spending orgy at Washington," declaring that he was "opposed to mortgaging the future welfare of our children, grandchildren, and even generations to come." A final Byrd amendment to reduce the appropriation to $1.9 billion failed, and the relief act passed the Senate, 68 to 16, with both Virginia senators joining four other Democrats in opposition. Roosevelt signed the bill on April 8, 1935. Plans were made to end the FERA and begin the WPA in mid-1935, but the conversion to a more complex work program proved difficult and it was not until December that the FERA was terminated.[3]

For Virginia the changeover was facilitated by a reorganization of the VERA in early 1935 and by the high proportion of FERA money already going into work relief. As in the nation at large, the WPA in Virginia was staffed with holdovers from its predecessor. Former VERA Director and now WPA Director William Smith defined his new objectives as "providing work for the many persons on relief and for improvements and accomplishments that will be of lasting benefit to the state and communities."[4] For administrative purposes Virginia was divided into six districts—Richmond, Norfolk, Fredericksburg,

Staunton, Lynchburg, and Roanoke—each with finance, projects, labor inventory, and social service divisions. These branches worked closely with the National Reemployment Service, which had offices in all counties and cities except Richmond and Roanoke, where the Virginia Employment Service centers were located. This cooperation was necessary since a work relief applicant first had to enroll with an employment center which would attempt to find him private employment before referring him to the WPA. The employment service could pull him off the WPA when labor shortages in the private sector occurred. Smith also worked closely with Colonel James Anderson, Virginia PWA director, and John Galleher, coordinator of all federal agencies in the state for the National Economic Council.[5]

In many respects the WPA mirrored the FERA on a much larger scale. Work continued on roads and schools, sewer and water systems, bridges and culverts, parks and recreational areas, airports, and public buildings, but the WPA emphasized new construction and additions as well as repairs and improvements, thus making its value more lasting. The following projects, included in a $2 million authorization for Virginia in November 1938, exemplify the construction work performed by the WPA: Hopewell, $22,794 for storm sewers; Newport News, $150,442 for storm sewers; Roanoke, $59,985 for improving streets; Alleghany County, $19,808 for construction and repair of roads; Brunswick County, $10,282 for construction of schools; and Elizabeth City County, $53,924 for improving Fort Monroe. There were, of course, jobs of lesser importance designed primarily for individual relief: Danville, $2,868 to cut timber; Alexandria, $1,934 for matron services in girls' rest rooms in public schools; Lancaster County, $2,397 for sidewalk construction in the village of Lively; and Portsmouth, $4,271 for renovating toys, furniture, and household articles for distribution among the needy. Almost any type of project was acceptable, and, in fact, the construction of two golf courses was approved. The use of WPA workers and money in emergencies, such as the flooding of the James River, was also authorized.[6]

Some Virginia projects had direct links to those begun under the FERA. The Fort Eustis transient camp was transferred to

WPA control, while the state camps were allowed to take in no more transients and were gradually closed down. Unemployed teachers were utilized in adult education classes, while the National Youth Administration (NYA), affiliated with the WPA, carried forward the college student aid program. Rural rehabilitation was placed under another federal agency, but the WPA maintained the surplus commodities program by distributing food received from the Federal Surplus Commodities Corporation (FSCC) to indigent Virginia families.[7]

A Women's Work Division, again under the direction of Ella Agnew, became a vital component of WPA work as it had been under the FERA. The projects for women included children's nurseries and camps, school lunches, canning, sewing, landscaping, bird and wild-flower sanctuaries, and clerical work. From January 1937 to April 1939 they preserved or canned 353,000 containers of food, served 9 million lunches, produced 1.7 million clothing items, and cared for 5,500 children in day nurseries. Regarding the sanctuary projects, one sponsor wrote: "Those women have transformed a section of our City from a jungle type swamp into a very beautiful place, and large numbers of people visit the area regularly. . . . We hope you will approve the project for its continuance." The Norfolk Azalea Gardens also were the creation of WPA women, who, recalls Mary Roberts, "did the planting in hip boots and work gloves—and they worked!"[8]

Public health and education in the Old Dominion received a considerable boost from the WPA. The agency spent several million dollars on tuberculosis and venereal disease clinics, sewer and water systems, health camps for undernourished children, and community sanitation. Assisted by state and federal departments, hundreds of WPA workers drained and cleaned swamps in many Virginia counties to reduce the hazard of disease-carrying mosquitoes over thousands of acres. Dr. I. C. Riggin, state commissioner of health, praised the work of the WPA in instituting health control measures and educating people in the field of public health. The WPA's major contribution in education was the construction and modernization of schools. In its first four years of service, it built 67 new schools and 63 new athletic fields and improved 894 other school buildings.

The introduction of inside running water, hot lunches, and libraries into many schools alleviated unsanitary conditions and lifted student morale. Writing in the *Virginia Journal of Education*, G. Watson James rhapsodized, "Future historians . . . will acclaim its contribution to upbuilding the public school system in the State."[9]

The WPA added a new dimension to relief assistance through its programs for white-collar workers who were among the last people affected by the depression. Once protected positions and middle-class savings were now gone, and their return to former jobs awaited full recovery. Amazingly, as the nation began to recover, between 1935 and 1937, the number of white-collar workers on relief in Virginia rose.[10] Some professional people were used in the education and health programs of the WPA, while many others found work in the special art, drama, music, library, and writers projects and in the multitude of surveys and studies made by the agency.

The Virginia Writers Project (VWP) was begun in November 1935 under the direction of Hamilton J. Eckenrode, a noted Virginia historian. Employing only those registered for relief and in need of work, the VWP took on researchers, writers, editors, proofreaders, and clerks. The project was slow getting underway because Eckenrode did not give it his full attention and his assistants were inadequately prepared for publication work, but eventually it produced two noteworthy books: *Virginia: A Guide to the Old Dominion*, part of the American Guide series, and *The Negro in Virginia*, sponsored by Hampton Institute. Supervised by Roscoe Lewis, a Hampton chemistry teacher who had become interested in oral history, the latter was very well received; Jonathan Daniels called it "one of the most valuable contributions yet made to the American Negro's history."[11] Subsequent efforts of the project were devoted to local histories and guides.[12] The VWP also compiled collections of Afro-American folklore and Virginia folk songs, and it was one of the first state groups to begin interviewing former slaves in an effort to preserve that priceless historical source. Initially a part of the Writers Project, but later an independent office, the Historical Records Survey inventoried and cataloged unpublished historical materials in the state. It produced several volumes on county and church archives and two volumes on the U.S. Departments of Agriculture and Justice.[13]

Under the Virginia Library Project, the WPA expended $1 million to "extend and expand library services" in the state. Not only was book availability increased, especially in the rural areas through the use of bookmobiles and "foot-back" librarians who tramped the hills providing service for the mountain people, but books were bound and repaired by other needy unemployed. The WPA constructed five libraries, including two regional libraries at Tappahannock and Radford. Several hundred people were employed, and 75 percent of the state's population was served by the expanded facilities.[14]

The Virginia Art Project never employed a great number, but it did provide a degree of cultural stimulation in the Old Dominion. Beginning in 1935 with fifteen artists in six areas, it eventually gave work to sixty-five employees in seventeen localities. Galleries in Fairfax, Richmond, Lynchburg, Big Stone Gap, Middlesex, and West Point displayed the 370 paintings, dioramas, and maps produced by Virginia artists. The project also conducted classes in art appreciation and inventoried works of art in Virginia, including early American furniture. The Virginia Handicraft Project was related to the art project since its wares were often displayed in the galleries. Weaving, sewing, and carving, 500 unemployed women created articles of beauty and utility that were often sold to defray the costs of the program. Two of their more noteworthy handicrafts were the table linen for President Roosevelt's yacht, the S.S. *Potomac*, and the draperies for FDR's Hyde Park study.[15]

Also of limited employment value but of considerable cultural benefit to Virginians was the Federal Music Project. Hoping to stimulate the understanding and love of good music, scores of musicians on relief toiled under WPA auspices. Working in symphony orchestras, choral groups, and mountain string bands, they presented hundreds of concerts and recitals. The largest operation was the state orchestra at Richmond, which for reasons of economy merged with the North Carolina symphony in 1937. Unemployed music teachers also found jobs giving instruction in music to several thousand youngsters across the state, most of whom were the less culturally privileged. Band projects were financed in Staunton and Norfolk, and in keeping with southern attitudes on the race question, a separate orchestra for Negroes was formed in Richmond. In one six-month period, 175,000 Virginians heard 497 programs given by WPA-employed musicians.[16]

Less successful in Virginia was the Federal Drama Project, which aimed at employing jobless actors. The WPA approved theaters for Henrico, Dickenson, Wise, Campbell, and Northumberland counties, appointed a state director, and made an initial allotment of $16,000, but the project was terminated because not enough professional actors were on the relief rolls in Virginia. A second attempt was made to form regional recreational drama groups not associated with the federal project, but funds were withdrawn from these groups in April 1936 because of the "scandalous" operation of the project. The WPA's national theater program also led a checkered career. Investigated in 1939 by the Congressional Subcommittee on Appropriations because of its "leftist" productions, it came to an inglorious end. The chairman of the subcommittee was Congressman Clifton Woodrum of Virginia's Sixth District, who incorrectly concluded that the project had "produced nothing of merit." When the last curtain came down on the New York performance of *Pinocchio*, the actors left the theater carrying placards reading, "Wanted—Representative Clifton A. Woodrum for the Murder of Pinocchio."[17]

A more successful theatrical venture in the Old Dominion unrelated to the WPA was the Barter Theatre of Abingdon. Originated in 1932 by Robert Porterfield, an actor out of a job, the theater presented performances in return for produce as the price of admission. Profits in the first year totaled $4.30, assorted jellies, and a 305-pound weight increase among the troupe. An instant success, the theater became the largest professional company in the country outside of New York. Attempting to obtain federal funds for his theater, Porterfield wrote to Mrs. Roosevelt explaining his idea, but the WPA refused his request because of its private enterprise nature. He eventually was subsidized by the state in 1946.[18]

With an increasing number of white-collar workers going on relief in 1936, the Virginia WPA earmarked $1 million for thirty-

94

four additional research projects that employed almost 1,000 persons. Unemployed clerical workers took real property and land use surveys designed to improve city planning and reduce crime and disease rates in Winchester, Norfolk, Portsmouth, Newport News, Hopewell, and Martinsville. Other WPA surveys included traffic surveys in Norfolk, Roanoke, Petersburg, and Portsmouth, farm mortgage and land value studies, land assessment surveys, historical building surveys, the rural relief studies of B. L. Hummel and C. G. Bennett, and the rural life studies of W. E. Garnett of VPI. Although these research projects satisfied the WPA requirement of being "socially beneficial," many people considered them to be "make-work" in nature.[19]

One of the most active New Deal agencies in Virginia was the National Youth Administration (NYA), established in June 1935 as an affiliate of the WPA to assist the youth of America find jobs or stay in school. Aware of the frustration the depression had created among young people, the New Deal, from the beginning, had attempted to find them productive work. Of Virginia's 450,000 youth between the ages of sixteen and twenty-four, it was estimated that 250,000 were out of school and that 80,000 to 100,000 were unemployed or had little income. Except for a recreational program operated by the state Department of Education, little had been done for them before the New Deal. The NYA did not have enough funds to employ all of them, but in 1935–36, 10,000 were given part-time work; five years later the number had risen to 16,000. Out-of-school youth worked forty-five to seventy hours a month, earning $11 to $13 on jobs ranging from construction to conservation to library and home economics projects. In the high school phase of the student aid program, students in 650 participating schools earned about $6 a month for work that was not to interfere with their schooling. In the college program, forty-two schools of higher education in the state participated; undergraduates earned about $13 a month, while graduate students received $22 for work that included research, library service, and building and grounds maintenance.[20]

Initially, the NYA tried to dispel boredom and despair, and the quality of projects in the early years reflected this thinking.

However, much of this "make-work" philosophy soon disappeared, and greater emphasis was placed on vocational training. Virginia's NYA director, Walter Newman, later president of Virginia Polytechnic Institute, was instrumental in expediting this shift. Convinced that job training and an environmental change would be of lasting benefit, Newman established an experimental program at Fort Eustis to teach 200 young men from southwest Virginia a new trade. Recalling these years as among the happiest of his long career in education, Newman witnessed "a spirit there that delighted me." His success led to an expansion of facilities in Virginia and was soon copied by other states.[21] Resident training centers for boys were located at Manassas, Norfolk, Danville, and Blacksburg, with a center for Negroes at Virginia State College. The centers for girls, which introduced young women to nursing, sewing, waitressing, and beautician training, were at Abingdon, Charlottesville, Harrisonburg, Norfolk, and Salem, with Aberdeen Gardens set aside for blacks. With the advent of war, these resident centers became valuable training grounds for the defense plants in Virginia. Of greater consequence was the continuation of the vocational concept by the Trade and Industrial Division of the state Department of Education after the federal agency died.

Like the CCC, the NYA had few enemies. Principals and pupils alike endorsed the program as valuable for preparing students for work after graduation, improving attitudes toward schoolwork, and promoting overall efficiency. Most desired its continuation. One student from Portsmouth commented: "When I was just about to give up in despair, then came the NYA to my rescue. NYA means a great deal to me. It means employment for which I have been seeking long; it means encouragement; it means a new and brighter outlook on life. All these things—and many others—it means to me because it has brought me a source of gainful employment." Some opposition was generated by NYA's association with the "leaf-raking" WPA and its meddlesome officials. Even Director Newman became exasperated by the interference of Washington bureaucrats: "I stayed as far away from Washington as I could but couldn't stay very far away. . . . Somebody would get an idea up there and bang, bang, bang, they'd want you to put it into effect."[22]

The final report on the NYA in Virginia was impressive. One NYA director called it "the prettiest story I ever heard." Over $8.3 million was spent in the state during a six-year period to employ 45,000 youth in the out-of-school program and to keep thousands of others in school. Concluded Newman, "In Virginia, through the close cooperation of the educational forces and the National Youth Administration, it has been demonstrated that work experience, supplemented by training, is a practical, efficient, and functional experience for young people." When he resigned as Virginia NYA director in 1942 to take a job with the state Department of Education, he wrote to his boss Aubrey Williams, "I am going to miss greatly . . . working with a group of young men and women in the State of Virginia who prior to the advent of the National Youth Administration had never been satisfactorily reached by any other agency."[23]

The almost unanimous endorsement tendered the NYA in the Old Dominion was not duplicated for the WPA. Although it was highly praised by local officials, sponsors, and workers, the WPA was not without its critics in Virginia.[24] Fiscal conservatives, distressed by its costs, its bureaucracy, and the potential for waste and corruption, desired a return to the dole or at least a reduction in WPA appropriations. Undoubtedly there were a number of goldbricks who reduced WPA efficiency. Years later many Virginians "fondly" remembered WPA as standing for "We Poke Along." One recalled a "directive" for the proper use of a privy by an eight-man mowing unit—"two coming, two going, two sitting, two mowing." Another claimed WPA work crews shoveled gravel from one side of the road to the other in the morning and reversed the operation after lunch. The white-collar jobs were especially susceptible to boondoggling charges because their immediate value was limited; the indictments appeared justified when the writers project began compiling recipes for Virginia foods. However, H. G. Parker, Norfolk's director of public relief, claimed that WPA workers, contrary to their image of being "shovel leaners," were "too darned efficient," getting work done so quickly that the men were forced to go back on relief. Workers also knew that there were plenty of jobless willing to take their places if work was not performed.[25] On one occasion, Director Smith challenged the *Times-Dispatch* to investigate any city in the state for evidence of boondoggling. Selecting Suffolk, the newspaper discovered little inefficiency, many useful projects, and a population highly appreciative of the WPA work. In spite of its general opposition to work relief, the *Times-Dispatch* praised Smith for his fine performance and the Virginia WPA for the absence of waste and graft among its work projects.[26]

Politics was not present in the state WPA machinery except at the local level where some favoritism was displayed in the selection of projects. A few cases of minor embezzlement were uncovered, but there were no major scandals. Occasionally charges of impropriety surfaced and jobs for "friends" were requested, but the dominance of the organization ensured that there would be little politicking with relief in Virginia. In a one-party state where the electorate was small and voter apathy high, there was no need to buy votes with jobs. Furthermore, there was no opposing Democratic faction of any size to battle the machine for patronage from Washington. The organization had a reputation for integrity, and state relief administrators Smith and Anderson lived up to that ideal.[27]

Although Virginia was devoid of any irregularities, their appearance elsewhere did little to endear the WPA to its enemies. Charges of mixing relief with politics were rampant during the 1938 congressional elections. Scandals were uncovered in Ohio and New Mexico, and when Assistant WPA Administrator Aubrey Williams called on relief recipients to reelect their "friends," the *Times-Dispatch* demanded Williams's dismissal. The Lynchburg *News* was highly critical of Williams and Hopkins, and after the election it called for an investigation of the WPA's involvement. The Woodrum-Taylor House Committee, which examined the activities of the WPA, found nothing that impugned the integrity of WPA officials in Washington.[28]

Nevertheless, the WPA had many problems, even in Virginia. It received a constant stream of complaints from the very men it was employing, who cited poor supervision, harsh treatment, and favoritism or discrimination when jobs were lost. Organized labor was a frequent critic. The Roanoke Central Labor Union, as it had with FERA work, often protested that WPA wages were not at prevailing levels, and the leftist Workers Alliance of

America was continually demanding wage increases and threatening strikes against the WPA. Although most grievances of this variety were ignored, in one instance when a Norfolk painters' union objected to WPA wages being below the prevailing wage, the WPA wage was increased. Other workers disliked arduous jobs such as snow shoveling and street cleaning, a resentment which strained relations between WPA administrators and city officials who expected the work to be done. In spite of these protests, the final state report concluded that labor problems among WPA workers were "at a minimum in Virginia," a result attributable in part to the weakness of organized labor in the state.[29]

Charges of racial discrimination by WPA were substantiated by the maintenance of segregated programs and facilities and unequal distribution of funds and skilled jobs. Nevertheless, blacks, who were hurt worst by the depression as whites shifted down and took jobs in the lower economic stratum traditionally reserved for the Negro, discovered they were not refused relief because of their color. Most projects for whites had corresponding programs for blacks, which, officials believed, revived hope for them and contributed to better race relations. Blacks should have had a larger percentage of relief work because of their high number on the relief rolls, but the politically expedient New Dealers refused to challenge southern custom on the issue. T. C. Walker of Gloucester, who served as consultant and adviser on Negro affairs in Virginia for the WPA, as he had done for the VERA, acknowledged the existence of discrimination, but he believed the lives saved and transformed, the homes purchased, and the schools constructed softened the blow. It was Walker who suggested a Negro studies project under the writers program that led eventually to publication of *The Negro in Virginia.*[30]

Individual requests for relief were countless. Often written by people in debt who were threatened with foreclosure or failing crops, the appeals for aid underscored the necessity of WPA work in Virginia. Indicative of the faith the less fortunate had in their leaders were the many letters sent directly to President and Mrs. Roosevelt. A seventy-six-year-old unemployed carpenter from Richmond entreated: "We are expecting to be put in the street. Now Mrs. Roosevelt will you please give us a little help, it will be highly appreciated and May God bless you. We certainly in need." And a lady from Clinchport wrote, "Now mr president you write to the one that you know is supposed to do this work an tell them to make us a road an we will all help you."[31]

Congressmen often received similar letters and forwarded them to the Washington offices of the WPA along with their own requests for action on pet projects. Even when objecting to relief appropriations and the supposed waste of the WPA, Virginia representatives were not above pressuring Hopkins and his assistants to approve these requests. Senator Byrd and Representative Robertson were staunch advocates of farm-to-market roads, which the WPA was authorized to build. Urging the development of such a road in his district, Robertson wrote to Democratic National Chairman James Farley, "In my opinion, it will help us both economically and politically to press relief work of this character with the greatest vigor. I will not discuss the pros and cons of other previous relief activities. . . . they have been far from satisfactory." Byrd, whom Aubrey Williams called one of the "worst" in trying to arrange appointments agreeable to him, made a similar request for a road in Rockingham County. Williams told Virginia Director Smith: "Glass is calling on that [the road] and Byrd. I think Harry wants very much to do it. If I give you an exemption of the fifty non-relief, non-skilled, do you have the money to do this with?" Smith replied affirmatively, the exemption from the WPA guidelines was granted, and the road built.[32]

The paperwork of the WPA at national and state levels was enormous. Requests and complaints were submitted and had to be answered, referred, approved, or investigated; inspections were conducted, reports submitted, and directives issued. This avalanche of red tape complicated the administration of the WPA. The dismissal of one Petersburg worker ran into tens of letters, while the correspondence of another reliefer, Marion Merryman, was so great that he had his own personal file in Washington. Merryman, a seventy-six-year-old former contractor, was given a WPA job painting roof directional signs for airport projects in Virginia. Thereafter he faithfully wrote Hopkins and Roosevelt suggesting additional work to be accomplished by the WPA. While praising his benefactors, he frequently criticized the two Virginia senators: "They are so insane as to be talking of bringing impeachment proceedings against you. I won't say they ought to be put in the penitentiary but I do think they should be given mental treatment." When he lost his job because of his age and the hazardous nature of the work, Merryman continued to write the WPA, blaming his dismissal on Byrd.[33] Another incident produced the following letter from a resident of New Castle: "I respectfully request you to investigate why the . . . relief workers moved about two railroad carloads of junk from a junk pile near the town of New Castle, Virginia, to a . . . tract of our land one mile north of the town." WPA Washington referred this to WPA Richmond, which placed the blame on local authorities who were responsible for the completion of projects.[34]

Despite all the protests, red tape, and inefficiencies, WPA was well received in Virginia. The opposition of Old Dominion politicians contrasts sharply with the responses of the aid recipients, who were less preoccupied with preserving the status quo and balancing budgets. An early survey of sponsors testified to its acceptability at the local level, and in 1938 a more independent study by the National Appraisal Committee on Community Improvements discovered overwhelming nationwide acclaim of the program. The NYA and the PWA were also commended. The Virginia Appraisal Committee, composed of prominent Virginians and sponsored by the League of Virginia Municipalities and the League of Virginia Counties, uncovered similar sentiments in the Old Dominion. It was one of twenty state committees giving full approval to the continuation of the WPA or a similar federal program. The committee report declared: "The quality of the projects and the increased voluntary activities of the public bodies in the planning and operation of projects of their choosing all indicate that the Works Program is headed in the right direction and the combined efforts of Federal and local governments will continually improve the quality of the program. . . . Some program of the nature of the WPA was necessary in order to take care of them [the unemployed] and in our judgment will be necessary as long as there is a relief program." It believed the only weak link in the Virginia admin-

101

istration lay in the lack of training for unskilled workers. The committee also discovered that the financial contribution of Virginia sponsors (27.3 percent of the total cost) was above the national average.[35]

The WPA came to an end in 1943 as the war and returning prosperity drastically reduced the number of unemployed. Its cost in Virginia was $107 million, of which $78.8 million was federal money. The Old Dominion did not rank among the leading recipients of WPA money (being thirty-second), primarily because of a lesser relief need in the state. Since it was a federally operated program requiring no matching state funds, organization leaders could do little to obstruct its work other than to admonish Washington for its excesses. Byrd and Glass did not like New Deal spending, but they always tried to get a fair share of it for Virginia. Roosevelt and Hopkins may have reduced the WPA's contribution to Virginia somewhat in order to discipline the Virginia senators for their lack of support, but the main reason for the low ranking was economic, not political. WPA money was distributed on the basis of 40 percent for population, 40 percent for unemployment rates, and 20 percent on a discretionary basis, considering such factors as the number on direct relief, those receiving unemployment compensation, and the number employed on other federal projects. Since the number of unemployed and those on direct relief in the state was low, WPA funds entering Virginia were low. The incidence of WPA workers in Virginia ranged from 75 to 115 per 10,000 population, about half the national average for 1935–39. During the recession year of 1937–38, the Old Dominion had one of the lowest unemployment rates in the nation and the second lowest incidence of WPA workers. By March 1940 Virginia was one of six states where less than 10 percent of the labor force was unemployed or on emergency work. Furthermore, the rural nature of Virginia and its faster recovery from the depression inhibited the work of the WPA, which was less oriented toward rural relief than the FERA had been and poured money into the hard-hit states of the urban, industrial Northeast.[36]

Even so, there was unquestionably a large segment of Virginia's population in need in the late thirties. It is estimated that 95,000 Virginians worked for the WPA at one time or another during its eight-year existence, earning $66 million. Rolls peaked early at 40,000 in December 1935, fluctuated between 16,000 and 32,000 as economic conditions improved or worsened, and finally dwindled to a few thousand by 1942. In the Old Dominion the WPA produced 5.2 million garments in the sewing rooms, served 32.8 million school lunches, and constructed or improved 7,602 miles of highways, roads, and streets, 695 bridges, 1,000 schools, and 135,056 sanitary privies. The quality of projects was proportional to the interest and effort of the sponsors. Fortunately for Virginia, administration was decentralized and the localities played an active role in the planning and direction of the work. The major weakness was the uncertainty of the WPA's continuation from year to year, which limited planning and caused some of the best projects to be cut.[37]

The psychological impact of the WPA in Virginia was also substantial. Along with the CWA and the FERA, it awakened a social conscience in the state and helped restore the confidence of Virginians in the future. Said an Albermarle farmer: "WPA built an addition to our local school. The major advantage was that it gave some of the local people a chance to work. This relieved many tensions [that] were gaining momentum during these times." A Richmond social worker claimed that WPA work not only provided employment but "maintained a measure of dignity and self esteem." Concluded the Virginia WPA employment division: "The closing of the program leaves Virginia communities both intangibly and tangibly enriched. Not only has the personal integrity of its people been safeguarded, but the improved road systems, public buildings, airports, stadiums, etc., stand as concrete monuments to the efforts of the unemployed citizen."[38] If the WPA was not as pervasive in Virginia as in some states, its impact on those in need in the Old Dominion was just as great. Said Representative Woodrum: "You do not have to look far to find very many fine things about this relief program. . . . Much of a notable character has been accomplished that will remain all through the years . . . every Congressman saw that as he went through his district. . . . Why it sounds almost like the accomplishments of King Solomon."[39]

Searle Charles has said of the Roosevelt relief program, "In maintaining the health and skills of millions of people, in supporting public education, and in renewing faith in the American democratic system, the relief program was as important as any other program of the New Deal."[40] Certainly this was true in Virginia, where it accounted for more federal money spent and directly touched the lives of more Virginians than any other administration measure. It mitigated depression conditions and educated, entertained, and trained thousands of citizens. Nevertheless, once it had passed from view, there were few reminders that it had been a prominent New Deal effort. Poverty— especially in rural areas—racial discrimination, and political indifference remained. The state made improvements to its welfare program, but they were contrived to avoid embarrassment, not bring social uplift. This failure was partially the responsibility of the Byrd organization, which was opposed to widespread reform for political and economic reasons, but it was also the fault of the relief programs themselves, for they were not dynamic enough to alter the social condition. Designed to restore the status quo, the CWA, the FERA, and the WPA arrived on the scene, effectively carried out their work, and departed, leaving a grateful populace but one which was little better off than it had been before the depression.[41]

6

The New Deal and
the Farmer

Next to the unemployed, no group drew as much attention from the New Deal as the farmers. Living in straitened circumstances since the end of the world war, they had long endured the ineffectual attempts of politicians to solve their basic problem of overproduction. The depression only worsened their situation. By 1932 farm prices had dropped to half of what they had been three years earlier and farm cash income declined to its lowest point in twenty-six years. Confronted with prices that did not cover their production costs, farmers permitted their crops to rot rather than market them. Faced with foreclosures on their farms, they often resorted to violence to save them. Conservative American farmers were now susceptible to almost any course of action that would bring favorable results, even to plowing under cotton and slaughtering little pigs!

That the New Deal would kill baby pigs in order to raise prices reveals the gravity of the situation and the extent to which Roosevelt's farm advisers were willing to go to combat the depression. Formulated to appeal to the several wings of the farm bloc, Roosevelt's first farm bill gave the executive branch broad discretionary power to restrict farm acreage and negotiate marketing agreements. The president established the Agricultural Adjustment Administration (AAA) to administer the program and placed it under the Department of Agriculture, where it soon became the key agency in the New Deal's attack on the farm problem. Henry Wallace, following in the footsteps of his father, was appointed secretary of agriculture, and George Peek was named to head the AAA. Wallace advocated reducing production through acreage allotments and benefit payments to contracting farmers, whereas Peek championed marketing agreements and the dumping of surpluses abroad as remedies for overproduction. Their differences came to a head in late 1933; Peek resigned and Wallace's domestic allotment plan became the basis for AAA policy thereafter.[1]

The farm bill was passed too late to prevent planting for 1933, thus necessitating the "plow-up" and the "kill." Because cotton surpluses were already enormous, Wallace advised the uprooting, which resulted in the turnover of ten million acres of cotton and the payment of $100 million to cotton farmers. Similar market conditions prompted the slaughter of six million pigs. Neither was of great consequence in the Old Dominion since cotton and hog production were not vital sectors of the state's agricultural economy. Although small amounts of tobacco were also plowed under, the AAA attempted to raise tobacco prices in 1933 through marketing agreements made with the buyers, who agreed to purchase at a stable price. Farm officials exhorted producers of other commodities to curtail the quantity marketed.

Wallace's domestic allotment plan was fully implemented in 1934. Contracts were signed with cooperating farmers who agreed to reduce their acreage of the specified crop in return for monetary payments supplied by a tax levied on the processors of agricultural commodities. The payments provided an incentive for reducing production and increased the purchasing power of the farmers. There was no enforced control of production for most of the basic commodities, only the inducement of receiving extra money if production was curtailed. There were two exceptions—cotton and tobacco. AAA officials feared that too many cotton and tobacco growers would remain outside the program and destroy its effectiveness by increasing their production while contract signers were cutting back. To prevent this, Congress passed in the spring of 1934 the Bankhead Cotton Control Act and the Kerr-Smith Tobacco Act, which imposed taxes on cotton and tobacco production of nonsigning farmers and contracting farmers who exceeded their allotments.[2]

In spite of its crop diversity, the agricultural sector of the Virginia economy reacted to the depression much like farming in the nation did. Farm prices, crop values, and cash income hit new lows in 1932. Such conditions encouraged Virginia farmers to cast aside their traditional conservatism and welcome the AAA. Old Dominion cotton growers plowed under part of their crop; thousands of wheat and tobacco farmers scurried to sign pledges reducing their 1934 acreage; and peanut growers entered into a marketing agreement which covered 75 percent of the Virginia and North Carolina peanut crop. When it became evident that tobacco prices would remain low in 1933, the AAA obtained a guaranteed minimum price from tobacco manufacturers by threatening drastic future production regulations. Utilizing publicity drives and educational meetings, state extension service agents and field representatives of the AAA conducted sign-up campaigns in which the farmers selected base acreages for determining their assigned allotment. For the crop year 1934 a 30 percent acreage reduction was assigned flue-cured tobacco farmers, who produced two-thirds of the state's tobacco crop; a 33 percent reduction was recommended for Virginia's cotton growers. The government agreed to pay $17.50 for each acre of tobacco removed from production.[3]

The first full year under the AAA program witnessed phenomenal gains in prices, crop values, and cash income. With production reduced by 13 million pounds, the state's tobacco crop doubled in price to twenty-three cents a pound and was valued at over $18 million, a gain of $6.6 million. All Virginia farmers benefited from the price increases, but only about 48,000 of them, one-fourth of the total, were under AAA contract.[4] In the first ten months of 1934, participating farmers in all but two counties received $2,232,000 in benefit payments. For this same period, $8,814,000 was collected in processing taxes in Virginia. Said extension agent S. B. Surber: "1934 . . . is a red letter year for the farmers of Alleghany County. I believe my farmers are really beginning to appreciate this effort our government is making to put farming on a level with other industries." However, one Virginia farmer remained suspicious of government grants, depositing his payments in a separate bank account because he knew they were "going to come and get it."[5]

This was also the year of Senator Byrd's public disavowal of the New Deal. The initial break came over agricultural policy. This was rather surprising because Byrd had endorsed the first farm act and had worked vigorously in early 1934 to have peanuts included in the basic commodity program.[6] But he did not like the coercive and bureaucratic features of the legislation, and

107

when a new AAA bill was introduced which extended the licensing power of the secretary of agriculture and permitted stricter production controls, Byrd rebelled. He believed the bill gave the secretary the power to determine what and how much was to be produced, power "inconsistent with the ideals of the Democratic Party [that] will . . . menace, if not destroy, the broad program of economic recovery sponsored by the President." "We do not want," he declared, "a Hitler of American agriculture." At the same time, he charged that the Bankhead Cotton Act was confiscating property without due process, claiming it made "criminals of those who plant in excess." In the face of New Deal arguments to the contrary, the senator led the fight against many of the amendments to the AAA. His tactics were also responsible for the inclusion in the Kerr-Smith Act of a provision stipulating that two-thirds of the farmers had to approve the program before it became operative. Finally, Byrd opposed the nomination of brain truster Rexford Tugwell as undersecretary of agriculture on the ground that "he has no proper conception of the principles of this government." Tugwell, however, was confirmed over Byrd's objections.[7]

Fellow Virginians were not in complete agreement with the senator regarding the AAA. Its benefits seemed to outweigh the liabilities. Representative John Flannagan of Bristol declared: "I am not in sympathy with those who seem to think the Agriculture Department is trying to Hitlerize the farmers. The farm program with one exception is a voluntary program. It hasn't been imposed upon the farmers, it has been worked out in cooperation with the farmers. I do not know of any farmers who think they are being Hitlerized."[8] Another Virginian wrote to Tugwell: "I do criticize him [Byrd] for masquerading under false colors. He belongs in the old line Republican ranks whose program includes no money experiments, the balanced budget, no direct relief, no public works, in fact the program followed between 1920 and 1932."[9] A survey of the Southside tobacco region gave Byrd mixed support. A Nottoway farmer said: "Byrd is about right. Wallace is a good man but I don't like the idea of him having complete say over what I must do on my farm." Commented an Amelia merchant, "Byrd hit the nail on the head when he said we'd be like Russia if more power is given

Wallace." However, a Southside assemblyman represented the majority opinion when he accused Byrd of "obstructing farm recovery. . . . I hope he cannot stop the passage of the amendment to the AAA."[10] Much of the senator's private support, in the form of typewritten letters and telegrams, came from large producers, packing companies, and shippers such as the Eastern Apple Growers Council and the American Association of Creamery Butter Manufacturers.[11]

While refraining from attacking Byrd, other Virginians enthusiastically supported the farm program. A Gainesville farmer wrote R. Walton Moore, undersecretary of state, "I have been so well pleased with the improvement in agricultural conditions since the beginning of Mr. Roosevelt's administration, that I am writing to outline some of them to you." The head of the Virginia Farm Bureau Federation, G. F. Holsinger, called the Adjustment Act "the most important piece of legislation ever enacted in behalf of agriculture." Writing to Wallace, Holsinger stated: "I wish to express my hearty approval of your crop-reduction program. I believe our farmers are very largely behind your program and are pleased to know of your continuing the work." Holsinger apparently spoke for most of the 4,000 farmers in the Virginia Federation.[12]

The director of the Virginia Extension Service at VPI, John Hutcheson, also was an ardent defender of the AAA, attributing the rise in farm prices to New Deal policies. Hutcheson called the AAA "the greatest educational experience that farmers have ever had."[13] The extension service in Virginia and across the nation played an active role in implementing the AAA. Administration at the local level was theoretically in the hands of elected farm committees (control associations), which were responsible for the sign-up campaigns, determining individual allotments, and assuring compliance, but they relied heavily on the county agents of the extension service. Much of an agent's time was now taken up with AAA work—explaining programs, benefits, and methods—but the federal program compensated for this, said the Amelia County agent, by "strengthening the position of Extension work with many farmers who have never before been interested in it." Responsibility for distributing benefit checks further enhanced the image of the agents.[14]

The best indication of the popularity of the farm program in Virginia was the action of the farmers themselves. At the end of 1934 there were 171 county production control associations in the state representing 50,000 farmers. Cotton planters in the South voted by a nine-to-one margin to retain the Bankhead Act in 1935, while those in Virginia were thirty-to-one in favor. The vote on the Kerr-Smith Tobacco Act was just as conclusive, with 99 percent of the flue-cured farmers approving; Halifax farmers responded affirmatively, 3,000 to 9. The 1935 vote on continued acreage control of tobacco in Virginia for the 1936 crop year produced a 19,229-to-293 endorsement. Votes of Virginia farmers producing wheat and the other types of tobacco (dark air-cured, fire-cured, and burley) also favored the controls.[15]

However, Senator Byrd was not deterred. Disregarding his constituents, he continued his fight in 1935 against amendments giving more power to Wallace, especially over commodities not then under contract, such as fruits and vegetables. Being an apple grower himself, he was not entirely disinterested. Sarcastically he prophesied, "Only the person who eats the food will escape this Federal dictatorship." He won amendments to the bill requiring 75 percent of the producers of a commodity to approve controls before they could become effective; he had fruits prepared for canning exempted from control; and he was successful in preventing the passage of a rayon-processing tax. Byrd was assisted by Senator Glass on one occasion when, in reference to a proposed marketing arrangement for honey, the venerable statesman claimed he did not want to go to jail because he could not "control the activities of my queen bee." The amendment was laughed down. With the objectionable sections having been removed, both Byrd and Glass were paired in favor of the final bill, which passed the Senate, 64 to 15. Besides giving additional powers to the secretary over new commodities, the legislation banned the reclamation of processing taxes if the AAA was declared unconstitutional, extended the Bankhead and Kerr-Smith control acts for two years with producer approval, and enacted a potato control measure. Proving the value of an opposition voice, Byrd's successful struggle strengthened the final bill and benefited several interests in the Old Dominion.[16]

Virginia potato farmers played an important role in the enactment of the potato control measure. Failing to enjoy the returning prosperity experienced by their neighbors and influenced by the apparent success of the cotton and tobacco control bills, the potato growers of the Eastern Shore petitioned Congressman Otis Bland, demanding a potato control bill. The farmers took more drastic action in July when 500 armed men in Painter forced the unloading of potatoes from the vehicles transporting them to market. Potatoes purchased at a higher price were allowed to go through. This action prompted legislation that led to the assignment of production quotas and the imposition of taxes on excess production. However, the potato program never was fully implemented because of a lack of enthusiasm for it within the AAA and the forthcoming court decision striking down control legislation.

Congressman Flannagan pushed through one final piece of legislation to benefit Old Dominion tobacco growers. The fascinating but bewildering process of the tobacco auction frequently disguised deals among warehousemen, speculators, and manufacturers' agents that bilked the grower of a fair price for his leaf. Flannagan called for a federal tobacco inspection and grading service to protect the interests of the farmers and the small warehousemen who were at the mercy of manufacturers' price discrimination. With the support of tobacco state congressmen, the bill passed in August 1935.[17]

The AAA proved itself once again in 1935 as gains were made in prices, crop values, and cash income. Eighty-seven percent of the Virginia tobacco farms were now under contract; 67 percent of the peanut farms; 61 percent, cotton (93 percent of the acreage planted); 12 percent, wheat; and 5 percent, corn-hog. Over two years these farmers received benefit payments totaling more than $7 million, an amount which placed the state thirty-first in the nation in receipts—a low ranking attributable to Virginia's agricultural diversity and large proportion of subsistence farms that did not produce for a market. One-crop agricultural states were the major recipients of AAA payments. The cotton states of the South and the wheat and corn states of the Midwest far outdistanced the Old Dominion in amounts received; Texas farmers received $133 million; Iowa farmers, $93 million; Alabama growers, $30 million. Of the $7 million paid

111

out in Virginia, cotton growers received $770,209; wheat growers, $1,451,631; tobacco growers, $2,430,404; corn-hog farmers, $1,914,857; and peanut growers, $507,392. The AAA also conducted a soil conservation program in the Old Dominion which retired over 100,000 acres planted in the basic crops. Price increases in Virginia between 1932 and 1935 showed the full measure of the improvement in farm conditions: tobacco, 8.9¢ to 17.9¢ a pound; cotton, 6.4¢ to 11.4¢ a pound; peanuts, 1.5¢ to 3.2¢ a pound; wheat, 58¢ to 88¢ a bushel; and corn, 52¢ to 81¢ a bushel.[18]

There is debate as to what extent the AAA was responsible for this improvement. Nationally, farm income improved 58 percent, but it was still only 66 percent of 1929 figures; farm prices were higher, but so were the prices of goods that farmers had to buy; $1.2 billion in benefit payments had reached the farmers, but this was a small percentage of farm income. While most commentators agree that the AAA was of some benefit in combating the emergency, they point out that the farmers were also aided by advances in the total economy and the severe droughts of the thirties, which curtailed production. Even the AAA report acknowledged the contribution of these forces plus dollar devaluation in boosting farm prices.[19]

Although Virginia's agricultural situation precluded a large inflow of federal farm money, the impact of the AAA in the Old Dominion was substantial, primarily because the cotton and tobacco control programs were the most effective in raising prices. The Kerr-Smith tobacco control act was particularly effective in reducing production because it forbade transfer of the tax-exemption certificates on the farmer's contracted allotment. The droughts did not appreciably affect these crops as they did the wheat harvests in the West, leading Harold Rowe to conclude that tobacco production would have been substantially higher, thus negating better prices, if the AAA had not been in existence. Virginia farm experts John Hutcheson and H. N. Young conceded the influence of currency changes and the droughts but attributed the rising prices to the AAA. Commenting on the AAA in Virginia, economist Leland Tate said, "It appears . . . that the adjustment program at least had a positive influence on the prices of the commodities with which it was directly connected, and probably had some influence on the prices of related commodities." Federal monetary policy, farm credit policy, relief grants, and, indirectly, the droughts all were factors in the return of better times to the farms, but it was the curtailment of production promoted by the AAA and the corresponding price increases that were most responsible for restoring dignity to farm life.[20]

Nevertheless, the AAA had its liabilities. Designed primarily to control the production of the large producers, it had little effect on small subsistence farms and farms producing noncontrolled commodities like vegetables and dairy products. This reduced its influence in the Old Dominion where 44 percent of the farms were under 50 acres and 20 percent were under 20 acres. In 1936 only 3 percent of Virginia farms of less than 20 acres were participating, while 62 percent of the 220-to-499-acre farms were involved. Crop controls were detrimental to tenants and laborers who were evicted or lost jobs because acres were taken out of production. Moreover, the tenants who remained to work the contracted acreage were lucky if they received payments from the owners in whose name the land had been contracted. The AAA estimated that in the high-tenancy counties of Virginia, such as Southampton (cotton) and Halifax (tobacco), most tenants received no benefits. Even one of the best features of the New Deal farm program was counterproductive. The AAA was teaching farmers how to take better care of their farms—educating them in the use of fertilizers, conservation methods, and better farm management techniques—all of which led to increasing the production that the AAA was desperately trying to control. Charged with waste and dishonesty, the New Dealers unquestionably made mistakes, but much of the criticism reflected disappointment with programs that were oversold or with allotments that favored the larger farmers.[21]

Although it had substantial support from the beginning, the AAA did have to overcome the reservations of many farmers who worried about its innovative nature and coercive tactics. The AAA challenged time-honored agrarian ideals and methods. Independent, self-sufficient farmers, of which Virginia had a notable breed, rejected dictation and were suspicious of outsiders importing change. Recalled one extension agent: "Farmers detested the program; they did not like to be told what they could or could not do. They tolerated it because they secured increased prices." Believing it sacrilegious to destroy crops and let land lie fallow, some Old Dominion farmers quoted the Bible to extension agents who were explaining the plow-up. Others resorted to hidden fields and incorrect acreage bases to circumvent the system. Most dissenting farmers, however, eventually resigned themselves to federal intervention. Older voluntary programs had proved unsuccessful; other alternatives had not presented themselves. At that point, said agent John Freeman, farmers "would have accepted most any measure designed to help them regain a market for their produce, provide emergency credit, and aid in putting production . . . in line with demand."

When the coercive methods proved successful in raising prices and putting money in pockets, principles were forgotten and cooperation followed. Those farmers not complying were soon revealed to the compliance checkers by their neighbors. The conversion of the Danville *Register* typified this change in opinion toward the agricultural program. Initially opposed to "legislating . . . prosperity for the American farmer," this tobacco-land newspaper became a defender of the AAA, criticizing industry and the "old guarders" who objected to a "political machine that is finally delivering to farmers." Concluded Lee County agent Homer Eller, "The only people who cursed the program were a few diehard Republicans who couldn't stand to see the Democrats get credit for doing a needed job." Continued participation was proof that Old Dominion farmers had accepted a new way of life on the farm.[22]

On January 6, 1936, the AAA program in its existing form came to an end. In *U.S. v. Butler*, or the Hoosac Mills case, the Supreme Court in a six-to-three decision invalidated the two major features of the program—the processing tax and the acreage reduction contracts—because they went "beyond the powers delegated to the Federal Government." It was not an entirely unexpected decision. The Kerr-Smith Tobacco Control Act had already been held unconstitutional by a federal district

114

court; the collection of the processing tax on peanuts had been halted by a federal district judge in Norfolk; and hundreds of industrial concerns, including several in Virginia, were waging war against the collection of the tax on their products. A Gallup poll, taken just before the decision was announced, showed the nation opposed to AAA, 59 percent to 41 percent, in part because it was "sinful to kill hogs and plow crops under." The South, benefiting from the cotton and tobacco control acts, was the only section to favor the AAA, 57 percent to 43 percent.[23]

In Virginia, in spite of the hope of one farmer that the AAA be "throwed out the window," there was genuine dismay at the decision. The *Times-Dispatch* thought it a "stunning blow," a "strait jacket" decision devoid of common sense and "as heedless of public welfare as the Dred Scott decision." The editor concluded, "Certainly it is clear that some form of control must be devised to prevent the loss of all that has been gained through the AAA." State officials, including Governor Peery, believed the decision a blow to the farm program in the Commonwealth and immediately sought new legislation. Agricultural Commissioner George Koiner thought Virginia farmers would even support a constitutional amendment continuing the program. Bitter toward the companies that worked to kill the AAA, Koiner did not think they would pass the tax reduction on to the consumer but "do just what they always have done in the past—charge the consumer a good fat price and pocket the difference."[24]

Almost at once a new farm plan was put into effect. The Soil Conservation and Domestic Allotment Act was approved February 29, 1936, "to promote the conservation and profitable use of agricultural land resources by temporary Federal aid to farmers." Although couched in language designed to appeal to everyone, including Senator Byrd who voted for it, the new program had as its primary objective production control. It would pay benefits of up to $10 an acre for shifting from" soil-depleting" crops (the basic commodities) to "soil-conserving" crops that would rebuild the soil. Additional smaller payments would be available for the use of approved soil-building practices such as seeding legumes, planting trees, and controlling erosion. An advantage of the new program was its availability to all farmers, not just to those planting the basic commodities. Commenting on the pretense of this bill, the *Times-Dispatch* said, "Congress must resort to subterfuge . . . and is justified in doing so."[25]

Virginians were generally pleased with the replacement. The Department of Agriculture estimated that 10 percent of Virginia's harvested acreage would be retired and $4 million in benefits paid to the farmers. Nevertheless, tobacco farmers, concerned that the loss of the AAA would adversely affect prices, called for a regional tobacco control plan for the six leading tobacco-producing states. The General Assembly and Congress approved such a plan creating a tobacco commission to determine demand and set state quotas. Some agreement was reached among the various state leaders, but the failure of the Georgia and South Carolina legislatures to enact similar legislation a year later destroyed any chance for a quick renewal of strict crop controls and clearly demonstrated the need for federal legislation.[26]

Conservation was not a new phenomenon in Virginia. The Department of the Interior had established a Soil Erosion Service in 1933 to educate farmers on the need for and the benefits of erosion control. It had been transferred to the Department of Agriculture in 1935 and formed into a new bureau, the Soil Conservation Service (SCS). Working with the extension service and the state Department of Conservation in what was primarily an educational capacity, the SCS set up three demonstration areas in Virginia—on the Banister River (Pittsylvania County), on the Sandy River (Henry County), and on Wreck Island Creek (Campbell and Appomattox counties)—and eleven smaller emergency conservation work camps in cooperation with the CCC, all to work with farmers in demonstrating proper erosion control practices. These included crop rotation, contour tillage, strip cropping, terracing and run-off control, repairing gullies, use of pasturage, and reforestation; all were designed to prevent erosion, preserve soil and water resources, and retire land that could not be farmed profitably. By March 1936, when the new AAA conservation act went into effect, 168,000 acres were under cooperative agreement in the SCS program to prevent erosion. There was, however, no reimbursement for the improvement of these acres.[27]

In comparison, the new program (which did not terminate the SCS) paid out large sums for the retirement of lands usually planted in basic crops and lesser amounts for soil-building procedures similar to those supported by the SCS. In its first year, 46,219 Virginia farmers applied for grants; 167,000 acres were diverted from soil-depleting crops; and soil-building practices were carried out on nearly one million acres. Although the conservation program was less effective than the allotment plan in controlling production, the continuation of federal funds helped Virginia farmers enjoy another good year in 1936. A drought (for which Virginia received federal aid) also assisted in keeping production low even without compulsory controls, and prices, crop values, and cash income once again rose. Tobacco production dipped slightly, but prices and values were up; potatoes tripled in price and doubled in value, while advances were also made in corn, wheat, peanuts, and cotton.[28]

In 1938 Congress passed the long-awaited "permanent solution" to the farm problem—the "ever normal granary" bill. It was designed to provide parity for the farmer by balancing crop supply and demand through a combination of production and marketing controls. The AAA would estimate the crop need for the coming year, allot acreage among the states on the basis of these estimates, and, as a part of the conservation program, pay benefits to the farmers who remained within their individual allotments. In the event of oversupply, the Commodity Credit Corporation, established in 1933, would store the excess and grant loans to farmers, using their surplus crops as collateral. This gave the farmers a percentage of the crop value for their immediate use and kept the surplus from flooding the market. If production still proved excessive, the secretary of agriculture could place marketing restrictions on the growers of the crop involved if two-thirds of them approved. Any sales above these restrictions would be taxed. If supplies proved too small, the government would release part of the stored crop. Senator Byrd was paired in favor of the final bill after opposing an earlier version; Representative Robertson was the only Virginian to cast a dissenting vote.[29]

Secretary Wallace immediately foresaw a surplus in cotton and tobacco and moved to poll these farmers to obtain approval for the establishment of marketing quotas. Virginia farmers once again overwhelmingly endorsed the new controls of the AAA, but the new allotments dissatisfied many Southside tobacco farmers who believed the reductions from the 1937 acreage were too great. Small growers were particularly aggravated. One Bedford farmer angrily cried, "I don't think we . . . need a dictator to say what we should do."[30] Halifax and Pittsylvania farmers charged that those who had not participated in the conservation program were being discriminated against by having to take the largest reductions. They ignored the fact that those already in the program had reduced their acreage in previous years while others had continued to produce without restrictions. The farmers also disliked the increase in Florida and Georgia allotments while Virginia's had been cut. They petitioned Wallace for adjustments in the allotments and asked Senator Byrd to have the state quotas increased. AAA and extension service officials defended the allotments and asked for compliance, pointing out that individual adjustments could be made through the local county committees. J. B. Hutson, an assistant AAA administrator, warned, "The allotments are small as compared with what farmers desire to grow, but it may be better to grow the smaller acreage at favorable prices than to grow a larger acreage at whatever price would be obtained in the market."[31] After Byrd obtained a small increase in the quotas, farmers reluctantly accepted their new allotments. In July a marketing quota of 65.5 million pounds was set for Virginia flue-cured tobacco, down 6.5 million from 1937 production.[32]

The result was disappointing. While prices rose slightly for the 1938 crop, the cut in production caused a $2 million loss in the value of the total tobacco crop. At year's end, in spite of an increase of 5 million pounds in their quota, Virginia tobacco farmers, along with those in other states, rejected the control program. The defeat was attributed to dissatisfaction with the supposed inequities of the 1938 apportionments, poor administration, and a restlessness with a control system. They were "tired of being told what to do," said William Daughtrey of the extension service. Farmers foresaw higher prices and envisioned the profits a larger crop would bring them.[33]

It was not long before they were to regret their decision. With unrestricted production and selling in 1939, production jumped 50 percent but prices declined to their lowest level since 1933. This overproduction and the suspension of British buying at the opening of the European war glutted the market. Only through the efforts of the Commodity Credit Corporation were prices maintained at the fifteen-cent level. In a late-year referendum the growers quickly adopted the quota system again for a three-year period.[34]

Although farm income declined in state and nation in 1938 due to the recession, AAA payments and price supports softened the impact. Over 100,000 Virginia farmers received $4.4 million, of which $2.5 million was for soil-building practices. The following year a similar amount was received by a like number of farmers, who constituted over half of Virginia's producers. Compared to amounts received elsewhere, these figures attest to the small dollar contribution of the AAA to the Old Dominion, a majority of whose farms were not oriented to large commercial production. But they overlook the accomplishment of the primary objectives of the program, which were of great benefit even in Virginia: the raising of farm prices and—a much more intangible contribution—the restoration of hope among a people who only six years earlier had questioned their existence as the nation's providers. The AAA did not restore the halcyon days of 1910–20 to the American farm. In fact, it was struggling to raise prices and income to predepression levels when the war arrived with its full employment and high exports to bring prosperity to the farmer once again. Nevertheless, this should not obscure the AAA's achievements as a harbinger of hope and recovery. Wrote P. H. DeHart of the Virginia extension service: "It is my opinion that if our government had not taken action we would not have the type of government in this country we have today. One great value of these new deal programs was to let the people know that someone cared and was doing something to try to help. This provided the courage and motivation to keep on trying and not give up."[35]

In addition to its efforts to control production and raise prices, the New Deal aided the farmer in three other fields—credit, rehabilitation, and electrification. The Farm Credit Administration (FCA) was created by executive order on March 27, 1933, to coordinate all farm credit activities, including the federal land banks, the office of the Land Bank Commissioner, the federal Intermediate Credit Bank and, after passage of the Farm Credit Act in June, a system of regional banks for cooperatives and a system of twelve production credit corporations. The primary objective of the land banks, which had been established in 1916, was the refinancing of farm mortgages, which were being foreclosed by the thousands in 1932 and 1933. With private credit restricted, the government was the only remaining source of funds with which to save farmers' homes and lands. Within three years over $2 billion in land bank and land bank commissioner loans were granted to 760,000 farms in the country. In Virginia, during the same period, farmers were granted 2,967 land bank loans worth $11 million and 5,237 land bank commissioner loans totaling $9 million. The relatively small number of loans suggests that foreclosures were not a major problem for Virginia farming. By the end of 1938, Virginia farmers had 16,472 loans outstanding with the land banks and the land bank commissioner that totaled $35.3 million (twenty-fifth in the country). Iowa had $263 million outstanding in loans, and Texas had $254 million outstanding on over 100,000 loans.[36]

The other credit facilities provided farmers with short-term loans for the financing of annual crop production and marketing. The banks for cooperatives loaned to individuals through their farmer co-ops. In the first year of operation they reached 10,700 Virginia farmers with $757,000. The production credit corporations assisted farmers (ten or more) by organizing local credit associations, investing in their stock, and facilitating the flow of money from the intermediate credit banks to the farmers. Fifteen such associations were formed in Virginia, and in the first decade of operation, 38,022 loans were made averaging $881 per loan. The FCA also aided in the adjustment of farm debts by encouraging the establishment of local and state farm debt adjustment committees that assisted creditor and debtor to reach agreement. Within three years, mortgage debts were reduced by almost $1 million in Virginia. There were few objections to the work of the FCA, which, according to Virginia farm economist H. N. Young, "put the lending of money to farmers on a sound basis [and] prevented many foreclosures."[37]

One of the most ambitious and humanitarian schemes of the New Deal, yet one which never achieved its full potential, was the rural rehabilitation program. Initiated by the FERA as an adjunct to regular rural relief, the program attempted to remove farm families from the relief rolls and make them self-sufficient by providing them loans with which to buy draft animals, seed, and fertilizer. Back taxes were paid, farms were remortgaged, and in a few instances, families were relocated on more fertile land. About 3,500 rural Virginia families were being supervised by the FERA in this manner when the program was turned over to the newly formed Resettlement Administration (RA) in June 1935. The RA instituted a four-point program which expanded the FERA effort: (1) rural rehabilitation—credit for farm families to purchase necessary stock, equipment, and land; (2) land utilization—the purchase of land unsuited for farming for other uses; (3) rural resettlement—development of farms on profitable farmland for families presently on unsuitable land; and (4) suburban resettlement—the creation of new communities that combined the best of rural and urban living.[38]

Virginia was ideally suited for participation in such a program, which was directed primarily at the marginal farm family. The acknowledged expert on Virginia's rural poverty in the 1930s, W. E. Garnett, rural sociologist at VPI, estimated that half of the rural population, some 875,000 people, was marginal—even in normal times! In general, they had gross incomes of less than $600, had less than a fifth-grade education, lived in poor housing, suffered poor health, and paid little or no taxes. His estimate included 325,000 rural Negroes, 118,000 white tenants and families, 150,000 mountain whites, 164,000 white farm laborers and families, and 118,000 farm owners and families.[39] Furthermore, the state had a high percentage of self-sufficiency farms (25.9 percent)—those farms "where value of the farm products used by the family was 50 percent or more of the total value of all products of the farm." Concentrated largely in the tobacco-growing area and in the mountainous western region, these small, unproductive farms had dotted the Virginia countryside since the Civil War. Because of their self-sufficient nature, the depression had little impact on them, and their owners were probably better equipped psychologically to endure the

Crash than those on more prosperous farms and in the cities. Nevertheless, since the New Deal did not demand to know the cause of a man's poverty, these families were eligible for resettlement aid.[40]

While the majority of poor farmers continued to live at or below subsistence levels without assistance, many "marginals" found their way to the relief rolls from which those eligible for rehabilitation were selected. During the first two-and-one-half years of rehabilitation, the Resettlement Administration aided 7,519 Virginia families with loans totaling over $3 million; 1,284 debt adjustments were made, reducing the debt load by $737,537; and the average worth of the rehabilitated families increased $233. Counties with the largest number of participants were Charlotte, Halifax, Patrick, Carroll, Grayson, Mecklenburg, and Pittsylvania. The RA and its successor, the Farm Security Administration (FSA), made determined efforts to ensure that blacks received a proportional share of the loans. On occasion the agency encouraged groups of farmers to pool their resources and take cooperative action to improve their situation. These community service centers, ten of which were in operation in Virginia by late 1937, used resettlement loans to purchase machinery and build laundry and canning centers to serve cooperative members.[41]

The RA's land utilization and rural resettlement plans proposed to take lands too poor for farming out of agricultural use and employ them for conservational and recreational purposes while assisting the families then on the land to relocate on more profitable soil. On most of these sites, conditions were wretched—marginal farm income, high tax delinquency, soil erosion, deteriorating housing, and a poor mortgage situation. A project report for the Appomattox-Buckingham region revealed "a sad picture of present living conditions, which have resulted from the uninformed selection of land for agriculture in the first place, and of the mining of the timber crop and of the soil in the second place. The result is a deplorable situation, which must be met and solved by the Government, or else the people will continue to live in subnormal conditions and be dependent upon the public relief rolls in years to come."[42] Purchases of fallow and eroded land in Virginia included the Surrender Grounds forest in Appomattox and Buckingham counties (23,000 acres) from which was developed the Appomattox Court House National Park, the Prince Edward Forest in Prince Edward County (6,000 acres), Cumberland Forest in Cumberland County (16,000 acres), and Swift Creek Park in Chesterfield County (7,500 acres). In some of these forests and parks the WPA constructed recreational facilities that were turned over to the conservation commission to become part of the state park system. The RA also purchased land in Shenandoah National Park and along the Blue Ridge Parkway and relocated the families living in these recreational areas. The projects received widespread support from local officials. Commented a member of the Board of Supervisors of Prince Edward County, "I am very optimistic about the good I think this type of relief is going to accomplish, and I believe it merits the approval and support of all the citizens of the county."[43]

The most visionary of the resettlement programs was the subsistence homesteads project, which was designed to resettle in small communities people who had little hope of escaping their impoverished environment. One hundred of these communities were built as a part of the collective experiments of the early New Deal. At first set up under the Department of the Interior, the subsistence homestead division was eventually transferred to the RA. The program had a rather tortured existence, being subject to charges of waste and communism, and no new communities were begun after the FSA took over the work of the RA.

Two of these settlements were established in Virginia. Aberdeen Gardens in Newport News was the first Negro subsistence homestead community in the country, consisting of 158 units constructed by black WPA workers at a cost of $1.4 million. It was surrounded by a "greenbelt" of farms and gardens which served more to maintain racial separation than to provide idyllic living. Upon its completion, an attempt was made by local citizens to convert the Gardens to white occupancy, but Will Alexander, the new resettlement director, prevented this.[44]

The other more controversial project was Shenandoah Homesteads, a group of seven communities totaling 160 units spread over five counties, which was designed to take care of the farmers forced off land in Shenandoah National Park. Opposition came from farm and mountain folk who did not want to move and from newspapers who portrayed them as the pawns of bureaucratic government. The loudest objection came from Senator Byrd, who charged the RA with erecting "a permanent monument to waste and extravagance such as has never been known in a civilized country." Byrd believed "simple mountain people" could do without the extravagances of "electricity, refrigeration, factory-made furniture, and indoor privies." Irate at the discovery of a cooperative farm at one community site, he demanded that Secretary Wallace order an end to the expensive project. Wallace contradicted Byrd's figures on the cost of the homesteads and refused to withdraw, but Byrd believed himself vindicated when the RA was abolished and replaced by the FSA.[45]

Rural rehabilitation work was continued by the Farm Security Administration, but the major emphasis of the new agency, created in September 1937, was the granting of loans to tenant farmers, sharecroppers, and farm laborers for the purchase of their own farms. Senator John Bankhead of Alabama had long desired legislation to benefit these forgotten producers, many of whom never received AAA benefit payments because the lands were not contracted in their names. Bankhead's farm tenant bill authorized $10 million in loans in the first year of operation, to be increased to $50 million within two years. Interest was a low 3 percent, and repayment could be spread out over forty years. In the initial year of operation in the Old Dominion, loans averaging $4,500 were given to just forty-six tenants, an indication that, despite its good intentions, the FSA would barely dent the nation's tenancy problem.[46]

If the rural rehabilitation program was limited in scope because of small appropriations, improved conditions among those assisted attested to its effectiveness. Little change in land tenure occurred, but their farms increased in size, crop yields increased, management practices and health conditions improved, and school attendance rose. Although recipients continued to produce 82 percent of their own food and consume two-thirds of their production, their net worth was increasing. Only 14 percent were adjudged not making satisfactory progress toward self-sufficiency. In seven years of rehabilitation work in Virginia,

14,198 farm families received over $7 million in loans and grants, almost half of which had been repaid by June 1941. In tenant purchase loans (1938–40), 256 tenants borrowed $1,455,853, an average of $5,687 per loan. Rural rehabilitation work adjusted 1,916 debts downward by over $1.2 million and paid $27,507 in local taxes; it operated seventeen group medical care units and one dental care unit in the state; and it provided over a thousand families with environmental sanitation grants to screen windows, construct privies, and protect water supplies.[47]

Such philanthropy cannot be overlooked in judging the merit of this program, but neither can the failure of the rehabilitation agencies to touch the lives of a majority of the rural poor be disregarded. Although the magnitude of the related problems of tenancy, sharecropping, and the decline of the small family farm demanded innovative approaches and massive funding, the RA and the FSA were inadequately financed and their programs were too tentative both in scope and implementation. Despite good intentions, the resettlement work was of questionable value since its perpetuation of small farm units ran counter to the growth of large-scale commercial agriculture; the farms on which families were relocated were not large enough to make the residents competitive farmers. Moreover, resettlement created problems for rural people, whose reluctance to change further complicated the effort. In the South, confrontation with the race issue and the crop lien system also militated against reform. Beleaguered by conservative opposition that continually sniped at their funds and philosophy, the agencies felt compelled to select their rehabilitation and tenant families with care and stress their high repayment rate rather than attack the problem on a broad base. The result was a minor experiment in social engineering which passed away under the pressures of wartime.[48]

Far less controversial was the electrification of rural America, one of the most lasting and widely hailed accomplishments of the New Deal. Through the efforts of the Rural Electrification Administration (REA) and the competition it furnished the private utility companies, practically every farm in the country was electrified within two decades. Roosevelt created the REA in 1935 to carry electricity to the rural areas (only 11.5 percent of the farms had electric power in 1936), but it was not until 1936 through the Norris-Rayburn Act that enough money was provided to make it a meaningful venture. Under the new program REA made loans at low interest rates to states, municipalities, and nonprofit farmer or citizen organizations (cooperatives) to build and maintain cooperative power lines and, if power could not be obtained cheaply from public or private sources, to build cooperative generating stations. The cooperatives then sold the power to the farmers to pay off the loans. Money was not available for the REA to electrify the country on its own, but by threatening competition with the private companies, it forced them to reduce electric rates and expand the power system across the nation.

In Virginia, although the utilities were making periodic rate reductions with the approval of the State Corporation Commission, electrification lagged in the farm areas. Only 7.6 percent of Virginia farms had electricity in 1934, and the private companies were unwilling to move into regions where they believed returns would be limited. In January 1936 the first REA cooperative was set up at Bowling Green; within fourteen years it had borrowed $3.4 million and had brought electricity to 9,000 consumers. Within two years additional cooperatives were established at Dayton, Crewe, New Castle, Warsaw, Lovingston, Chase City, Millboro, Culpeper, and Jonesville, many of which purchased power from Virginia Electric and Power Company at wholesale rates. Electricity brought the benefits of modern living to the farms: lighter work loads, improved living standards, entertainment, and the movement of industry and business into untapped regions. Said Henry McGehee, "Getting electricity in 1937 made Fluvanna a nice place to live."[49]

The REA encountered some initial difficulty in Virginia because there was no state legislation authorizing the organization of the cooperatives. Rectifying this in 1936, the General Assembly also passed legislation that threatened the future of the REA in Virginia. The State Corporation Commission was given the authority to order power companies into difficult-to-reach areas upon the request of farmers. The commission claimed that the REA had no right to keep the private companies out even though the cooperatives were already there. When it ordered Vepco to extend lines into REA territory, REA administrator Morris Cooke countered by ordering all activities in the state stopped until the commission displayed a friendlier attitude toward the REA. He hinted at a two-year delay that might cost the state $10 to $12 million. The dispute was quickly cleared up, and private electric power companies pledged cooperation in bringing electricity to rural Virginia.[50]

The impetus given the private companies by the REA was phenomenal. Within three years they were putting up line at the rate of a thousand miles a year, a 100 percent increase over the 1925–35 average. One Virginia farmer described it as a "mad rush." Homer Eller, extension agent of Lee County, recalled organizing an REA project in 1940: "The power companies wouldn't talk to you before we had a countywide meeting. There wasn't standing room in the courtroom for this organization meeting. The next day the power companies had men in the small towns or villages taking deposits on meters and promising electric power. Rural Electrification was one of the best programs for rural people. . . . Prior to this program the power companies only skimmed off the cream." By 1939, 21 percent of Virginia farms (40,893) were electrified, placing the state third in the South, behind Texas and North Carolina. Half of these customers were serviced by the REA, which had strung 5,165 miles of line and allotted $5.6 million to cooperatives in the state. Ten years later 91 percent of Virginia farms would be electrified, a lasting tribute to the farsightedness of the New Dealers. "REA," said Arthur Eure, "brought the farmer out of darkness at a price he could afford."[51]

New Deal farm programs left an ambiguous legacy in Virginia—much good was done; much was left undone. Significant departures from past farm practices had an enduring impact on state and national agriculture for several decades. Through the efforts of the New Deal, farmers accepted controlled production. The parity system, benefit payments, and large-scale conservation practices, while not new in concept, were new in implementation and were largely responsible for the farmer's recapturing a sense of dignity and an income on which he could sustain himself and his family. Through the expanded credit agencies of the New Deal, farmers saved their farms; through relief and rehabilitation programs, farmers saved their very lives. If conditions were not measurably different from those of ten years earlier (except for the benefits of electricity), they were remarkably improved over those of 1932. The farmer was no longer the "forgotten man." The New Deal had ensured that in the future his problems would be carefully considered and solutions attempted with little regard for traditional methods.[52]

This transformation in farm life was tempered in Virginia by the peculiar nature of Old Dominion agriculture, whose crop diversity and large number of small farms made it less well-suited for the crop control programs of the AAA than farming in Iowa and Nebraska. Furthermore, Virginia's low real estate taxes and high percentage of mortgage-free farms kept foreclosures low and lessened the demand for land bank loans and farmer "activism." Concerned with farm prices and income rather than equality in agriculture, New Dealers offered no assistance to the state's small, independent farmers who were losing the battle to the new agribusinessmen; and the federal rehabilitation and resettlement projects, which could have done so much for Virginia's marginal people, were compromised by inadequate financing and their own conservative orientation. Much like the relief programs, New Deal farm measures permitted survival and brightened horizons, but they did not upset the social and economic bases of rural Virginia.[53]

7

The Politics of
Status Quo

As the New Deal concentrated on relieving the urban and rural poor, Virginia focused attention on the promising signs of recovery. A psychological tonic for the state's citizenry was the changing of the guard in Richmond. On January 17, 1934, Virginia inaugurated a new governor, George Campbell Peery, who had defeated the Republican nominee in November as easily as he had captured the Democratic primary in August. A tall, distinguished-looking lawyer from Tazewell, former Ninth District congressman, and member of the State Corporation Commission, Peery was the ideal choice to carry forward organization policies. Since he had campaigned on the Byrd-Pollard record of balanced budgets without tax increases and additional indebtedness, his victory was interpreted as an overwhelming endorsement of the organization's course of fiscal responsibility.[1]

In his farewell address, Governor Pollard defended this record, pointing to Virginia's sound financial condition, which, he predicted, would bring a quick return to prosperity while avoiding future tax burdens. His recommended budget continued the economy trend and minimized capital outlays. Having received the plaudits of his fellow Virginians for commendable achievement under the most difficult circumstances, Pollard retired to a position on the Veterans Board of Appeals. He had been, in many respects, a Virginia Herbert Hoover: "a cautious man," says biographer John Hopewell, "choosing to be moderate and conservative, never daring." Although sympathetic to the needs of his fellow citizens and willing to participate in available programs, he was too conservative to initiate measures that would have satisfied those needs. In Pollard's defense, few others had conceived of such far-reaching plans before the New

129

Deal, and the organization probably would have restrained any attempt at more active direction.[2]

The new governor appeared to be a carbon copy of his predecessor. Forecasting a deficit of over $2 million, Peery advised in his inaugural address: "There is evidence that in many ways the old order has changed. We may, in some respects, have gone too fast and too far, and readjustments will have to be made. . . . Business methods are challenged. . . . We need economy in government today, as we have never needed it before." There would be no attack on the depression by the Peery administration. He accepted the Pollard budget with one notable exception. Reflecting his personal concern for public education, Peery asked for a $2 million increase in the educational appropriation to be financed by a corresponding increase in taxes. "Schools must be continued however deep the depression may be," the governor argued. His proposal experienced difficulty in the Assembly, but thanks to his forceful leadership it eventually passed. The legislature also modified the fee system for compensating local officials, partially replacing it with a salary scale, instituted a statewide trial justice system, redistricted the state, and created a liquor control board whose supervision of the sale of alcoholic beverages marked the end of Prohibition in the Old Dominion. Following an FERA announcement that Virginia would have to begin providing funds for direct relief, the Assembly considered but rejected an additional appropriation.[3]

Although business and farm indexes continued to show improvement, Virginia was not yet out of the depression. Unemployment was estimated to be over 125,000. The Virginia Alberene Corporation at Schuyler went into receivership, putting 450 men out of work, and a rayon strike at Hopewell threw hundreds onto the relief rolls. From the tobacco districts of the state, relief appeals came in to the VERA from farm laborers who had been laid off because of AAA crop restrictions. Curry Hutchinson wrote to his brother: "There is much dissatisfaction in the country, especially among the farmers. I hope that this season will bring better prices for our people of the Southwest. It seems all the attempts to help farmers have cost our people here more than it has benefitted. Everybody is discouraged." In

June, Governor Peery ordered a 5 percent cut in general fund expenditures to prevent a deficit for fiscal year 1935.[4]

As Virginia moved into the second half of 1934, however, most evidence suggested that economic recovery was well underway. A *Times-Dispatch* man-on-the-street survey found that ten of twenty people questioned were better off since the New Deal came into being, six in the same condition as before, and four worse off. A Broad Street merchant replied: "I'm a whole lot better off. My business is better, I feel better. My friends feel better. Better times are coming, and you just bet your life the average man is one hundred percent for Roosevelt."[5] Manufacturing employment in the first six months of 1934 increased 23 percent over 1933 with the textile and chemical industries and the automobile and railroad repair shops registering the strongest gains. Unemployment dropped to 85,000, and the value of manufacturing output was approaching 1930 levels. Wages lagged behind but were improving. The number of bank suspensions had been reduced by half, retail sales were up 18 percent above 1933 figures, and Virginia farm prices and cash income moved to their highest points since 1930. The state incurred a $2.3 million deficit at the end of the 1934 fiscal year, but within two years this would be converted into a surplus because of improved business conditions and the revenue from liquor sales. The state debt had increased little since 1930, whereas in North Carolina and West Virginia it was up $9.5 million and $28 million respectively. Virginia businessmen were extremely optimistic for 1935—if, said one, the ideas of "theorists, parlor bolsheviks and college professors" were abandoned.[6]

Most of Virginia escaped the clutches of depression in 1935. Every economic index registered advances, and many exceeded those of 1930. The number of industrial wage earners surpassed that of 1929, while in the nation it was only 84 percent of the predepression figure. Virginia had recaptured 83 percent of its 1929 income, a figure surpassed by only four states. Douglas Southall Freeman, editor of the *News-Leader*, proclaimed the end of the depression and concluded that Virginia experienced less unemployment and suffering than all other states but three. He credited this to diversified agriculture, the nature of

131

Virginia's industry, federal crop control, fiscal conservatism, and the stoical temperament of Virginians. A regional analysis by the *Times-Dispatch* substantiated Freeman's findings. The resurgence of tobacco had returned prosperity to town and country in the Southside. Southwest Virginia was feeling the effects of recovery to a lesser extent, but conditions in Tidewater and the Valley confirmed the view that Virginia had "settled itself down to enjoy a degree of prosperity not experienced since 1929."[7]

For the leaders of the organization, Virginia's relative success in the early thirties vindicated their fiscal conservatism. They believed the failure of the depression to bring great hardship to the state was attributable in large measure to their frugal policies of reduced expenditures and balanced budgets. In late 1935 Senator Byrd declared: "I confidently predict an era of prosperity for Virginia which may not come immediately, but it is certain to come in strong measure if we adhere to the general policies that have stood so successfully the acid test of the most serious financial emergency ever experienced by the American people. . . . Let us continue to keep our budget in balance and to live within our income. . . . Let other states go the way they prefer, but we in Virginia can continue the less spectacular paths of industry and thrift; paying as we go and then pay just as little in taxes as necessary for our essential functions of government."[8]

Juxtaposed against the New Deal's more liberal bent and its willingness to use the resources of government to serve those in need, the organization philosophy partially explains the opposition of Virginia's political leaders to almost every facet of Roosevelt's program. Advocating strict economy for the state, they could not honestly vote for large federal expenditures. Their adherence to states' rights also forced them to reject legislation that, they predicted, would lead to widespread federal interference in the affairs of Virginia. Ironically, their failure to respond to depression-caused conditions only encouraged greater federal intervention.

Organization opposition to the New Deal was motivated not only by conservative economic dogma but also by a desire to safeguard the social and political status quo in Virginia. The organization's ability to remain in office on a record of minimum service relied on maintaining and manipulating a small electorate. From 1925 to 1945 only 11.5 percent of those eligible voted in the Democratic gubernatorial primary, where victory was tantamount to office holding. Through the application of tight-fisted spending policies and stringent suffrage restrictions, such as the poll tax, the organization perpetuated the indifference, ignorance, and poverty that allowed it to rule. Such apathy, along with the traditional deference that the Virginia working class showed its "betters," precluded the development of a competitive political system. In the minds of Old Dominion leaders, New Deal policies threatened to change this situation.

The Democratic party's political machine, the organization as it was more commonly called, had controlled state politics since the late nineteenth century. Long under the command of Senator Thomas S. Martin, the organization was taken over by Harry Byrd in the years following Martin's death in 1919. It was, according to its members, "an association of like-minded men." To V. O. Key, Jr., the distinguished student of southern politics, it was "an oligarchy" which "subverted democratic institutions and deprived most Virginians of a voice in their government." But, he continues, it also had "a sense of honor," a "degree of sensitivity to public opinion," a "concern for efficiency in administration, and, so long as it does not cost much, a feeling of social responsibility."[9] Loyalty and longevity were the requisites for success in the organization. With rare exception only those who had served a lengthy apprenticeship and had demonstrated fidelity to organization principles and leaders were allowed into the inner circle or tapped for high public office.

In its domination of state politics, the organization remained flexible within the bounds of fiscal conservatism. Permitting a degree of internal strife, it accepted persons who, while not wholly in accord with its social philosophy, were supportive of balanced budgets and low taxes. The selection of John Garland Pollard, who had only recently made his peace with the organization but whose antimachine past and prohibitionist present made him the ideal choice to head the ticket in 1929, was an example of pragmatism triumphing over ideological purity. So, too, was the belated endorsement of James Price, who appeared unbeatable for the governorship in 1937. Rather than withhold support and risk party division, the leadership gave him tepid recognition. On the other hand, if members demonstrated too much independence, they faced political oblivion—ostracism from the inner circle, defeat at the polls, or loss of appointment. Although fittingly molded in the cavalier tradition, without the trappings of bossism, the organization was a powerful and relentless political machine.

The machine hierarchy placed much of the burden for maintaining its hegemony on the county "courthouse ring." Consisting of the Commonwealth's attorney, treasurer, commissioner of revenue, clerk of the circuit court, and sheriff, and abetted by the circuit judge, this group was responsible for getting out the vote and dispensing local patronage. Since the judge appointed the electoral board, which supervised the election machinery, the organization could effectively control the electoral process from the choice of candidates to the size of the vote. Indeed, machine personnel were not above paying the poll taxes of "dependable Democrats" and tampering with absentee ballots. The organization secured the loyalty of the ring through the fee system, which allowed the state Compensation Board to determine the income of the county officials. The circuit judges were appointed by the General Assembly and, therefore, had to be sympathetic to Richmond if they were to retain their positions.

In election campaigns, organization candidates avoided issues that might unite the opposition, concentrated on discrediting opponents as racial liberals or spendthrifts, and emphasized their own record of honest and frugal government, low taxes, and opposition to organized labor. These tactics attracted the support of the first families of Virginia and the wealthy professionals, farmers, and businessmen, who provided the organization with money and candidates. The record also appealed to rural interests, who were overrepresented in the Assembly and who liked Byrd's spending and road policies. A conservative press and a large state bureaucracy supplied additional backing.[10] Furthermore, a "reputation for invincibility" discouraged competition and contributed to voter apathy. Reflecting an elitist vision of the public interest, machine policies satisfied the desires of the few while ignoring the needs of the many. Says

historian Raymond Pulley, "During the late 1920's the tradition-
alist ruling class of the Old Dominion simply lost interest in
creating better social services for the people."[11]

Although the organization was an oligarchy which relied upon
the efforts of hundreds of lesser officials to maintain its power,
its consummate director was Harry F. Byrd. A self-made newspaper man and orchardist from the northern Shenandoah Valley, Byrd became the dominant force in Virginia politics when
he was elected Democratic state chairman in 1922. His personal
magnetism, driving energy, and political heritage, along with
his successful advocacy of a pay-as-you-go plan for public road
building, enabled him to seize control of the Democratic machine and establish a reign which lasted over four decades until
his death in 1966. His accomplishments as head of the party and
as governor made him one of the most respected and popular
men in the state, and his selection as Swanson's replacement in
the Senate was well received. In his new position, Byrd
solidified his control of Virginia politics through his use of patronage and his attainment of a national reputation.

The cherubic-looking, soft-spoken man from Winchester was
an image-conscious politician. He projected the appearance of a
selfless public servant who did not run for office but was sought
by the office, who did not dictate policies but consulted experts
and suggested solutions. However, behind this facade, Byrd was
a Machiavellian—a hard-nosed politician who was ambitious,
power-conscious, pragmatic, and discreet. Not shy about
pursuing office, he waged a vigorous, albeit belated, campaign
for the presidency in 1932; and using his own influence with
FDR as well as that of his brother, Admiral Richard E. Byrd, he
probably orchestrated Swanson's cabinet selection so that he
could be appointed to the Senate. His correspondence is replete
with suggestions to others—Billy Reed, Ebbie Combs, and
newspaper publishers and editors among them—to publicly
support him and his policies without disclosing his own involvement. The phrase "Do not mention that I have written you" was
not an uncommon charge to his confidants.[12]

Byrd was a tough, demanding political leader. Referring to
the 1932 General Assembly session, he wrote to Reed, "It seems
to me that we must deal with all matters with a firm hand."[13]

While capable of flexibility on some issues, he could tolerate no compromise regarding deficit spending. Obsessed with his reputation for budget balancing, he advocated reducing appropriations and manipulating bookkeeping procedures to maintain the appearance of state surpluses. So concerned was Byrd about the small deficits incurred during Pollard's term that on one occasion he prevailed upon bankers not to extend loans for road building that had been arranged for by the governor.[14] According to a friendly biographer, this obession stemmed from his "pathological abhorrence for borrowing."[15] It may also have reflected Byrd's sensitivity to criticism. He feared that any policy failure, such as a deficit, might be attributed to him personally, and he interpreted opposition to his proposals as the equivalent of a personal attack on him. He once stated to Reed: "All of us of course recognize that the worst thing that could happen to us now would be to have a deficit. It has been heralded over the country that we do not have a deficit, and if we have one it will result in very bad advertising for the State, and our enemies will attack us on all sides, especially the Richmond newspapers."[16] Nor could he tolerate any talk of revising Virginia's segregated tax system, the reorganized executive branch, or the short ballot, all of which had been major innovations of his governorship. Those who "betrayed" him felt his retribution. Charles Harkrader, editor of the Bristol *Herald-Courier*, who had been on the Byrd presidential bandwagon in 1932 but who had become enthusiastic about the New Deal, was denied party support in his quest for a state Senate seat in 1935; for a time thereafter, Byrd's letters to him were no longer addressed "My Dear Charlie," but "Dear Mr. Harkrader." Other "defectors" were not so fortunate and lost their state jobs or had their salaries reduced.[17]

Unusually pessimistic about his political fortunes, Byrd left no stone unturned in his efforts to secure personal victory and preserve his power base. Candidates for office in Virginia were selected for their loyalty, length of service, geographical balance, and electability; they not only had to win, but by margins large enough to preclude any suggestion that organization strength was waning. Even after he left the governor's mansion, Byrd felt it necessary to maintain his Richmond connections.

Reed and Combs, his closest confidants, were in constant communication with him regarding legislative programs and executive action. A close personal friend, Reed was president of Larus and Brother Tobacco Company in Richmond. Everett Randolph "Ebbie" Combs, who had begun a political relationship with Byrd in the early twenties, held influential positions as state comptroller and chairman of the state Compensation Board. Through these emissaries and by personal correspondence, Byrd offered his successors advice on policy and recommendations on appointments. In fact, Pollard relied so heavily on Byrd's experience, especially on fiscal matters, that he frequently appeared to be little more than a cipher. Byrd's relationship with Pollard and with subsequent governors was always a cordial, respectful one, but Harry was definitely the master. While his control was not total, his opinions carried great weight in the determination of policy. Commenting on Byrd's preeminence, Benjamin Muse wrote, "Governors of Virginia are appointed by Harry Byrd, subject to confirmation by the electorate." It was no mistake that the organization was frequently labeled the Byrd machine.[18]

It took almost a year for Byrd to articulate his opposition to the New Deal. The severity of the depression, party loyalty, and political reality had dictated his support of New Deal measures during the Hundred Days. As a new junior senator, he had not wanted to challenge a popular president. Such an insurgency might have jeopardized his own election chances and encouraged an intraparty struggle in the Old Dominion. Privately, however, Byrd was already worried about the direction of the New Deal. He wrote to Billy Reed at the end of the congressional session, "Many things have been done here that I think will have a very bad effect."[19]

In the spring of 1934, having won election and believing the economic emergency over, Byrd openly attacked the Roosevelt regulatory policies as efforts "to control the daily activities of our people." Rarely thereafter did he vote with the administration on domestic programs, and in later life he even denied that he had ever supported the New Deal. Byrd did like to say that he was the "last of the original New Dealers," meaning that he had supported the 1932 platform calling for balanced budgets and reduced spending and nothing more. As economic conditions improved, he called for a return to the sound principles of reasonable taxation, a stable currency, and the protection of property, which, he believed, would restore business confidence. Later in the decade he cited the Roosevelt administration as "the most wasteful and bureaucratic form of government that has been known in our history," and he predicted a "rude awakening" when the nation was called upon to pay the national debt.[20]

Byrd's castigation of the New Deal was temperate when compared to the scathing attacks of Carter Glass. A Lynchburg newspaper man, Glass had entered Virginia politics as an opponent of the machine. A congressman, then Woodrow Wilson's secretary of the Treasury, he had been appointed to a vacated Senate seat in 1920 by Governor Westmoreland Davis, himself a political independent, who hoped to establish a beachhead for Virginia progressives in Congress. Shortly thereafter, Glass made his peace with the organization and went his independent way, thenceforth considered Virginia's irreproachable elder statesman.

Few men owned a more caustic tongue than the senator from Lynchburg, who taunted his adversaries with language reminiscent of that of an earlier Virginian, John Randolph of Roanoke. Small in stature and easily provoked, Glass was a proponent of states' rights and limited federal power. He was a nineteenth-century liberal whose progressivism did not extend beyond a desire to restore the competitive economic order, an objective which, he believed, required minimal involvement by Washington. New Deal bureaucracy and coercion, therefore, were anathema to him. Writing to Charles Harkrader, he ruminated, "I am seventy-six years old in genuine Jeffersonian Deomocracy and I do not care to mar the record before I die by embracing brutal and despicable bureaucracy." Josephus Daniels, who had worked with Glass in the Wilson cabinet, described him as "a sad illustration of an old man who has lost faith in his early dreams and surrendered to the status quo."[21]

Glass was among the first to excoriate the New Deal. In July 1933 he wrote to Russell Leffingwell, a Wall Street banker, that Roosevelt was following in the steps of Hoover in leading the country to disaster. A true goldbug, he labeled devaluation and departure from the gold standard "immoral" and "worse than anything Ali Baba's forty thieves ever perpetrated"; he was the only Democrat to vote against the devaluation bill. Avoiding open condemnation of FDR, with whom he was on very good terms, Glass denounced the Seventy-third Congress as "a curse to this nation."[22]

The two Virginia senators rarely detoured from their course of opposition to New Deal domestic programs. They repeatedly cast votes against relief bills, farm bills, labor bills, housing bills, social security legislation, tax programs, and administration appointments. Glass topped all Democratic senators in opposition to the New Deal, voting against major administration legislation 81 percent of the time; Byrd opposed 65 percent of the legislation.[23] On anything resembling an economy measure, such as the refusal to pay veterans' bonuses, or on matters of national defense, they voted with the administration. While they were not always in agreement, Glass usually being the more independent of the two, their consistency was remarkable.

For their votes against the regulation of utility holding companies, the "soak-the-rich" tax scheme, and spending measures in general, Byrd and Glass became the favorites of the business community and the American Liberty League. These conservative elements of American society, uncertain of the direction of the administration, critical of the benefits granted labor, and fearful of losing their positions of influence, constantly attacked Roosevelt and the New Deal. Virginia businessmen joined the negative chorus. In 1934 the Virginia Manufacturers Association called for a stable national debt, an end to extravagant spending, and a revision of the NRA, particularly section 7a. The president of the Richmond Chamber of Commerce pronounced the emergency over and declared: "I believe government should permit industry to take care of itself, . . . Such a course would give us more confidence in the future."[24] The Liberty League, formed in August 1934 to combat the "leftist" tendencies of the "Brains Trust" and to return the nation to sound constitutional principles, courted both Byrd and Glass, but the Virginia senators refused to join. Although they would not bolt the party or criticize the president personally, their words and deeds continued to bring joy to the "loyal" opposition.[25]

Conservative elements of the Virginia press also applauded the independent course taken by the senators. *News-Leader* editor Freeman called their philosophy a marriage of "fiscal conservatism" and "political liberalism," the balancing of the attainable with the desirable.[26] Even the more liberal *Times-Dispatch*, which had approved most of the New Deal legislation, saluted Byrd and Glass as men of conviction who provided healthy opposition to the new programs. The approbation given the senators often was translated into condemnation of the New Deal. Taking issue with Roosevelt's annual message in 1935 asking for social security and multibillion-dollar relief legislation, Glass's Lynchburg *News* queried: "Is it any purpose of government to guarantee all these securities (security of livelihood, against major hazards, of decent homes)? Is there no responsibility resting upon the individual to secure himself against the 'major hazards' and vicissitudes of life?" The *News* objected to unemployment insurance and old-age pensions and cautioned of the dangers of bureacracy, dependency on government, unbalanced budgets, excessive borrowing, and high taxes.[27]

And yet the New Deal was not without its prominent defenders in Virginia. Former Governor Westmoreland Davis, Undersecretary of State R. Walton Moore, Secretary of the Navy Claude Swanson, secretary of the Democratic state committee Martin Hutchinson, and future governor James Price all praised its efforts. Hutchinson wrote to Representative Clifton Woodrum: "I trust that all friends of the administration will accept the challenge of Wall Street just as you have done. The people of Virginia have gotten tired of Al Smith, [Jouett] Shouse, and [John W.] Davis and from what I hear a great majority of our people are behind President Roosevelt."[28]

The New Deal also had support within the state's congressional delegation. While Representatives Otis Bland, Thomas Burch, Colgate Darden, Patrick Henry Drewry, A. Willis Robertson, and Howard Smith were more inclined to vote with their colleagues in the Senate, Woodrum and John

Flannagan were staunch New Dealers. Representative Andrew Jackson Montague divided his loyalties evenly, but ill health frequently prevented his taking public positions. The two senators had little regard for Flannagan, whose independent constituency, the "Fighting Ninth," ruled out the possibility of removal by the organization. Byrd characterized him as "a thorough demagogue of the first water." Woodrum, who believed the New Deal's goal was "equality of opportunity for every man," was often the House floor leader for New Deal legislation, defending it as necessary for recovery and reform. When he exuberantly declared that March 4, 1933 (Roosevelt's inauguration day), should subsequently be celebrated like July 4, Byrd remarked to Glass, "I assume that he means by that that our freedom was given us on July 4 and taken away on March 4."[29]

Certainly none of the representatives was a sycophant, and all evidenced the independence typical of Virginia congressmen. However, their allegiances generally lay as indicated above. Tied for first among Democratic representatives opposing the administration, Robertson voted against major New Deal legislation 60 to 65 percent of the time. Burch and Smith were in opposition on 45 to 49 percent of the measures; Bland, Darden, and Drewry, 35 to 39 percent. In the late thirties Woodrum, who was voted one of the ten ablest congressmen in a 1939 *Life* magazine poll, divided his loyalties more evenly between the New Deal and the organization, voting against Roosevelt's executive reorganization and wage and hour legislation and for reductions in WPA appropriations and investigations into its activities. These votes left him with an anti–New Deal percentage of 25 to 29 percent. Perhaps Woodrum no longer saw the need for excessive spending, or as the *Times-Dispatch* suggested, he was beginning to hear voices from his constituency. In the 1936 and 1938 election campaigns, strong challenges were made upon his seat by Republicans.[30]

The *News-Leader*'s opinion that "we had rather have a senator wrong with convictions than right without them" was not universally accepted in the Old Dominion. The Portsmouth *Star*, seconded by the Bristol *Herald-Courier*, observed, "Senator Byrd is not truly representing his constituency when he so frequently places himself out of step with the Roosevelt administra-

141

tion at Washington." Committing the final heresy, the Danville *Register* suggested that Senator Glass should retire because of his advancing age and inability to adjust to changing times.[31] Organized labor in Virginia was openly critical of the "unfairness and unreasonableness" of the senators' attitudes on New Deal legislation. Noting their votes against the interests of working-men, R. T. Bowden claimed they were "absolutely worthless to the labor movement. Both are anti-everything." An equally ardent critic of Senator Byrd was Westmoreland Davis, who had campaigned actively for FDR in 1932. Davis, whose ideas for systemization and centralization of the state government had been implemented by Byrd, applauded the progressive nature of the New Deal. His *Southern Planter,* a farm journal with 240,000 subscribers, became a mouthpiece for administration measures and condemned Senator Byrd for his obstructionism.[32]

Davis was one of a growing number of Virginians who were already or soon to be labeled antiorganization or "antis"— enemies of the organization. They eventually included former Governors Davis and E. Lee Trinkle, James Price, Congressman John Flannagan, Martin Hutchinson, and editors Norman Hamilton and Charles Harkrader. Although they remained loyal Democrats, their political ambitions and personal philosophies were incompatible with organization objectives. While a few of the "antis" had liberal backgrounds, most of them were fiscal conservatives who simply believed more money should be made available for services other than highways. However, their primary differences with Byrd were not over policy but control. The allegiance Byrd demanded precluded their kind of independence, and while many of them remained on the fringes of the inner circle because there was no alternative, they chafed at their forced subservience. Theirs became an opposition of "quiet desperation," united by a clandestine sharing of ideas until the New Deal arrived to offer promise of a political emancipation.[33]

The presidential election of 1936 indicated how correct Congressman Woodrum was when he confided to Martin Hutchinson, "I am thoroughly convinced that the people of Virginia are with the Administration."[34] Once it became clear that Byrd and Glass would not bolt the party, Virginia Democrats joined the Roosevelt bandwagon. Calling Roosevelt a "great Democrat, a courageous, humanitarian President," Governor Peery, along with Lieutenant Governor Price and former Governors Davis and Trinkle, took to the campaign trail in support of the New Deal. Virginia labor leaders also worked for Roosevelt's election, predicting the workingmen of the state would cast their ballots solidly for the president. The newspapers of the Old Dominion, with perhaps a little less enthusiasm than in 1932, contributed their support to the administration as well. Among black-owned newspapers, the Richmond *Planet* supported Alf Landon, the Republican nominee from Kansas, declaring it found no lure in the "boondogglers, office holders, Santa Claus enthusiasts, college professors, [and] dreamy-eyed social workers," but the *Journal and Guide* backed Roosevelt, accurately reflecting the shift of black voters from Republican to Democrat. Even Harry Byrd campaigned for the ticket, praising Roosevelt for steps taken that "won the unqualified approval and praise of men and women of all parties." Glass, however, remained, in FDR's own descriptive phrase, the "unreconstructed rebel." Writing to Byrd on the eve of the election, the senator remarked, "I hate the New Deal just as much as I ever did and have not the remotest idea of making any speeches for it."[35]

The victory of Norman Hamilton over Colgate Darden in the August Democratic primary for the Second District nomination to the House confirmed the popularity of the New Deal in Virginia. Hamilton, editor of the Portsmouth *Star* and an ardent New Dealer, defeated an incumbent whose opposition to much of the administration's program was well known. His victory was attributed to the urban-labor texture of the district, which had never been a powerful organization stronghold. He won easily in the November election.[36]

The 1936 results belie the intensity with which the campaign was waged and mock the validity of pollsters' predictions. Until the last few weeks of the campaign, the Gallup Poll envisioned a very close race, perhaps the closest since 1916, while the hapless *Literary Digest* forecast a Republican success. The question in Virginia, however, was not who would win but the margin of Roosevelt's victory. Commented one citizen: "Roosevelt couldn't possibly lose Virginia. Every section of the state has been so well watered with Federal benefits and Federal money that potential voters are out there in bunches." Assessing the situation for Jim Farley, Representative Pat Drewry predicted: "Virginia is safely Democratic. Roosevelt should carry the State, as of today, with a majority of one hundred thousand. . . . The only trouble that I can see is with the businessmen in the cities and some towns who are upset because of what they call 'the extravagances' of the Administration. We are working on this condition."[37]

The state campaign was enlivened by the withdrawal from the party of a segment of the conservative community. Calling themselves Jeffersonian Democrats and affiliating with a national group of the same name, these conservatives declared, "[The] preservation of the principles of the Democratic Party, the welfare of Virginia, of the South and of the nation can best be assured by the defeat of Mr. Roosevelt at the November, 1936 election." Thomas Lomax Hunter, a *Times-Dispatch* columnist, directed publicity for the Jeffersonians and urged either a vote for Landon or an unmarked ballot. Some of Hunter's literary efforts were entitled "Something Rotten in PWA," "Are You in Jim Farley's Bag?", and "Who Pays the Bill?" Utilizing a biweekly radio show and the largest direct-mail campaign in the state's history, the Jeffersonian Democrats charged that the administration was associating with Communists and Socialists. S. D. Timberlake of Staunton claimed that "no true Democrat" would recognize the New Deal if he met it on the street but "might recognize it if he met it in Moscow."[38] Although the Jeffersonians predicted a Landon victory nationwide and a greatly reduced Roosevelt margin in Virginia, the *Times-Dispatch* confidently stated: "Virginia is strongly pro-Roosevelt. This has been shown in every poll of the State. It is very evident when one interviews the voters. Farmers are almost solidly for the President in most sections, as is union labor and the great bulk of those who have received real or fancied benefits from this administration. The 'economic royalists' in Virginia are comparatively few."[39]

Since state leaders had predicted an 80,000-vote margin for Roosevelt in Virginia, the magnitude of the landslide was unexpected. In the largest turnout for a presidential election in the Old Dominion since 1888, Roosevelt smothered Landon by 137,000 votes, winning 70.2 percent of the ballots cast and carrying all Virginia Democratic congressmen into office with him. The *Virginian-Pilot* saw the election as an affirmation of government's responsibility for the economic security of the country, while the Danville *Register* called it a "mandate" for the continuation of a program of "practical Americanism." The *Times-Dispatch* and Lynchburg *News*, however, were apprehensive about the size of the victory, which, they believed, placed too much power in the hands of one man.[40]

The 1936 election was the high-water mark of the New Deal in Virginia. The margin of the victory—Roosevelt won over 90 percent of the vote in some rural counties—Norman Hamilton's triumph, and the popularity of the federal agencies combating the depression, particularly the CCC and the AAA, all testified to the acceptance of leader and program by the Old Dominion. But no foundation for further progress had been created. The New Deal had not disturbed the hierarchical nature of Virginia society or located a political voice in the state as liberal as that in Washington. The president had done little to cultivate opposition to the machine by directing patronage away from the Byrd-Glass faction because the senators were deemed too powerful and influential and their Virginia adversaries too few and ineffectual. As Virginia emerged from the depression—earlier than most other states—there was no demand for a continuation, much less an expansion, of the programs that soon would be equated with waste and interference. Finally Roosevelt's own political missteps—court packing and the purges—generated additional resentment and contributed to the ebb of the New Deal.

Roosevelt's 1936 mandate apparently convinced him that he could pursue a more authoritative course of action with his new Congress. The major obstacle to his legislative programs had been the Supreme Court, whose conservative majority had repeatedly found New Deal legislation unconstitutional. In addition to the NRA and the AAA, the Court had thrown out the railroad retirement act, the Frazier-Lemke Farm Mortgage Act, and the Guffey Coal Act. Consequently, in February 1937

Roosevelt presented Congress a federal judiciary bill which included a provision for increasing the size of the Supreme Court by up to six new justices. Designed to liberalize the high tribunal, the proposal triggered a debate which had marked consequences for the Court and for the future of the New Deal.

Public criticism of this plan in Virginia was immediate and sharp. Predictably, the Lynchburg *News* called it "immoral," a "scheme . . . to destroy the judicial branch," a "conspiracy against democracy." Even normally pro–New Deal newspapers labeled it a deception because it had not been presented during the 1936 campaign. Bar associations in almost every city passed resolutions opposing the plan; the State Bar Association was "unalterably opposed" to it, 125 to 49. Seeing in the court plan an intention to revive the NRA, Richmond business leaders protested the "unwarranted governmental interference with legitimate business."[41]

However, within a month support for the president's plan surfaced in the Old Dominion. Representatives Flannagan and Woodrum voiced their approval, and a *Times-Dispatch* survey indicated Virginians favored it by a two-to-one margin. Flannagan saw it as an attempt "to keep special interests from using the court to transform an unglorious defeat at the polls into a glorious victory by judicial fiat." Labor generally endorsed the plan, and the Virginia Farm Bureau Federation, after a talk by Secretary Wallace, announced support for it as a means for meeting the "social and economic needs of the people."[42]

The pressing need for judicial reform was soon obviated by the action of the Court itself, which suddenly reversed its position on New Deal measures and upheld a Washington State minimum wage for women, the new Frazier-Lemke Farm Mortgage Moratorium Act, and a railroad labor act sustaining collective bargaining. The Wagner Labor Act and the Social Security Act received similar approval in subsequent weeks. This reversal, combined with the resignation of conservative Justice Willis Van Devanter and a letter to Congress from Chief Justice Charles Evans Hughes disputing the administration's charge of Court inefficiency, effectively killed Roosevelt's effort to reorganize the Court. In July the Senate returned the bill to committee, with both Byrd and Glass voting for recommittal.[43]

Although Roosevelt lost the battle, he may have won the war. Certainly his plan put pressure on the "swing" members of the Court, Justices Hughes and Owen Roberts, to reconsider their positions. The retirement and death of two other conservative members enabled the president to replace them with men whose views were consistent with his own, so that by the end of the decade liberal domination of the court was assured and New Deal legislation secure. The political price of the victory, however, was high. The "court packing" scheme cost FDR the sympathy and allegiance of many voters in Congress and in the country at large. This obvious ploy to realign the Court gave credence to charges of former Liberty Leaguers that the president was usurping the power of the other two branches and acting like a dictator. Most importantly, the issue forged a conservative coalition in Congress consisting of longtime opponents of the New Deal and men of conservative leaning who had supported the president through the emergency but who now had an excuse for returning to their philosophical home. Strengthened by other examples of Rooseveltian imperiousness, such as the executive reorganization bill and the 1938 "purge" attempts, this coalition would delay, sidetrack, and finally halt the New Deal legislative train.[44]

Senator Byrd led the opposition to Roosevelt's 1937 reorganization plan, which proposed the addition of two new federal departments and six presidential assistants and the replacement of the comptroller general with an auditor general without authority to pass on the legality of expenditures. Byrd objected to what he called "mere regrouping" as well as the loss of the auditor's watchdog function. Having dedicated himself a year earlier to the "drastic reorganization and simplification of the Federal government," the senator felt upstaged by the president and retaliated with a plan of his own. Roosevelt's handling of the reorganization bill, particularly his failure to consult Byrd, the acknowledged authority on waste in government, may have triggered a final personal break with the Virginian and contributed to the bill's eventual defeat in 1938.[45]

Shortly after this failure, the president, encouraged by primary election successes of New Dealers, set out to remove some of his prominent congressional opponents from office by endorsing their more liberal opposition. It was only natural that the home state of two of the most vociferous antagonists of the New Deal would receive attention. Indeed, the year before, Byrd had written Glass that Roosevelt was "actively supporting in Virginia all forces hostile to us."[46] However, the only Virginian who incurred the administration's wrath in the ill-fated 1938 "purge" attempt was Howard Smith, whose opponent was William E. Dodd, Jr., a self-declared 100 percent New Dealer. Avoiding issues and refusing to debate Dodd, Smith accused him of willingness to be a New Deal rubber stamp and of being a favorite of the CIO. Dodd, son of the former ambassador to Germany, claimed labor support but denied the CIO endorsement and countercharged that Smith was a tool of the organization. Late in the campaign, Interior secretary Ickes injected himself into the race by accusing Smith of trying to ride the "coat-tails of PWA" while voting against all but one PWA appropriation. Smith retaliated, reproaching Ickes for "muscling" in on a Democratic primary. The charge of outside interference worked to Smith's advantage, and he ran up a three-to-one victory over Dodd. In another blow to New Deal prestige, Colgate Darden, benefiting from the exploitation of some racial material, won a close rematch over Norman Hamilton for the Second District nomination. In November, plagued by a recession and his own high-handed methods, Roosevelt suffered serious reverses in the congressional elections. Thereafter, the strengthened conservative coalition, although unable to dismantle what the New Deal had wrought, prevented further innovation. With his domestic program effectively thwarted, Roosevelt directed his attention to the worsening foreign crisis and, ironically, with the aid of many of the conservatives prepared the nation for the coming war.[47]

While organization leaders were attempting to curtail federal expansion and spending, they were suddenly confronted with a challenge to their domination at home. James Price, lieutenant governor for two terms, announced in July 1935 that he would be a candidate for governor in 1937. Formerly a Richmond lawyer and member of the House of Delegates, Price was an extremely popular figure in the state. Handsome, gregarious, and active in several fraternal organizations, he declared early primarily to disrupt the organization's normal selection procedure, which he believed would deny him the nomination. Although he had always been acceptable to the leadership, he was not among the inner circle and had frequently taken positions at variance with those of the organization, including advocacy of a state work relief program in 1931 and support of the New Deal. His candidacy, labeled the first serious threat to the machine in years, was quickly endorsed by former Governors Trinkle and Davis, but Byrd and Glass withheld comment. The failure of potential organization candidates to elicit enthusiasm and Roosevelt's overwhelming election victory, which strengthened Price's bid, forced Byrd to capitulate. On December 23, 1936, organization men joined the Price bandwagon. Mollified by a statement that Price favored a "sound and conservative fiscal policy," Byrd declared he had "no desire whatsoever to exert a personal influence over political affairs in Virginia except to lend my support as a citizen to a more efficient and progressive government in the State." The senator had suffered a reverse.[48]

The lieutenant governor's platform was a mixture of organization and New Deal objectives. He endorsed a sound fiscal policy, pay-as-you-go highway construction, social security, fair hours and wages for labor, adequate teacher salaries, a nine-month school term, and federal farm assistance. He smashed independent Vivian Page of Norfolk in the Democratic primary and easily defeated Republican and Communist candidates in November. Price's failure to openly endorse candidates sympathetic to him, an indication of his reluctance to press his advantage too far, allowed organization men to win the offices of lieutenant governor and attorney general.[49]

Price's first session with the General Assembly proved to be the pinnacle of his success against the machine. In his inaugural address he declared, "We are living in a new day, one filled with splendid opportunities for service to our fellow man; and while I am not disposed to extravagance or ill-advised liberality, I am in hearty sympathy with the present trend of government toward humanitarian ideals and I am pleased to see it make a more substantial contribution to the fullness of life."[50] Much of his legislative program was passed—social security, a more liberal hour law for women, and increased aid to schools. Even as the Assembly sat, Price began removing longtime organization stalwarts, replacing them with his own friends. E. R. Combs, a staunch ally of Harry Byrd and one of the most powerful men in the state because of his positions as comptroller and chairman of the state Compensation Board, lost his jobs. The governor eventually replaced the head of the Division of Motor Vehicles, the director of the Division of Purchase and Printing, and the commissioners of public welfare, labor, and fisheries. In a belated attempt to check him, the House of Delegates withdrew the governor's right to appoint the chairman of the Compensation Board, but Price, insisting on retaining "the prerogative exercised by my predecessors," won a sizable victory when the Senate voted 23 to 15 in favor of the budget bill without the disruptive House amendment. The House then concurred, 49 to 44, and Price appeared ready to challenge Byrd's control of the state.[51]

Long denied their place in the sun by the Byrd machine, the "antis" savored this assault on the organization. Walton Moore, who would be Price's contact in the Roosevelt administration, wrote the governor, "I do not wish to be in the Virginia political picture except for my very strong desire to prevent the continued control by an organization that is antagonistic to the Roosevelt Administration and the Price Administration, and is thus so definitely illiberal." The two men exchanged ideas on how Roosevelt, through the patronage system, could strengthen Price's position. Price was forthright in asking that the men he had just fired not be given federal jobs in Virginia with which they could befriend the organization and embarrass him. He entreated Moore, "If the Federal administration will back us up in the individual cases, it would be a tremendous help." Roosevelt now appeared ready to assist the new regime when he reportedly told Jim Farley that he was "not going to let Glass or Byrd make any appointments in Virginia."[52]

Price's success and the popularity of the New Deal alarmed organization leaders. Roosevelt's large pluralities in Southside suggested that Byrd's opposition to federal farm programs had reduced his popularity. More significantly, the appointment of Martin Hutchinson as the new chairman of the Compensation Board threatened the internal courthouse network on which organization power relied. Hutchinson's predecessor, E. R.

Combs, anxiously wrote Byrd, "Price has sent out his agents over the State with a view of bringing out candidates against members friendly to us in districts where he thinks he would have some prospects of victory." At the national level it was no secret that the president wanted to "purge" disloyal Democrats from office, and Byrd and Glass were potential targets.[53]

Although Byrd's congenital pessimism heightened his concern, his fears were groundless. The new governor had risen to power primarily on his personal popularity, not widespread antipathy to Byrd's policies. Therefore, the power bases of the organization—the courthouse ring and the General Assembly— were undisturbed; Price had no base of his own on which to forge a separate machine. More importantly, says biographer Alvin Hall, Price had neither "the desire nor the aggressiveness" to carry on the fight, especially after suffering some reverses at the hands of the organization. He seemed more interested in governing than in building a machine, not realizing that in Virginia the latter was a prerequisite for the former. Furthermore, Price's meetings with Roosevelt and Farley and the announcement by state Senator Charles Harkrader, a Price supporter, that the governor would have "veto power on all appointments of any consequence in Virginia" were not enthusiastically received in the Old Dominion, whose citizens traditionally had been hostile to outside interference. The abortive purge attempt later in the year against Representative Smith demonstrated this resentment dramatically.[54]

In July 1938 the appointment of Judge Floyd Roberts of Bristol to a federal judgeship in the Western District of Virginia widened the breach between Price and the organization. Roberts's nomination, endorsed by Flannagan and Price, was termed "deliberately offensive" by Carter Glass, who claimed the president had disregarded his and Byrd's recommendations. In the next congressional session, the two Virginia senators employed senatorial courtesy to reject the nomination, demonstrating once more their power over federal patronage in the state and the weakness of the governor's position in combating the organization.

It is clear that the New Dealers, using presidential and gubernatorial popularity, patronage, and purges, belatedly tried to undermine Byrd's rule in Virginia. Glass wrote to Byrd that Woodrum "told me to warn you that Price and his miserable gang, abetted by the White House, were surely after you." How involved Price was in this effort is unclear. Hall says he was a "passive instrument" of the "antis" and the New Dealers, who desperately wanted to break up the machine, but his letters to Walton Moore indicate that he was not an innocent bystander. In any event, these attempts to alter Virginia's political scene proved ineffectual. Throughout the thirties there was never a formidable enough opposition to the organization on which to build a challenge to its power. Although it was rumored that Price would run against Byrd in 1940, the senator had no opposition that year. The progressive Price legislative program was rejected by the General Assembly in 1940, and when he stepped down in 1942, the organization once again reigned supreme over Virginia politics.[55]

Virginians, in a surprising display of impartiality, divided their loyalties between the New Deal and the organization. Other than the political leadership and the business community, there were few groups in the state hostile to the national program; most interest groups openly endorsed it. Roosevelt was particularly beloved as "a God-sent man," a president who supplied the "psychological fillip to halt negative momentum and start positive action," a man whose "personality and promise gave most people new hope." Yet the people also returned organization men to office whose philosophies were diametrically opposed to those of the New Dealers. Senator Byrd and his pay-as-you-go program were equally well liked. Indeed, loyalty to the Byrd name bordered on idolatry. Fellow Virginians remembered him as "a great Virginian to whom the State should be forever grateful," the "greatest Statesman Virginia ever produced," and a man who was "honest, frugal, and very wise—an honest to goodness real American."[56]

Of great significance in explaining the coexistence of New Deal and organization was the class structure of Virginia society. The people to whom most of the New Deal money was going and to whom removal of the organization was most desirable were the poverty stricken—the blacks and rural poor—whose disfranchisement and inferior educations prevented their having an effective political voice, thus preserving Virginia's deferential one-party politics. Furthermore, southern racial attitudes, which were endorsed by Virginia's leaders, albeit with greater gentility than elsewhere, precluded a coalition of white and black poor which might have challenged upper-class rule. Therefore, those who controlled political life in Virginia and benefited from organization policies—state and local officeholders, professional people, and the wealthy—were allowed the luxury of indulging their conservative preferences while admiring and, for a time, supporting the energetic activities of an administration which had pulled the nation out of the despair of 1932.

In addition, the infrastructure of Old Dominion politics prevented a confrontation between these competing ideologies. The electorate remained small and controllable, and the state's off-year election arrangement kept state elections from being influenced by the heat of a national contest. The "courthouse crowd," provided with jobs in a period of great scarcity, remained intensely loyal to the leadership. Urban interests, which tended to favor increased spending for educational and welfare facilities, continued to be grossly underrepresented in the legislature and, thus, powerless. Finally, there was rarely an alternative to vote for. Virginia was a Democratic stronghold, and party loyalty demanded the dual allegiance to differing philosophies at separate political levels. Old Dominion Republicans were hard to find, and the "antis" were often as critical of the New Deal as the organization, offering little more than watered-down reforms of conservative policies.

Coexistence, however, did have its limitations. Price's mild effort to end organization domination died as FDR's popularity waned in the late thirties and Senator Byrd's economy drive received greater support. Virginians still liked Roosevelt, but his spending policies and political maneuverings made it unlikely that they would depose their favorite sons, who were trying to protect them from the high taxes and federal interference that had always been anathema to them. Once better times returned to the Commonwealth, Virginians were more receptive to traditional sights and sounds. They would not turn their backs on the federal largesse, but neither would they reject the time-honored clichés of states' rights, rugged individualism, and economy and efficiency. Such an attitude permitted Byrd and Glass and others to follow their independent course of attacking the New Deal while maintaining their personal hegemony over the Old Dominion.

8
Virginia's
"Little New Deal"

If the New Deal was unable to change the conservative politics of Virginia's leaders, it did transform the social welfare system of the Old Dominion and indirectly improve the position of labor in the state. Through coercive legislation the federal government forced Virginia to abandon its policy of "no direct relief" and implement social security and unemployment insurance programs. Long negligent in providing adequate care for the underprivileged and dependent, Virginia, by the end of the decade, had upgraded the quality of its relief facilities and was paying greater attention to the needs of these people.

Characteristically, however, this was a long overdue achievement in Virginia. A 1922 law had encouraged counties and cities to establish local public welfare units, but by 1932 when RFC aid began entering the Commonwealth, only half of the state's population was being served. Thirty-five counties still had almshouses. The Department of Public Welfare was providing minimal service for the mentally deficient, the criminal, Confederate veterans, and some dependent children, but the burden of relief for the unemployed fell on the localities and private charities. Their resources were inadequate to meet the demands of the depression, and had it not been for the injection of vast sums of federal money, the situation in Virginia could have become critical. The reluctance of state leaders to materially aid the destitute contributed to this crisis.

Under the influence of the RFC, CWA, FERA, and WPA, a statewide welfare system began to blossom. These agencies required the formation of a state relief administration as well as the presence of supervisory bodies in the communities to distribute funds and administer the programs. Emergency relief committees in the cities and counties became the foundation on

155

which future state welfare machinery was built. While a sub-structure of relief facilities developed, Virginia's involvement remained meager. The public welfare and highway departments had cooperated with the RFC in sponsoring a road-building program that employed several thousand jobless, but when Washington assumed the major burden of relief, these departments ended their contribution.[1]

A nationwide study of state relief expenditures revealed the extent of Virginia's welfare commitment. As of December 31, 1935, of the major areas of relief—aid to the aged, the blind, dependent children, and the unemployed—Virginia appropriated funds only for dependent children through its Mothers' Aid program. Georgia and South Carolina financed none of the needy groups; North Carolina, like Virginia, aided only one; all other states provided funds for at least two or three of the groups, with twenty-nine states financing all four. Forty-three states had an unemployment relief program. The failure of Virginia to provide funds also reduced the amount of matching federal money entering the state, thus pinching relief needs two ways. Even Virginia's Mothers' Aid plan was not considered substantial enough to justify matching funds; with only 4 percent of those eligible receiving aid, it was judged among the "most inadequate" in the country. Furthermore, the Old Dominion was far behind other states in the performance of its schools, libraries, and crime prevention agencies, while half its counties had no public health services. Lamentably, a blind devotion to fiscal conservatism was depriving citizens of necessary services.[2]

To compensate for such state apathy as well as to provide a buffer against future economic disasters, President Roosevelt presented a national social security program to Congress in January 1935. It encountered a strong challenge from Senator Byrd, who disliked the expense and permanence of the plan. He estimated its cost to Virginia at $21 million a year, a sum which would force the state to raise taxes drastically. Echoing the senator, Governor Peery believed the cost precluded adoption of the system in the immediate future. Organization leaders received sympathetic support from the Virginia Manufacturers Association and the *News-Leader*, which hoped such a system would not replace "filial duty" or be overly expensive. The *Times-*

Dispatch, however, took exception to Byrd's cost estimates and fears of federal control, believing better standards could be ensured through supervision in Washington. The editor was indignant: "But the most disturbing aspect of Senator Byrd's statement is to be found in the fact that nowhere in it does he indicate that he regards social security legislation as either necessary or desirable. . . . There is the apparent lack of interest on Senator Byrd's part in these humanitarian measures. The United States is the only major nation in the world except India and China which has no social security laws. Does Mr. Byrd wish this country to continue to trail along with the backward nations of Asia instead of going in the van with the socially enlightened nations of Europe?"[3]

The editorial elicited an immediate response from the senator, who declared that he was not "opposed to any reasonable plan of economic security for the individual citizen which contemplates joint contributions," but that he would continue to oppose disastrous fiscal policies even if it made him unpopular. The governor likewise clarified his position. He said he was not opposed to a sound program, but he believed it could not be promoted by financial extravagance. He expressed a willingness to appoint an advisory commission to study the old-age pension plan and its implications for Virginia.

Washington officials quickly rebutted Byrd's major objection to the plan. They estimated the annual cost to Virginia at $1.3 million and indicated that states would have great control over the size of the program since they would be determining eligibility within their borders. Other estimates by John Hopkins Hall and the VERA predicted a cost of $2 to $3 million, far below Byrd's projections. The Old Age Pension League of Virginia contended that the senator was "more concerned with public expenditures than he is with private suffering; [he] thinks more of property rights than he does of human rights."[4]

The security bill passed the House, 372 to 33, with four Virginians—Bland, Burch, Darden, and Robertson—joining nine other Democrats in opposition. The Senate approved it in June, 76 to 6, with Byrd and Glass paired against it. The act had several features: (1) pensions for the existing aged (sixty-five or over) to be paid for with state and matching federal money; (2)

future social security payments to be paid for with taxes levied on employers and employees to be repaid as annuities when the employee reached sixty-five; (3) unemployment insurance to be paid for with taxes on employers, the money to be paid into a state insurance fund if the state passed the necessary enabling legislation; and (4) aid for dependent children and their mothers, for the blind and the crippled, and for public health services, also to be paid for with state and matching federal funds. The bill was far from perfect. Its taxation was regressive; it did not cover many classes of workers, particularly the domestics and farm laborers who needed the assistance most; and, to quote the *News-Leader*, the bill opened "Pandora's Box" since it set no national standards and permitted the states great leeway in establishing their plans. Nevertheless, it was a step toward more security for those less able to provide it for themselves; it was a break from the limitations of rugged individualism; and it acknowledged that government had a responsibility for society's less fortunate.[5]

Immediately after passage of the social security bill, Governor Peery indicated that Virginia would adopt the pension plan in the 1936 Assembly session. Two months later, however, he declared that no appropriation was being considered to implement the plan. Reiterating the oft-repeated cry of Virginia conservatives, he said: "Virginia is committed to a balanced budget. Under our law we cannot borrow money for anything except to meet a casual deficit." In lieu of a legislative proposal, the governor launched a new study of the cost of a pension plan in Virginia which predicted an annual cost to the state of $2.5 to $11.4 million. The low figure was based on the experience of seven states with the program; the maximum was based on FDR's estimate that half the people over sixty-five were dependent. The report also noted that costs would increase with the years and that Virginia's costs would be larger because of the high percentage of dependent Negroes on the relief rolls. Armed with these facts, Peery timidly asked for a legislative commission to study further the prospective costs of a plan. On other parts of the security bill he was less cautious. Following the recommendation of an earlier commission study on unemployment, he offered the Assembly an unemployment insurance bill along with a $2 million relief request to care for the unemployables who were no longer receiving direct assistance because of the termination of the FERA.[6]

The failure of the Assembly to adopt a broad welfare plan was regrettable. Accepting the advice of the Virginia Manufacturers Association, which lobbied against the bills, the delegates scuttled old-age pensions, unemployment insurance, and a reduction in the working day of women from ten to eight hours. Rejection of the unemployment plan was especially illogical. The federal act required payments by employers for unemployment compensation, regardless of state action. If a state joined the program, 90 percent of the money was "returned" to the state to provide unemployment benefits for its workers. If a state elected not to participate, employers would still pay, but the unemployed would receive no compensation. Incredibly, the Assembly chose the latter course. The House of Delegates passed the eight-hour bill and a small old-age pension plan only to see them die in the Senate. The Senate, on the other hand, after bitter debate, passed the unemployment insurance act, 18 to 17, only to have the House veto its decision. Fortunately for the needy unemployables, Peery's relief bill slipped through the Assembly along with authorization for a commission to study social security costs.[7]

This legislative session was remarkable for its negativism. In addition to the defeat of the three major pieces of social legislation, due in part to the governor's failure to support them actively, the legislators rejected an antinepotism bill, a more liberal criminal probation bill, and a more equitable redistricting bill. One senator called the Senate a "monkey house." The *Times-Dispatch* remarked, "The General Assembly of 1936 will go down in history as one of the most reactionary legislatures which has sat in Virginia since the first parliamentary gathering in the New World convened at Jamestown in 1619." The Petersburg *Progress-Index* exclaimed, "We confess we had not realized that there was such a strong element in Virginia opposed to legislation based upon considerations of humanity as well as of justice." More restrained was the conservative Roanoke *World-News:* "It [the Assembly] has done its part to keep Virginia sound; it has imposed no new taxes; it has kept appropriations within fairly anticipated revenues." Clearly, however, government in the Old Dominion was not responding to the economic and social demands of the day.[8]

Even the relief bill paid homage to a balanced budget. The Assembly permitted no expenditure for relief over $580,000 if it would cause a deficit. Allocations to the counties and cities were to be made on the basis of population with the localities matching 60 percent of the money coming from the state. The new program implemented the old idea of a statewide welfare organization. Supervised by the state welfare department, localities were to take over responsibility for direct relief and the traditional welfare functions in addition to administering CCC enrollments, surplus commodities distribution, and WPA certification. By October 1936 eighty-six of the counties and twenty-three of the twenty-four cities had operating units. Even with this step forward, Virginia still lagged behind the rest of the country in caring for its indigent. The incidence of Virginians on general relief in 1936 (52 per 10,000) was only 40 percent of the national average, eighth lowest in the country, and the state ranked thirty-second in the amount of state funds obligated for relief.[9]

Stirred to action by the defeat of the security legislation, moderate forces in the state formed the Virginia Consumers League to lobby for its passage. The group included Richmond editors Virginius Dabney and Douglas Southall Freeman, Labor Commissioner Hall, Francis Pickens Miller of Fairfax, and William Garnett of VPI. They were assisted in this effort by Roosevelt's overwhelming triumph in November. When it became apparent that Virginia would lose the benefits of unemployment compensation if it did not act, a clamor arose for a special session of the Assembly. Governor Peery responded to a majority of the legislature and called the session for December 14, 1936. Presented with a program similar to the one defeated earlier in the year, the same Assembly membership passed it, 39 to 1 in the Senate and 93 to 1 in the House. Applying to firms with eight or more employees—thus benefiting 320,000 workers in the state—the bill established an Unemployment Compensation Commission consisting of the commissioner of labor and two other appointees of the governor. Unemployment insurance quickly proved its worth during the recession of 1938 when it put millions of dollars into the hands of the jobless.[10]

Virginia was even more dilatory when it came to aid for the elderly, being the last state to join the basic pension program. For two years older citizens of the state had to rely on Confederate Veterans Aid or the limited resources of the new Public Assistance Act. Both Welfare Commissioner James and his successor, William Stauffer, justified the delay on the grounds that it gave Virginia time to investigate thoroughly all possible programs and avoid the expense and inefficiency encountered in other states. Westmoreland Davis was unimpressed. His *Southern Planter* retorted, "The explanation of Virginia's lag lies not in a lack of need for her aged, but in a lack of interest of a machine-controlled legislature in matters of human welfare."[11]

In December 1937 the Commission on Old Age Assistance in Virginia reported its findings to the governor. The commission estimated the cost of old-age pensions for the needy at $5 million, with Virginia's share being $2.9 million the first year and rising to $3.3 million by 1947. Of 141,432 persons over sixty-five in the state, it estimated 39,000 were eligible for assistance. Suggesting a $30 maximum, it foresaw an average payment of $11.48 a month for whites and $9.05 for blacks. The commission recommended that the localities put up 37.5 percent of the state's share of 50 percent. Three members disagreed with the cost findings, believing future costs would be much higher than estimated.[12]

Confronted with the Supreme Court's decision upholding the social security legislation, the 1938 General Assembly consented to have Virginia join the other forty-seven states in the program, but it approved participation on a more limited basis than that recommended by the commission. Aid to the aged was lumped together with general relief and aid to the blind and dependent children in a $3.3 million relief bill. The maximum contribution per person per month was to be $20. This Public Assistance Act required every city and county to have a welfare department and stipulated the additional amounts to be paid by the locality for each category of aid. If the locality declined to participate, the state was to direct the program and deduct the cost from funds already allotted to the community. Maintaining organization control, the Assembly dictated that the new welfare boards were to be appointed by the circuit judges; the boards in turn would appoint the superintendents of public welfare with the approval of the state welfare department.

This program began operation on September 1, 1938, over three years after the social security bill passed Congress. The new public welfare commissioner, William Stauffer, former state economist, ran a taut adminstrative ship, maintaining complete records, taking periodic audits, and employing more professional social workers. From an initial monthly total of 4,564, the number of persons over sixty-five receiving aid grew to 19,646 by December 1940. With an average payment of $10 per person, the state ranked twenty-ninth nationally in number of recipients, thirty-eighth in total payments, and forty-second in the average amount of payments—further indications of Virginia's persistently parsimonious nature. Realizing the inadequacy of Virginia's program, Commissioner Stauffer predicted, "Failure to make reasonable progress in these fields is not characteristic of humanitarian statesmanship, and may in the end rebound to the disadvantage of the Commonwealth."[13]

While Virginia's first efforts in the field of large-scale public welfare were hesitant and niggardly, the advances made in the thirties were significant. Before the New Deal the state welfare department had a very limited program which reached a small percentage of the people and operated only through persuasion in the localities. By 1938 it supervised a large domain of welfare activities and its authority had become law. Ten different security programs were in effect in the state, seven of them having coming into being since 1937: (1) old-age insurance with 600,000 workers making payments, (2) old-age assistance for 20,000 aged, (3) unemployment insurance, (4) aid to the blind, (5) aid to dependent children, (6) maternal and child health care, (7) child welfare, (8) aid for crippled children, (9) public health work, and (10) vocational rehabilitation. Combined with the activities of the many federal agencies in the state (the WPA, CCC, and NYA), these programs demonstrated the striking progress of welfare in Virginia since 1932. A new awareness and responsibility were also evident among the professionals in the department, a mood comparable to that experienced by all those who worked with the New Deal. Marguerite Farmer of the Richmond Family Service Society concluded, "The welfare program in Virginia received a shot in the arm with the institution of the Federal programs of the '30s."[14]

The General Assembly session of 1938 was noteworthy for several other events. It marked the end of the Peery regime and the accession to power of James Price. Although he left office in the midst of a recession, Peery had had the good fortune to govern during the years of recovery. Revenues had so increased that he estimated a surplus in general fund monies of over $5 million by June 1938 and a reduction in the public debt of over $3 million. He presented the largest budget in the state's history, with major increases in expenditures for capital outlays, roads, education, and the Alcoholic Beverage Control (ABC) Board. As he stepped down, Peery drew praise for his service, especially for the advances in social reform and the maintenance of fiscal integrity. In the tradition of Virginia's leaders, he had governed honorably, fairly, and conservatively—a performance which enabled Harry Byrd to solidify his control of Virginia politics.[15]

In his inaugural address, Governor Price hinted at involving the state more actively in the lives of its citizens. He asked for funds for old-age assistance, increased aid to education, an eight-hour workday for women, and liberalization of the poll tax requirements. His requests were partially met. The Assembly, as previously noted, passed social security legislation, added a bare $600,000 for schools, and, over the objections of Virginia industrialists, approved a maximum forty-eight-hour week for women permiting no more than nine working hours a day. Passage of additional labor legislation—an improved Workmen's Compensation Act, a bill to exempt labor pickets from the provisions of Virginia's antilynch law (except in the case of murder), and the appointment of a commission to study labor relations in the state—drew praise from the Virginia Federation of Labor. The Assembly also approved a Price recommendation permitting the cities in the state to participate in the $500 million federal slum clearance program. Attributing much of the progress to Price's leadership, the *Times-Dispatch* congratulated the lawmakers on their long overdue successes.[16]

However, on other legislation the Assembly proved less enterprising. Liberalization of the poll tax died without much fanfare, as did a bill for free textbooks for schoolchildren. A penal reform bill, viewed as too costly, was also defeated, despite the fact that Virginia had a jail committal rate four times that of the nation. Although improvements in working conditions were approved, the legislators ignored other recommendations of the commissioner of labor, who for years had asked for better mine inspection laws, a minimum wage, raising the child labor age from fourteen to sixteen, and a labor mediation board. The failure to upgrade mine safety standards was tragically highlighted by an explosion in Grundy which took the lives of forty-five miners shortly after the Assembly adjourned. Rejection of a minimum wage law and a mediation board for settling labor disputes did not produce such distressing consequences, but the results were nonetheless onerous to thousands of Virginia workers. Many assemblymen apparently agreed with the Lynchburg *News*'s assessment that Virginia was "in danger of running wild with the idea that the state has to take care of the physical, mental and moral welfare of all its citizens."[17]

Organized labor in Virginia operated at a considerable disadvantage. As in the South generally, much of the industry in the state relied on cheap, plentiful semiskilled labor that was least susceptible to unionization. A paternalistic tradition in many mill towns either satisfied or intimidated a placid work force which was fully indoctrinated in the evils of "foreign" labor agitators and their unions. Employers also used race as a weapon to keep workers from upsetting the status quo. And in the rare event of unrest, management resorted to its hardline strategy of no mediation, the use of strikebreakers, and an appeal to the courts and public officials, from whom support was usually forthcoming. The mutuality of interests between businessmen and politicians in Virginia—maintenance of an apathetic work force and electorate, rejection of outside interference, low taxes, and limited government—created an imposing obstacle for labor to deal with.[18]

Despite the obstructions in the Old Dominion, labor made modest strides forward during the depression years. The collective bargaining clause (7a) of the National Industrial Recovery

Act had been an important breakthrough, but the major elements behind the victories of labor in the late thirties were the Wagner Labor Relations Act, which put teeth into the decisions of a new National Labor Relations Board (NLRB), and the split in the ranks of labor, which led to the formation of the CIO and the subsequent unionization of the mass industries. The competition between the AFL and the CIO for new members brought thousands of workers into the unions who now knew that the government would enforce their right to organize and bargain collectively.

Labor in Virginia benefited from these developments, which were opposed by the conservative hierarchy in the state. As it had fought the NRA, the Virginia Manufacturers Association criticized the Wagner Act, calling it "one of the most pernicious bits of legislation that has been enacted by a Federal Congress." The *News-Leader* said it was the "wrong means to a proper end."[19] Predictably, Senator Byrd voted against it. The legislation had an immediate impact in the Commonwealth when the Amalgamated Clothing Workers of America charged Friedman–Harry Marks Clothing Company of Richmond with discrimination against workers who joined a union. In March 1936 the NLRB found the owners guilty of such discrimination; it issued a cease-and-desist order and called for the reinstatement of the discharged workers with restoration of pay. A year later the Supreme Court, overruling a circuit court, decided in favor of the NLRB, five to four, thus upholding the constitutionality of the Wagner Act. Within a month Amalgamated had negotiated a three-year contract with Friedman-Marks recognizing the union, restoring lost jobs, and providing a thirty-six-hour week and a minimum wage of $14 a week.[20]

Further union success in the Old Dominion awaited the competition between the AFL and the CIO. John L. Lewis and his United Mine Workers (UMW) had unionized the Appalachian coalfields in 1933, but the textile and tobacco industries had remained largely unorganized. The United Textile Workers was so weak in Virginia that state union officials declined to participate in a nationwide strike in 1934. Seeking greater power for labor through organization of the large industries, such as steel and automobiles, Lewis broke with the AFL and its trade union policies and formed the Committee for Industrial Organization (CIO) in late 1935. After being formally ostracized by the AFL in September 1936, the CIO unions initiated their notorious sit-down strikes, which gave their new organization the necessary impetus to challenge AFL ascendancy. Virginia politicians and editors deplored the sit-down strike as a lawless violation of property rights, but they could not prevent its influence from extending to the Old Dominion.[21]

The first sit-down strike in the Commonwealth occurred at the White House Café in Ashland on March 19, 1937, when four employees demanded higher wages and shorter hours. All four were fired. The second work stoppage at a Richmond bag manufacturer resulted in a compromise 10 percent pay hike after a six-hour holdout. The largest and most important sit-down strike in Virginia took place at the Industrial Rayon Corporation in Covington. Seeking sole bargaining rights and higher wages, 250 to 400 members of the Synthetic Yarn Federation, an affiliate of the United Textile Workers, charged discrimination against union members and sat down at the job on March 30. After spending a peaceful ten days in the plant, the sit-downers left the factory to avoid conflict with the police, set up their picket lines on the outside, and continued negotiations. The strike proceeded in this manner into July when fighting broke out at the plant between strikers and nonstrikers who desired to return to work. Governor Peery, who had refrained from earlier involvement, ordered an investigation and dispatched twenty-five state patrolmen to the area where they were used to escort workers back to the plant. Peery justified his action on the ground that he was protecting the right of workers to return to their jobs, but whatever his purpose, the strike was broken. Although the plant was soon organized by the union through an NLRB election, no settlement with management was ever reached, and the workers drifted back to work.[22]

Just after the Covington strike began, competing CIO and AFL organization drives got underway across the state. The CIO through its Textile Workers Organizing Committee (TWOC) attempted to organize the textile mills in the South, a feat that had gone unaccomplished through the twenties and early thirties. The AFL, continuing its policy of signing up skilled craftsmen, approached such Virginia industries as shipbuilding. To counteract these activities and to avert prolonged and divisive strikes, many Virginia industries instituted wage increases. In a bandwagon effect, rayon plants in Waynesboro and Ampthill, cotton mills in Martinsville and Danville, and tobacco plants in Richmond raised wages before strikes could begin. Labor activity in the state reached a new intensity as labor unions were formed, strikes were threatened, and wage increases were granted.

In many instances strikes did occur, including those at the Covington rayon plant, in Virginia's coal mines, and at the tobacco stemmeries in Richmond. In the latter factories black women involved in the preparation of the leaf for manufacturing walked off the job protesting low wages, which for some of them was five cents an hour. The Tobacco Workers International Union of the AFL, which had been recognized by the large tobacco companies of Richmond, believed their case was "hopeless" and refused to represent them. Forming their own independent union with the support of the Southern Negro Youth Congress and the CIO, the workers won a wage increase, a forty-hour week, and recognition of their union.[23] Spawned by the interunion struggle, by confidence in the enforcement of the Wagner Act, and by improved business conditions, fifty strikes involving 18,743 workers occurred in Virginia in 1937, both high marks for the decade. The strikes increased union membership, brought higher wages to workers who had long been the victims of insensitive management, and probably influenced the General Assembly to approve legislation that enhanced the rights of working men and women.

The arrival of a recession in late 1937 tempered union gains that year and restored some calm to the labor scene in 1938. Although there were twenty-three strikes in the Old Dominion, only 2,412 employees were involved. Many strikes failed because conditions now favored management; with men being laid off, others could hardly ask for wage hikes. Organizing continued, but labor worked to consolidate the gains of the previous year. Late in the fall, as business activity picked up, labor regained its lost momentum and strikes became more numerous.[24]

Passage of the Fair Labor Standards Act highlighted labor activity in 1938. Proposed by President Roosevelt the year before to replace the old NRA wage and hour standards, the bill was delayed by the House Rules Committee, of which Representative Howard Smith was a ranking member. This rearguard action collapsed in May 1938 when Congress passed a wage and hour bill establishing a twenty-five-cent-an-hour minimum wage and a forty-four-hour workweek. Applying only to industries operating in interstate commerce, the law also set a minimum age of sixteen for children working in these firms. Representatives Smith, Robertson, and Drewry opposed the final version, while the remaining six Virginia congressmen voted for it.

Observers predicted Virginia would be less affected by the bill than most other southern states. The state labor department estimated that half of Virginia's industrial workers, including employees in the major industries of tobacco, shipbuilding, railroad repair, and textiles, were already earning the twenty-five-cent minimum or better and working a forty-four-hour week or less. Industries considered to be operating with marginal standards included lumber, fertilizers, tobacco rehandling, and clothing, some of which had the minimum wage but demanded longer hours. Although tobacco officials believed the stemming of tobacco for export might have to be abandoned due to the prohibitive costs, there were few shutdowns and few violations across the Old Dominion. The exemption for firms involved only in intrastate commerce saved many businesses from closing. The Fair Labor Standards Act, in addition to its benefits for workers, had the practical effect of moving the South and Virginia into the mainstream of the national economy by reducing wage differentials and stimulating better management techniques and mechanization. It was the last major piece of New Deal domestic legislation.[25]

As labor registered gains in the second half of the thirties, so too did every segment of the Virginia economy. Industry in the state took giant strides forward as 510 new manufacturing firms settled in the Old Dominion between 1935 and 1940. Virginia's enviable record during the depression and a favorable tax system were the primary lures, but an adequate supply of raw materials and cheap labor, a favorable climate, and excellent transportation facilities also made the state an attractive location. Among the largest new companies were a $500,000 silk printing and dyeing plant in Richmond, a $1 million Johns-Manville plant in Jarrett, a $2.5 million pulp and paper plant at Franklin, a $10 million American Cellulose and Chemical Company plant at Pearisburg in Giles County, and a Viscose Corporation rayon yarn factory at Front Royal. Although most of the new firms had headquarters outside Virginia, their entry absorbed surplus rural labor, increased tax revenue, and raised living standards for many workers in the state.[26]

By 1937 all manufacturing indexes exceeded those of 1929—salaries, wages, number of workers, and value of products. The billion-dollar year prophesied for 1930 arrived seven years later. Tobacco, paper and pulp products, metal machinery manufacturing, furniture manufacturing, and railroad repair work were making the most impressive strides forward. Coal production in 1937 reached 13.2 million short tons, highest in a decade. For the years 1929 through 1937 Virginia ranked first in the country in the increase in the value of its industrial products (21.8 percent); Richmond's increase of 44 percent made it the fastest growing industrial center in the nation. Imports and exports of tobacco, coal, lumber, and cotton into and out of Hampton Roads doubled between 1932 and 1936, and the total value of commerce through the port in 1937 was the second highest on record. Virginia farmers continued to improve their position, but they did not surpass 1929 income levels until the war years. The value of the tobacco and peanut crops, however, did exceed those of eight years earlier. On the relief front, the number employed by the WPA declined from 38,330 in March 1936 to 16,452 in September 1937. Although federal money continued to pour into Virginia, amounts were diminishing, and as recovery seemed assured, the president began making cuts in the budget in the spring of 1937.[27]

Roosevelt's optimism was unfounded. He had counted on business to take up the slack as government retreated from deficit spending and attempted to balance the budget. Although this was what commercial and industrial leaders had clamored for, they proved unwilling and unable to fill Washington's shoes. Apprehensive over the sit-down strikes and a tight-money policy instigated by the Federal Reserve, businessmen hesitated to undertake the expansion necessary to maintain economic growth. Government economists were among the first to predict the slump that began to take effect in September as new construction stalled and the stock market fell to new postdepression lows.[28]

Like the depression, the recession of 1937–38 had a more modest effect in the Old Dominion than in the nation. An unemployment census revealed that Virginia had one of the lowest jobless rates of any state (3.1 percent). In the first six months of 1938, Virginia employment declined 11.3 percent, compared to the national drop of 20 percent, and Virginia farm prices for the year did not plummet nearly so low as national prices. Roger Babson, nationally known economist, claimed Virginia and Richmond were among "the most favorable sales and credit territories in the Nation." In April editors of Virginia's business magazine, *The Commonwealth,* perceived the flattening out of the recession; by July they predicted its end. Most economic indexes for 1938 were lower than the year before, but the declines were nowhere near as drastic as in 1931 and 1932. The number of Virginians on WPA rolls increased, but federal expenditures for relief, unemployment compensation, and social security payments ameliorated the conditions of the needy. State Banking Commissioner M. E. Bristow reported that Virginia banks were in "as fine shape as at any time during my banking experience." The recession proved to be only a temporary brake on Virginia's industrial boom, and few doubted that 1939 would bring conditions reminiscent of 1929 before the Crash.[29]

In the last half of the thirties the Old Dominion recaptured the prosperity of the twenties and made significant advances in the fields of social welfare and labor relations, but it was New Deal legislation, not state innovation, that was the primary contributor to progress. Two of the most notable achievements of this legislative program were the development of a more liberal social conscience within the state and the stimulus given the labor movement. The protection of the rights of labor by the federal government—to organize, to bargain collectively, to obtain a decent wage, and to work under good conditions—was a milestone in the history of the workingman in the United States. It was reflected in the growing ranks of labor unions in Virginia, which during the decade increased their membership from 30,000 to 68,000. Although the state did take some steps to improve working conditions (e.g., the eight-hour law), the political establishment remained antagonistic to organized labor. The victories won by the workingman in Virginia were the result of individual sacrifice and New Deal support, not dynamic state leadership. Likewise, a sense of responsibility toward the unfortunate was slow to take root in the Old Dominion. The organization shifted its course only when it proved financially impractical and politically embarrassing for the state to remain without social security legislation. The new programs were immediately beneficial, demonstrating again the shortsightedness of doctrinaire fiscal conservatism. None of the relief programs threatened to bankrupt the state or erode the spiritual fiber of Virginia's citizens; aid to the aged, the destitute, and the unemployed became accepted functions of enlightened government.

Despite the successes, utopia had not arrived. Education in the Old Dominion continued to languish; efforts to upgrade the archaic penal system had been rejected; and conditions remained abysmal in the state mental hospitals—problem areas that, except for its construction programs, not even the New Deal was addressing adequately. The advances in social security and unionization, while commendable, were minimal compared to the progress in other states. The elderly could hardly be expected to make ends meet on $10 a month, and the number of workers in unions remained a small fraction of the work force. Virginia's "little New Deal" was very little indeed.[30]

9

The Enduring
Dominion

Although the events of the 1930s had an incalculable effect on American life, their impact in the Old Dominion was less momentous. The Virginia of 1939 was remarkably similar to that of ten years earlier. The organization suffered a reverse in 1938, as it had in 1928, but subsequent tests did not find its power and influence wanting; fiscal conservatism still dictated the policies of the state government; industry was making rapid advances while the farmer continued to tread water; and the gulfs between white and black, between FFVers and mountain "billies," and between urban and rural interests remained. David Shannon writes, "For about twelve years . . . the American people suffered from the Great Depression. Such an experience inevitably wrought many changes in American society—in politics, in economics, in social values, in formal culture."[1] Yet this generalization is not true for Virginia. Changes imported from the outside, notably those produced by New Deal agencies and their money, enlivened the landscape, but liberalism did not replace phlegmatic conservatism, Keynesianism did not replace the balanced budget, and rugged individualism remained the dominant social philosophy.

The two factors most accountable for the retention of the status quo were the relative mildness of the depression in the Old Dominion and the presence of a conservative political organization which thwarted New Deal attempts to change the social structure of the state. While the Old Dominion suffered industrial reverses, above-normal unemployment, and much hardship, its citizens did not experience, in the same degree, the wholesale misfortune that much of the rest of the nation endured. Virginia did not avoid the depression, but the balanced nature of the state economy mitigated its severity, permitting

172

Virginians to avoid major adjustments in adapting to the new conditions. Similarly, New Deal programs and money left their imprint on Virginia, but the impact was tempered by the milder depression shock, which reduced the demand for federal help, and by the opposition of a political regime which ruled with unusual monopoly and prevented liberal adversaries from seriously challenging its anachronistic policies.

Virginia had a delayed reaction to the financial catastrophe. The nature of its economy—the balance between agriculture, industry, and commerce, subsistence-level farming, and the support of federal money in the Washington and Norfolk areas—immunized the state from the immediate effects of the Crash. These buffers eventually broke down, but they did minimize the total effect of the depression in Virginia and contributed to its more rapid recovery by 1935. Although the business relapse experienced in the Old Dominion was severe, it compared favorably with that encountered in the nation at large. Most available statistics indicate that, compared to conditions in 1929, Virginia was relatively better off than most other states during the depression.[2]

Farm conditions for two decades were agonizing all across the nation, Virginia not excepted, but farming in the state survived the depression years in better fashion largely because of geographical location and agricultural diversity. Noted one farmer: "It was a rural area of rather diversified economic foundations. We did not have an immensely urban, industrial and service oriented economy. We were perhaps little changed from 19th century self-sufficiency and what was maybe even 'depressed' reconstruction rurality." Adjacent to the largest urban market in the country, Virginia found its truck crops and dairy products both readily accessible and in demand. Although the state experienced one severe drought, it did not have to suffer through the ravages of dust storms and drought in the mid-thirties as did the middle section of the country. Nor was it enslaved to one-crop agriculture. With truck crops, cotton, and peanuts in the Tidewater, tobacco in the Southside, and orcharding, wheat, and dairying in the north and west, Virginia farming did not face disaster when the price of one crop declined. Furthermore, many of its farms were small and self-sufficient and not reliant on the marketing of a single crop. Economist Treadwell Davison observed, "It is this diversity of agricultural interest that has made the impact of the prolonged agricultural depression less in this State than in the cotton states of the deep South and the wheat growing areas of the West."[3]

Nor was Virginia a highly industrialized state, which helped it avoid that phase of the depression which struck the nation hardest. Before the depression only 24 percent of Virginia's gainfully employed population was in industry, compared to 36 percent in the East and Midwest. Old Dominion manufacturing did not include the heavy industries of steel and automobiles that sustained huge national losses. Falling coal production did depress the southwest section of the state, but a major portion of its industry was consumer oriented, producing those necessities which even a poverty-stricken people could not do without—food, clothing, and cigarettes. Thus, industrial employment and wages in Virginia, compared to 1929 figures, remained at higher percentage levels than those of the nation. The 1933 value of Old Dominion manufactured products fell to 70 percent of the 1929 totals, but the nation's production declined by more than 50 percent.[4]

In matters of finance, there was no question of Virginia's superior position. Pay-as-you-go road building in the twenties had not overextended resources, and reduced expenditures in the thirties kept personal taxes low and the debt stable. The third lowest bond interest rate in the country could have allowed the state to undertake expanded services for its people had its leaders chosen to do so. This fiscal conservatism contributed to public and business confidence, which provided Virginia with an enviable banking record. Bank suspensions and commercial failures were held to a minimum.[5] Fortuitously, the General Assembly in 1928 had raised the minimum capital requirements for organizing a new bank and in 1932 had taken additional safeguards to prevent failures. From 1930 to 1935 Virginia had the lowest percentage of decline in per capita savings in the South, and its percentage of decrease in savings deposits was less than half that of the national average. These statistics prompted M. E. Bristow, state commissioner of insurance and banking, to credit Virginia with "one of the finest records among the entire forty-eight states."[6]

The depression had only a slight effect on Virginia's vital statistics, except for the suicide and homicide rates. From nine suicides per 100,000 population in 1929, the rate rose to 15.2 per 100,000 in 1932. The homicide rate was up from 10 to 14.5 per 100,000. The birth rate declined slightly, the marriage rate was up, and the death rate and divorce rate remained relatively stable. Virginia's population growth for the decade, 10.6 percent, was higher than that of the nation, 7.2 percent, and compared favorably with a 4.9 percent increase in the twenties.[7]

Relief statistics prove that Virginians were in need; they also suggest that the need was far less in Virginia than in the nation— although perhaps not so inconsiderable as the organization wanted to believe. At the peak load, the percentage of people on relief in Virginia was half that of the nation, with only two other states having lower figures. The Old Dominion, with 2 percent of the nation's population, received less than 0.6 percent of the money expended on direct relief by the federal government. While Cabell Phillips was generally correct when he wrote that less money went to those states which contributed no money of their own, several states provided less than Virginia yet received more federal funds. There is little doubt that the government would have disregarded the absence of a state contribution if conditions had demanded it.[8]

Virginia's low ranking in New Deal spending (twenty-seventh in total dollars; forty-third in per capita figures) reflected the state's peculiar economic situation more than political considerations. While Roosevelt was not averse to using propaganda and purges to combat the organization, there is little evidence that he manipulated New Deal programs and money to influence state politics or enhance his own prospects. Harry Byrd's fear of federal intrusion into the affairs of Virginia affected the state's participation in some federal programs, which caused Washington's contribution to be reduced, but relatively low unemployment, general farming, a sound home and farm mortgage situation, and an aversion to local spending and the indebtedness that federal money necessitated were more important factors in determining the Old Dominion's share of funds.[9]

Statistics, of course, do not tell the full story of how hard the depression squeezed the people of the Commonwealth. They do not tell of the food distributed to the hungry by local commissaries or private charities. There is no count of the letters crossing the desks of congressmen pleading for work, nor an accurate survey of the hundreds of children in need of shoes. These tragic situations existed in Virginia, but they were more common in other states where they often were transformed into more violent events. There were no mobs, no reported near-lynchings of judges, no milk poured out on the roads, and few labor disorders in the Old Dominion. Historical accounts of the depression do not refer to long breadlines or murdered laborers in Virginia, and there is little mention in local contemporary sources of the physical suffering or underlying discontent of the people. The Virginia economy had much to do with this, but the nature of the society and the strength of traditionalism also helped to insulate the state from the worst shocks of the Crash. Virginia was, in a sense, not only resistant to progressive innovation but impervious to regressive change as well. Ledger books in the black, an "abhorrence for borrowing," one-party politics, a stoical outlook, and a strong self-help ethic had a very stabilizing effect when times turned bad.

Virginia society proved remarkably resilient to depression because of its peculiar polarization between haves and have-nots. The ruling elite, composed of the aristocracy of old first families and big farmers, professional people and businessmen, and local politicians and white-collar workers dependent upon and sympathetic to the whims of the organization, subsisted on its accumulated wealth and protected positions, while the 875,000 marginal rural poor, the urban Negroes, and the low-wage-earning blue-collar workers, who were without political voice, endured as they had before the depression. Although textile workers and black domestics were among the first to face unemployment and the specter of starvation, they were also the first to receive private and public aid, and their depression standards of living were not that far removed from what they had been in 1929. The fact that Virginia reached its 1929 levels of production and employment by 1935 but still had thousands of citizens on relief suggests that many of these recipients had been poor before the Crash. What was absent in Virginia was a large, typically aggressive American middle class of "expectant capitalists," whose wealth was increasing and who were politically active for the purpose of achieving their goals. Now out of work, without credit, facing poverty for the first time in their lives, these people were the hardest hit by the depression, both economically and psychologically. The relative absence of such a class in the Commonwealth lessened the magnitude of the crisis in the Old Dominion.

Further cushioning its effect was the well-known stoicism of Virginians, who were prone to endure much hardship without asking for help or without rocking the foundations of their social order. One Red Cross official remarked during the 1930 drought, "Virginians are prouder and less willing to seek outside help than citizens of the other states in the drought areas."[10] Decades later, residents of the Old Dominion were using words such as "proud," "conservative," "thrifty," and "self-sufficient" to describe how they lived through the depression. For many, conditions in the thirties had changed little from the years of post-Civil War poverty. Said one ancient Confederate veteran, "The depression is paradise compared to the ten to twelve years following the Civil War." Douglas Freeman agreed: "If it be true, as many visitors affirm, that Virginians have accepted hard times with stoicism, it must be in part because they realize that their woes are less than those of their fathers in the years after the War Between the States."[11] From what they read in the newspapers about conditions elsewhere, Virginians concluded they were better off. A typical reaction was: "Everyone here . . . has suffered like the devil in this depression, but we are all getting used to it now and it is really not so bad. We work a little harder, drink a little less, and go to bed a little earlier at night. The net result is good—try it."[12]

Nevertheless, the depression did have a significant impact in the state. It brought undue misery to thousands of Virginians, impoverishing, disrupting, and scarring their lives—in some cases permanently. More positively, it revealed long-term subsistence-level poverty and precipitated New Deal legislation that benefited both the new and the old poor. Furthermore, the relative mildness of the depression in Virginia permitted a quick revitalization of the state's economy. Industrial productivity and employment moved upward rapidly in the last half of the decade. The negative agricultural trends of the early thirties— increasing tenancy and decreasing farm size—were reversed. The state reduced its bonded indebtedness by over $5 million and amassed a sizable surplus in the general fund. Income from 1929 to 1940 rose 20 percent, the fourth highest increase in the nation. Unfortunately, this economic picture was little more than a replica of the situation in 1930 at the end of the Byrd administration. Despite the state's solvency, Virginia had not appreciably increased its services to the people; agricultural cash income, although well above depression lows, was not yet equal to 1929 figures; and the industrial growth, while heartening, was still reliant on cheap-labor, low value-added industries. A new millenium had not arrived.[13]

Most importantly, the depression helped perpetuate the status quo in Virginia. The crisis was not overwhelming enough to overthrow the existing orthodoxies. In fact, the depression experience confirmed in the minds of Virginia's leaders the necessity of maintaining conservative fiscal policies at the expense of providing better services. They disseminated the idea that this conservatism was largely responsible for moderating the effects of the Crash. While balanced budgets and reduced expenditures preserved the financial integrity of the Old Dominion, these measures by themselves did not hold off adversity or smooth the path to recovery. Yet organization politicians became captives of their own propaganda and refused to recognize and correct existing conditions. Hardened into dogma, pay-as-you-go became the icon before which all future Virginia leaders had to bow. William A. Garrett, state senator from the Danville district, composed a proper epitaph for himself and the organization:

I would like to have the next generation know that I have stood steadfastly against the generation of Virginians passing on a heavy burden of debt to those who come after us. I believe that governments as well as individuals should live within their means and this has been the key note of my public life.

I count myself fortunate that my position as Chairman of the Finance Committee of the Senate of Virginia has enabled me to play an important part in blocking many movements which would have led to the extravagant use of public funds. The young people of the rising generation could learn no more important lesson than to live within their means and I have always thought the State should set them a good example.[14]

Commenting on such an "adding machine mentality," V. O. Key stated: "Attached to the fetish of a balanced budget, it takes a short-run view that almost invariably militates against the long-run interests of the state. Men with the minds of tradesmen do not become statesmen."[15] Ironically, saddling the state with balanced budgets and minimal expenditures, while presumed to be its salvation in the thirties, condemned Virginia to social backwardness for the next generation. The traditionalism that had permitted Virginians to endure bad times gracefully became a barrier obstructing the road to progress. This was the sterile legacy which the depression bequeathed Virginia.

Reinforced by a desire to maintain the political and social status quo, this fiscal dogmatism caused the organization to reject progressive courses of action proposed by voices of reason and moderation in both Washington and Richmond. For years the recommendations of Labor Commissioner John Hopkins Hall and Education Superintendent Sidney Hall for improved labor legislation and increased educational expenditures went unheeded. William Garnett, prominent Virginia rural sociologist, argued for more effective spending in education, the attraction of skilled labor in industry, and the development of a more sensitive social conscience as the solutions to the major problems of the state, but his perceptive analysis of Virginia's deficiencies received scant attention from the politicians.[16]

Organization leaders boasted of the soundness of state finances, yet they were unwilling to use that strength to support education adequately or grant relief to those in need. In 1936, in relation to its taxpaying ability, Virginia was expending less money for education than forty-three other states. One Virginia Education Association official declared, "It just doesn't make sense for us to boast the lowest tax rate in the nation when our crime average is so high. We are breeding criminals because our education facilities are not adequate." Concluded a student of Virginia's education expenditures, "Unquestionably the failure on the part of the State to meet its obligations in the adequate support of education is due more to political attitude than to the inability to pay."[17]

Other equally sound fiscal policies were available to state leaders had they wanted to choose them. The Commonwealth was financially capable of borrowing, raising taxes, or diverting money from the segregated special funds to the general fund. Borrowing on a large scale would have required a constitutional amendment, but this was not an insurmountable obstacle. Raising additional taxes would not have been a popular move, but it would have been a statesmanlike method for relieving the poor and improving education.

Diversion of special funds was the most rational alternative to pay-as-you-go. While general fund revenues declined from $22 million in 1929 to $13 million in 1934, the sources of money for special funds (e.g., gasoline and license taxes, which paid for highways) were not appreciably affected, and in fact these revenues rose from $25 million in 1929 to $30 million in 1934. State funds for public education fell from a high of $7 million in 1931–32 to $5.5 million in 1933–34. During this same period, highway revenue receipts rose by $3 million, a figure which did not include the increased millions the federal government was providing for road building.[18] In most years the highway department carried over a balance of several million dollars to the following year, while schools were cutting teachers' salaries and shortening terms because money was not available to them. To some it made sense to combine monies or divert funds from one source to other areas whose needs were more pressing. Arguing for an overhaul of the segregated tax system, the *Times-Dispatch* declared, "State taxes must be considered as a unit and the services rendered by the central government should be regarded in the terms of their social value." The Portsmouth *Star* queried, "Is it more important to build roads than it is to educate the future citizenry of the Commonwealth?" Even the rural Manassas *Journal*, which in 1932 had supported the Byrd county road bill, called for an end to segregated funds that permitted highways to prosper and schools to languish. Defenders of tax segregation re-torted that diversion would impair the highway system and un-fairly deprive motorists of the benefits of their gasoline taxes. They pointed out that some diversion had already occurred through highway spending for the relief effort. Representing business and rural interests, these arguments prevailed, making it necessary for schools, colleges, penal institutions, and welfare facilities to rely on the inadequate general fund revenues to con-tinue their already inferior services.[19] Years later, Colgate Darden admitted that the organization had been "too rigid" in pursuing pay-as-you-go. "We lacked imagination," he said. "We were not sufficiently abreast of the times."[20]

In some cases—direct relief, unemployment insurance, and social security—Virginia was forced to "modernize," but usually it was one of the last states to do so, and its eventual contribu-tions were often minimal. The leaders of the organization did not inquire what was good for the people but what was good for the state. To them the state was an autonomous entity with its own set of rights and duties, which included "living within its means." The concept of the state as a servant and protector of all the people was foreign to their minds; thus, their only conces-sion to the depression was to cut spending. That thousands of Virginians could get no relief or received less than they needed because of this policy did not seem to bother them. Critical of Senator Byrd's attitude on social security legislation, the *Times-Dispatch* declared: "Both Mr. Byrd and Mr. Peery seem to be living in the nineteenth century era of laissez faire, when any-body who advanced the idea that governments were socially re-sponsible for their citizens was regarded as a radical or a crank. . . . They are so intent on keeping Virginia's budget bal-anced or nearly balanced, and so anxious to maintain the State's credit at its present high level, that they seem to have lost their perspective. . . . The time has come for the political leaders in the State to wake up to the fact that they are not living in a by-gone era." Although the newspaper applauded the management of Virginia's financial resources, the editor, Virginius Dabney, concluded, "We cannot help wishing, however, that the state of Virginia had revealed a social conscience during the depres-sion."[21]

In addition to having faulty consciences and myopic vision, organization leaders had a propensity for delay, postponing action as if somehow the problem would cure itself. The road to penal reform illustrates this disposition to procrastinate. With a rising committal rate and a faulty jail inspection system, improvement of Virginia penal institutions was a topic of legislative discussion throughout the decade. In 1935 a Federal Bureau of Prisons report listed fifty Virginia jails as unfit for federal prisoners. This was confirmed by a state Jail Commission report in 1938 which claimed there were too many inadequate jails, too many committals, and too many pretrial detentions. Virginia's jail population in June 1937 was four times the national average. One-fourth of the jails were deemed fire hazards, and one-third had no night watchman. While legislators debated, four jails burned down in the mid-thirties, killing three inmates. Furthermore, Virginia had no parole system and an inadequate probation system. Several legislative commissions from 1932 to 1939 recommended action to remedy these deficiencies, but no legislation was forthcoming, a fact many commentators blamed on the politically advantageous fee system. The Newport News *Daily Press* editorialized: "Why the General Assembly has been so loath to take remedial action in this matter we do not know. . . . Our entire penal system is outmoded and is costing us a great deal more than it should. We prate about our enlightenment, yet we tolerate a criminal system which in itself is criminal."[22] Finally in 1942 the Assembly created a state Department of Corrections to supervise all jails in the state as well as a new parole system. A history of that system written years later concludes: "As has been true in so many instances, Virginia in the best traditions of conservatism moved with majestic slowness into the field of parole. By 1942 when the present parole system was established, this State stood practically alone in the United States in not having any system whereby prisoners were released under certain conditions and with supervision provided before their sentences had been completed."[23] Such tardiness was the result of a miserly aversion to spending combined with a politically motivated desire to deter social reform. Byrd's confidant, William Reed, put it best: "We must keep Virginia like she is without any changes."[24]

The uninterrupted domination of the organization over Virginia politics was secured by the loyalty of the courthouse ring and a rural-dominated legislature, the financial support of the upper classes, and the continued existence of a small electorate and an apathetic citizenry. These factors made it unlikely that a dramatic reversal in the policies of the organization would occur. Critics of the regime, including the "antis," had neither the money nor the power to challenge this political and social order. Secure in their positions, organization politicians expounded their conservative convictions in the national theater, opposed measures that were not in accord with those convictions, and disregarded the larger needs of the people. Although it provided honest and reasonably efficient government, the Byrd machine was one of the most self-serving regimes in the history of American politics.

While the organization refused to acknowledge the distress created by the depression and ignored the long-term social needs of the state, the Roosevelt administration attempted to address these problems. The immediate economic impact of the New Deal programs was quite noticeable in Virginia. Roosevelt never did solve the problems of unemployment and reduced business activity, difficulties which only wartime production cured, but limited pump priming was enough to restore the less sophisticated Old Dominion economy to normal levels of activity within five years. While New Deal standards of relief were lower than the normal living standards of people in the heavily industrialized states, in the South they more nearly approached the norm, especially among the marginal poor. Similarly, minimum wages and maximum hours had a far greater effect in those states, including Virginia, which had no previous legislation in these areas. The relative success of the New Deal in reviving the farm economy was also of great aid to Virginia, a predominantly agricultural state. Furthermore, the attraction of thousands of new faces to the expanding bureaucracy in Washington, D.C., and the huge expenditures on the sizable military establishment

in the state, even before war clouds began to gather, also benefited the Old Dominion. The combined effects of a milder depression shock and large amounts of federal money were enough
to restore 1920s prosperity to Virginia long before the rest of the
nation achieved it.

Aid to the unemployed constituted the largest portion of federal money entering the state during the decade. Since the
Commonwealth provided practically no money for relief and the
localities appropriated only meager amounts, the New Deal deserves the major credit for feeding and clothing Virginia's needy
during the depression. Even though the state was less affected
by the Crash, there were thousands of Virginians whose survival
depended upon money given by the FERA and the CWA. Once
the crisis passed, WPA work continued to sustain numerous
jobless and to maintain the level of purchasing power necessary
for the full recovery of the state's economy. Complementing the
rescue nature of these agencies were their socially redemptive
programs which educated and entertained citizens all across the
state, maintaining spirits in a difficult time and preparing men
and women for future jobs. The roads and bridges, schools and
post offices, hospitals and libraries of the PWA and the WPA
were more than concrete monuments to federal generosity; they
were the means by which thousands of Virginians began to live
better lives.

To the most despairing souls—the young and the aged—the
New Deal extended opportunity and security. Although essen-
tially relief oriented, the CCC and the NYA made lasting contributions to the American scene through their conservation work,
job-training programs, and "anti-drop-out" incentives. Having a
wealth of forest territory, Virginia took full advantage of the
CCC. Its proximity to the nation's capital enabled it to serve as a
testing ground for the entire program and to receive ample
funds for projects with which to impress visitors from
Washington. The development of a statewide park system was
one of the most beneficial contributions of the New Deal to the
Old Dominion. It was second only to the improved state welfare
system, adopted under the pressure of national social security
legislation, which incorporated general and old-age relief and
unemployment insurance into its older program of services.

184

Virginia's elderly had to wait two years longer than aged elsewhere before they could participate in the pension program, but
it eventually became a part of their everyday life.

Through the efforts of the Roosevelt administration, black Virginians were provided a separate but almost equal share of the
bounty. Fearful of antagonizing powerful southern congressmen, New Dealers made no attempt to break the segregation
barrier, a fact condemned by some historians as a sanction of Jim
Crow. However, a realistic appraisal suggests that in the thirties
only a gradual erosion of institutional racism was possible, and
the New Deal was in the forefront of this effort.[25] Had the administration tried more forcefully to get full equality for blacks,
its programs would have been defeated in Congress as the federal antilynching bill was. For the first time since Reconstruction the national government made more than a token effort to
ensure the Negro's participation in its work. The change was especially apparent in Virginia where the New Deal appointed
blacks to the staffs of the federal agencies and funneled FERA,
WPA, and PWA money into the black communities in the form
of new schools, hospitals, and community centers. Although facilities were segregated, Negroes found jobs with the CCC, the
NYA, and the Resettlement Administration housing projects,
and their percentage on the relief rolls approximated their percentage of the state's population. The friendship shown blacks
by the First Lady, demonstrated in Virginia with a visit to
Hampton Institute and an invitation to the White House for the
Hampton singers, was quickly reciprocated. Largely because of
these measures, a majority of Negroes for the first time in
Virginia history voted for the Democratic candidate in 1936.
This significant shift was an indication of the faith they had in
Roosevelt and their appreciation for the patronage coming their
way. But no change in race relations occurred. Indeed, the New
Deal's association with civil rights may have heightened racial
fears and cost it some support among white Virginia voters.[26]

For the farmer and the industrial worker the New Deal was
the catalyst by which they increased their share of the national
wealth, if only by meager amounts. Although there were inequities in the farm program and delays in the establishment of a
permanent program, the AAA alleviated the immediate problem

of overproduction through its allotment-benefit payment system, thus raising prices and restoring the farmer to a position of respectability. While Virginia's many small farms did not benefit directly from the allotment program, the state's major cash crop, tobacco, was covered by the most effective of the AAA's control bills. Through its resettlement and farm tenant programs the New Deal offered hope to a forgotten segment of the nation's farmers, but fund limitations reduced their effectiveness in the Old Dominion. Organized labor in the state improved its position through implementation of the NRA, the Wagner Labor Act, and the Fair Labor Standards Act. Union membership rose markedly, and workers received higher wages and worked under better conditions. However, despite intense labor activity in 1937 and the legislature's effort to improve state labor laws, unions did not become a major voice in Virginia's political life because of a traditional indifference to unionization, a deference to paternalistic ownership, and the continued presence of many "cheap-labor" industries.[27]

The limited success of the New Deal farm and labor programs in the Old Dominion is indicative of the problems the Rooseveltians faced in their efforts to rebuild and reshape American society. Part of the difficulty lay in the New Deal itself. Designed primarily to combat the depression, it was not radical enough, despite the charges of its conservative critics, to effect widespread social reform aimed at eradicating the inequities of wealth and position. In the words of Alonzo Hamby, "It gave the least to those who needed the most."[28] Much of its effort, such as the NRA, the Securities and Exchange bill, and the banking acts, preserved the predepression status quo with somewhat greater federal supervision. Agricultural policy was more concerned with higher farm prices than saving tenants and sharecroppers, while relief efforts often seemed preoccupied with the interests of private enterprise or state participation rather than employing the jobless. "Voluntary cooperation," restoration, accommodation, and the "American Way" were themes that dominated the thinking and thus the programs of the New Dealers.[29]

But even had it been more liberally conceived, it is unlikely the New Deal could have overcome the political opposition, local interests, and allegiance to an older ethic that it confronted. Several of the more transcendent pieces of legislation, such as the "soak-the-rich" tax scheme and the public utility holding company bill, had to be watered down or, as in the case of the TVA and the FSA, were restricted in scope or inadequately funded because of conservative resistance. Playing broker politics, Roosevelt was forced to balance the interests of southern barons and urban bosses against the needs of the disadvantaged, while his own political fortunes and those of his party also compelled him to compromise and intrigue. Politics may well have dictated New Deal spending policies in some states where political factionalism, especially among squabbling Democrats, frequently hindered the work of the national administration. Furthermore, many programs were administered locally, which limited the power of the Rooseveltians to impose their will. The innovative nature of these programs, which worked unevenly across the nation because of varying economic conditions, challenged the old federal-state relationship, arousing suspicion, jealousy, and hostility. Very simply, there were severe limitations on how much the New Deal could have accomplished.[30]

In Virginia the resistance was both structural and political. The same factors that moderated the depression shock— diversified and self-sufficient farming, minimal heavy industry, and a strong self-help ethic—inhibited the inroads of programs that had not been created with Virginia in mind. The absence in the state of an urban-labor-ethnic coalition—Roosevelt's strongest constituency—and a tradition of political apathy restricted the demand for more forceful action. So, too, did a pay-as-you-go disposition that permeated all levels of government and all classes of people and militated against the spending required by agencies like the FERA, WPA, and PWA. Finally, the philosophical opposition of the organization and its friends prevented full implementation of all that the New Deal offered Virginians. The programs were accepted—often reluctantly—but the most valuable gift of the Roosevelt administration, a sense of responsibility toward neglected elements of society, was rejected by Old Dominion leaders, who feared that such a revolution might jeopardize their rule. Conservative businessmen, editors, and politicians endlessly cast aspersions on the work of the

New Dealers, harping on waste in government, excessive spending, unconstitutional legislation, increased federal control, and the weakening of individual character through handouts. Stated the editor of the Farmville *Herald*, "Like a dreaded disease making slow inroads on the human body, we have developed a paternalism, a spirit to expect financial support from the national government, that has reached dangerous proportions."[31]

Such opposition, however, should not obscure the accomplishments of the New Deal or the popular support it received in the state. The overwhelming endorsement of Roosevelt through four elections reflected the confidence Virginians had in his leadership and policies. James Wright of Waynesboro declared: "All of the programs were idealistically conceived and as human institutions were probably unevenly administered, but their thrust was correct. Many went toward the solution of the most basic social problems. I was for them."[32] Even Governors Pollard and Peery claimed that the New Deal had played a prominent role in ending the depression. Peery applauded federal officials as men "driving back the depression, bringing needed help and succor and bringing greatly improved conditions." The comment of W. B. Barbour of South Boston represented the sentiment of most Virginians: "Even though some are loath to admit it, and some may not have increased their worldly goods in the same proportion as others, it is an undeniable fact the New Deal has brought prosperity to this section, and in a way that was undreamed and is apparently of a permanent nature."[33]

Nevertheless, force of habit, apathy, the lack of strong opposition candidates, and their individualistic philosophy prevented Virginians from endorsing the New Deal to the extent of removing the existing state leadership from office, an imperative step if greater reform was to be achieved. Their attitudes as much as the intransigence of their leaders were to blame for the failure of the New Deal to make a more enduring contribution to the future of the state. Yet the citizens of the Old Dominion should not be overly faulted for their adherence to more traditional means and rhetoric. Only where there was constructive leadership working in a progressive environment did the New

Deal redirect state policies and services on a more liberal course. Throughout the nation there was a reluctance to abandon conservative fiscal policies and the cult of self-help, a fact which caused historian James Patterson to conclude that there was "as much continuity as change on the state level." Ironically, the early successes of the New Deal lessened the need and demand for more drastic compulsory action, especially in Virginia where recovery was relatively rapid.[34]

The interplay of two-party politics in some northern and western states eventually advanced the causes of education, welfare, and labor in those states, but in the South and in Virginia, agrarian values, a more rigid social structure, one-party politics, and the Jeffersonian ideal of limited government all combined to resist the reforms of the New Dealers.[35] Such resistance, however, frequently eroded in the face of the economic crisis, allowing the New Deal to have a considerable impact on the region as a whole. Comparing Woodrow Wilson's administration to Roosevelt's, George Tindall comments: "If the influence of the South on the New Deal would be less than on the New Freedom, the impact of the New Deal on the South would be far greater. Unlike Wilson's New Freedom, Roosevelt's New Deal would shake the social and economic power structure of the region, and would thereby generate an opposition such as Wilson never had." The New Deal ended the enslavement of the southern economy to cotton, stimulated agricultural diversity and industrialization, revolutionized health conditions, liberated labor, and inaugurated a new era in race relations.[36] Obviously such an impact was limited in Virginia where cotton had a minor influence on the state's economy, farming was already diversified, industry was well established, and far less tension existed between the races. Virginia was sui generis, being neither a progressive industrial state nor a backward one-crop state. Protected from great economic dislocation, it incurred no political turmoil as experienced by other southern states; the power structure remained intact to insulate the Commonwealth from widespread social alteration.

In summary, the New Deal was very much in evidence in the Old Dominion. Its ubiquitous programs aided almost every segment of Virginia society, easing them through the calamity of depression. Nevertheless, although many of its benefits were long lasting, the New Deal was ineffectual in converting Virginia into a modern progressive state. Its advances in welfare, security, and labor legislation were blunted by a political machine whose attitudes on finance, the role of government, and federalism were diametrical to those of the Rooseveltians and whose power enabled it to flaunt its nineteenth-century philosophy in the face of twentieth-century demands. In a public letter to Senator Byrd, Marriner Eccles of the Federal Reserve Board contrasted the philosophical differences between the New Deal and the organization:

You stated that you are concerned about "the character of the individual citizen" and "the dignity and the rights of the individual." So am I. I believe, however, that the most basic right of all is the right to live and next to that, the right to work. I do not think empty stomachs build character, nor do I think the substitution of idleness and a dole for useful work relief will improve either the dignity or the character of the people affected. . . .

Further than the right to eat and the right to a position, I think the individual, whether rich or poor, has a right to a decent place to live. I think he has a right to security in old age and to protection against temporary unemployment. I think he has a right to adequate medical attention and to equal educational opportunities with the rest of his countrymen.

The Government expenditures which you condemn have in large part been the means of translating these basic rights into realities. . . .

I am convinced that your program [pay-as-you-go, etc.] is not only a defeatist one, a program of retrogression and not of progress, but that it would jeopardize the salvation of our democracy, which I know you are as sincerely desirous of preserving as I am.[37]

Although Eccles had stated the case for the New Deal clearly and concisely, it made no impression on the senator, who remained as convinced as ever, particularly in the light of Virginia's depression experience, that limited spending and a balanced budget were the proper objects of government. Fashioned by dogmatism and self-interest, this narrow vision of its leaders cost Virginia an opportunity to exchange the traditionalism of the past for the progress of the future. The state's industrial gains and financial soundness and an active federal government gave Virginia every reason to be optimistic in 1939, but for the next two-and-one-half decades the Old Dominion continued to slumber and suffer under ultraconservative leadership. It was a Gibraltar which not even depression and New Deal could bring down.

Appendixes

Notes

Bibliography

Index

Appendixes

Appendix A.   Employees, Earnings, Value of Production,
Virginia Industry, 1928-39

	Employees Wage earners and salaried	Wages and salaries (millions of dollars)	Output (millions of dollars)
1928	180,356	148	819
1929	188,142	185	897
1930	176,311	171	814
1931	164,910	151	679
1932	150,508	120	575
1933	160,834	122	616
1934	177,631	149	768
1935	192,763	165	845
1936	207,019	190	980
1937	218,416	215	1,103
1938	210,880	201	1,033
1939	228,160	229	1,195

Sources: *Annual Reports* of the Virginia Department of Labor and Industry, 1925-40.
Note: Included in the category of "Virginia Industry" are manufacturing, services (e.g., laundries), public utilities, coal mining, and other mining.

Appendix B. Value of Production, Selected Virginia Industries, 1925–39
(in millions of dollars except for coal production, which is in short tons)

	Tobacco	Cotton mills	Paper and pulp mills	Shipbuilding	Furniture	Auto Repair and assembly	RR shops	Rayon	Coal
1925	117	29	21	18	18	21	—	—	—
1929	192	25	30	39	30	54	29	30	12.1
1930	187	22	27	43	23	33	28	32	10.8
1931	188	17	32	40	23	22	28	24	9.5
1932	200	14	28	32	15	11	18	20	7.3
1933	215	22	32	28	16	4	18	27	7.9
1934	266	28	39	30	16	25	23	28	8.7
1935	278	26	41	35	22	42	22	29	9.3
1936	313	30	48	42	27	36	33	34	11.2
1937	359	34	56	41	30	38	36	33	13.2
1938	377	22	46	45	25	21	27	30	11.9
1939	410	26	56	65	30	34	30	45	12.8

Source: *Annual Reports* of the Virginia Department of Labor and Industry, 1925–1940.

Appendix C.   Virginia Farm Income for Selected Years, 1913–43
(in thousands of dollars)

	Cash Receipts	Consumed on farm	Gross income	Government payments	Total
1913	94,621	42,511	137,132		
1919	206,576	92,810	299,386		
1921	112,744	50,653	163,397		
1925	157,696	67,158	224,854		
1929	168,940	62,123	231,063		
1930	128,673	57,251	185,924		
1931	88,930	49,863	138,793		
1932	70,464	40,632	111,096		
1933	79,387	42,371	121,758	460	122,218
1934	96,218	44,408	140,626	2,322	142,948
1935	111,140	52,126	163,266	4,340	167,606
1936	120,589	54,758	175,347	1,656	177,003
1937	132,933	58,593	191,526	3,350	194,876
1938	121,216	53,046	174,262	4,083	178,345
1939	116,453	52,743	169,196	6,288	175,484
1940	122,873	54,508	177,381	4,724	182,105
1941	154,348	60,340	214,688	6,524	221,212
1942	213,124	69,706	282,830	5,860	288,690
1943	272,723	81,447	354,170	6,392	360,562

Source: *Virginia Farm Statistics*, bulletin 15 (1949), pp. 9-20, 150.

Appendix D.   Virginia Selected Crop Production and Prices, 1929–39

	Tobacco lbs(million)/cents	Corn bu(million)/cents	Cotton bales(1,000)/cents/lb	Peanuts lbs(million)/cents
1929	119/17.6	35/105	51/16.7	158/3.4
1930	113/8.8	16/97	46/9.6	99/3.1
1931	101/6.2	40/44	46/5.6	173/1.4
1932	54/8.9	26/52	34/6.4	147/1.5
1933	94/12.6	35/68	37/10.5	111/2.7
1934	81/23.0	31/87	36/12.1	144/3.5
1935	105/17.9	37/81	30/11.4	149/3.2
1936	97/21.4	30/106	33/12.4	148/4.3
1937	112/19.1	37/68	43/8.3	178/3.4
1938	99/19.4	35/64	12/8.6	136/3.5
1939	144/14.2	36/71	13/9.2	179/3.6

Source: *Virginia Farm Statistics*, bulletin 15 (1949), pp. 9–20, 150.

Appendixes

Appendix E. Index of Farm Prices for Selected Years, 1919–40
(1910–14=100)

	Virginia	United States		Virginia	United States
1919	233	213	1934	104	90
1921	152	125	1935	111	108
1925	154	156	1936	128	114
1929	151	146	1937	122	121
1930	120	126	1938	106	95
1931	89	87	1939	104	93
1932	71	65	1940	105	98
1933	87	70			

Source: *Virginia Farm Economics*, No. 42 (July 1942), p. 688.

Appendix F. Index of Personal Income in Selected States, 1929–40 (1929=100)

	U.S.	Va.	N.Y.	Ohio	Iowa	Colo.	Md.	N.C.	Tenn.	Tex.	Cal.	Wash.	Neb.
1930	90	89	93	86	88	94	93	89	87	87	92	89	88
1931	77	85	81	73	70	78	84	75	75	74	79	73	70
1932	58	66	63	52	52	59	68	58	54	57	61	55	52
1933	55	66	59	51	45	59	62	65	57	55	59	52	47
1934	62	74	64	60	47	62	71	77	68	63	65	61	43
1935	70	83	69	68	74	74	75	85	74	71	73	68	68
1936	80	93	77	78	68	91	85	94	85	82	88	81	65
1937	86	103	80	86	89	91	92	104	93	93	93	86	68
1938	80	97	76	75	80	88	89	97	86	91	92	85	66
1939	85	107	79	82	83	90	94	106	90	94	96	91	64
1940	92	120	83	89	90	96	104	112	101	101	106	99	71

Source: Schwartz and Graham, "Personal Income by States," pp. 12–22.

199

Appendix G. Index of Manufacturing Industries in Selected States (1929=100)

	U.S.	Va.	N.Y.	Ohio	Mich.	Mo.	Md.	N.C.	Ala.	Tex.	Cal.
No. of wage earners											
1931	74	86	77	68	70	77	82	86	71	71	70
1933	67	85	66	64	66	71	76	96	71	69	66
1935	84	103	81	79	101	81	92	110	82	80	85
1937	97	112	90	94	125	94	111	124	101	98	104
1939	89	113	87	81	98	90	108	129	98	96	95
Wages											
1931	62	76	67	54	54	67	72	74	60	65	63
1933	45	59	46	40	41	50	56	71	47	48	46
1935	65	82	62	61	83	67	74	94	64	64	65
1937	87	96	75	87	118	85	98	117	94	88	92
1939	78	98	71	74	94	80	95	124	90	85	87
Value of products											
1931	59	82	66	53	55	58	60	78	58	58	60
1933	45	70	46	40	45	47	47	67	45	48	49
1935	65	97	62	61	86	64	68	85	65	75	71
1937	87	124	74	85	114	80	99	106	103	111	95
1939	81	135	72	76	93	74	93	109	103	107	92

Source: *Statistical Abstracts*, 1937, 1941.

Appendix H. Index of Retail Sales in Selected States (1929=100)

	U.S.	Va.	N.Y.	Ohio	Mich.	Md.	N.C.	Ala.	Tex.	Cal.	Kan.
1933	52	60	54	51	43	63	56	48	48	54	45
1935	68	79	67	69	63	75	72	64	64	73	60
1939	87	106	80	86	83	101	98	84	90	101	65

Source: *Statistical Abstracts*, 1934, 1941.

Appendixes

State	A	B	C	D
Alabama	483,756	18.3%	$50.5	$156.7 (89%)
Arizona	91,971	21.1	17.6	92.5 (85)
Arkansas	350,380	18.9	47.0	142.8 (92)
California	717,130	12.6	164.1	786.0 (68)
Colorado	229,312	22.1	40.5	180.1 (78)
Connecticut	179,987	11.2	25.7	151.6 (61)
Delaware	17,028	7.1	2.4	18.0 (67)
Florida	301,970	20.6	49.9	132.3 (90)
Georgia	377,721	11.0	53.1	169.1 (91)
Idaho	82,038	18.4	15.5	94.4 (87)
Illinois	1,092,599	14.3	211.3	897.0 (71)
Indiana	447,098	13.8	52.3	306.9 (75)
Iowa	264,429	10.7	26.1	172.7 (66)
Kansas	297,646	15.8	43.3	176.9 (78)
Kentucky	483,559	18.5	36.4	169.9 (85)
Louisiana	270,195	12.9	49.8	170.5 (89)
Maine	78,945	9.9	13.7	69.2 (65)
Maryland	174,841	10.7	35.7	122.8 (74)
Massachusetts	695,204	16.4	121.8	602.6 (62)
Michigan	640,276	13.2	116.2	504.0 (73)
Minnesota	498,143	19.4	74.9	336.8 (74)
Mississippi	279,028	13.9	34.8	126.3 (91)
Missouri	581,193	16.0	71.0	310.0 (79)
Montana	100,805	18.8	25.7	94.9 (86)
Nebraska	171,682	12.5	29.5	125.5 (79)
Nevada	11,275	12.4	5.5	28.9 (90)
New Hampshire	41,573	8.9	6.7	52.9 (70)
New Jersey	596,930	14.8	93.3	439.2 (70)
New Mexico	128,094	30.3	19.8	75.9 (93)
New York	2,041,913	16.2	411.6	2,116.4 (61)
North Carolina	335,738	10.6	39.9	148.2 (92)
North Dakota	190,192	27.9	35.0	98.3 (87)
Ohio	1,122,941	16.9	172.3	750.4 (74)
Oklahoma	588,082	24.5	46.7	226.8 (83)
Oregon	115,676	12.1	21.2	129.3 (83)
Pennsylvania	1,721,820	17.9	298.1	1,252.4 (72)
Rhode Island	76,337	11.1	7.4	63.7 (58)
South Carolina	295,962	17.0	37.3	119.6 (93)

State	A	B	C	D
South Dakota	253,847	36.6	43.6	122.8 (88)
Tennessee	336,988	12.9	37.8	156.5 (85)
Texas	1,016,442	17.5	98.5	363.6 (80)
Utah	116,871	23.0	20.7	91.5 (80)
Vermont	28,598	8.0	3.9	49.8 (84)
Virginia	208,626	8.6	26.3	144.3 (92)
Washington	200,088	12.8	38.7	210.7 (78)
West Virginia	378,780	21.9	45.9	183.0 (87)
Wisconsin	429,323	14.6	77.0	386.0 (75)
Wyoming	31,877	14.1	9.6	44.3 (86)
Total U.S.	19,179,123	15.6	3,022.6	13,485.2

Sources: Columns A and B: Hummel and Bennett, *Magnitude of the Emergency Relief Program*, p. 16. Column C: *Final Report of the FERA*, p. 103. Column D: *Report on the Progress of the WPA Program*, June 30, 1938.

Appendix J. CWA and FERA Statistics—Virginia Cities and Counties
Column A: CWA wages, paid, Nov. 20, 1933–April 5, 1934.
Column B: FERA obligations incurred for general relief and special emergency programs, April 1933–December 1935 (approximately 90 percent of the total is the federal contribution).
Column C: Monthly average number of residents receiving relief under the general relief and special emergency relief programs, July 1934—June 1935.

	Population (1930)	A ($)	B ($)	C
Cities				
Alexandria	24,149	87,706	123,975	991
Bristol	8,840	79,876	197,742	1,799
Buena Vista	4,002	8,520	49,969	491
Charlottesville	15,245	82,797	139,296	1,260
Clifton Forge	6,839	36,557	101,417	716
Danville	22,249	116,485	390,073	2,925
Fredericksburg	6,819	29,464	58,527	448
Harrisonburg	7,232	39,316	102,978	893
Hopewell	11,329	56,469	195,888	2,265
Lynchburg	40,661	111,203	544,458	3,564
Norfolk	129,710	639,953	1,955,146	15,055
Petersburg	28,564	106,265	490,019	4,971
Portsmouth	45,704	296,002	511,573	6,206
Radford	6,229	21,413	85,387	1,000
Richmond	182,929	880,168	2,142,794	17,598
Roanoke	69,206	226,983	920,930	6,901
South Norfolk	7,857	76,838	84,308	1,083

Appendixes

	Population (1930)	A ($)	B ($)	C
Staunton	11,990	62,396	97,726	827
Winchester	10,855	27,727	82,223	736
Newport News	34,417		162,063	1,540
Suffolk	10,271		93,088	1,128
Counties				
Accomack	35,854	86,857	144,217	2,506
Albemarle	26,981	135,730	91,992	1,864
Alleghany	20,188	73,482	156,248	1,784
Amelia	8,979	24,496	51,792	1,127
Amherst	19,020	43,171	63,677	979
Appomattox	8,402	26,452	49,957	862
Arlington	26,615	170,208	18,983	26
Augusta	38,162	84,932	124,938	1,670
Bath	8,137	32,066	88,029	1,305
Bedford	29,091	57,513	80,231	1,764
Bland	6,031	25,249	31,036	557
Botetourt	15,457	8,307	87,017	1,997
Brunswick	20,486	61,624	27,281	327
Buchanan	16,740	50,176	104,247	2,672
Buckingham	11,000 (est.)	—	89,091	1,579
Campbell	22,885	45,998	83,950	1,029
Caroline	15,263	45,697	65,988	1,630
Carroll	22,141	33,816	86,721	2,293
Charles City	4,881	14,974	26,901	472
Charlotte	16,061	54,885	16,336	85
Chesterfield	26,049	80,102	46,593	779
Clarke	7,167	17,930	8,453	29
Craig	3,562	11,782	27,846	481
Culpeper	13,306	37,958	43,749	955
Cumberland	7,535	16,992	67,172	1,575
Dickenson	16,163	62,134	130,375	2,732
Dinwiddie	18,492	50,059	48,118	843
Elizabeth City	32,599	472,770	72,608	930
Essex	6,976	29,313	24,693	477
Fairfax	25,264	155,838	56,660	680
Fauquier	21,071	61,736	67,594	1,368
Floyd	11,698	25,109	37,452	950
Fluvanna	7,466	27,319	38,979	840
Franklin	24,337	40,636	116,039	2,572
Frederick	13,167	13,081	30,055	385
Giles	12,804	30,972	109,954	2,314
Gloucester	11,019	53,376	28,114	202
Goochland	7,953	33,284	43,197	744
Grayson	20,017	20,931	108,267	2,876
Greene	5,980	33,754	21,803	186
Greensville	13,388	42,488	43,453	993

Appendix J *(continued)*

	Population (1930)	A ($)	B ($)	C
Halifax	41,285	108,066	107,149	1,299
Hanover	17,009	74,021	33,502	571
Henrico	30,310	100,118	126,221	1,292
Henry	27,793	54,326	73,878	1,153
Highland	4,525	9,849	18,677	444
Isle of Wight	13,409	48,430	19,757	386
James City	11,357	41,686	10,707	186
King George	5,297	40,201	29,816	406
King and Queen	7,618	24,825	27,030	715
King William	7,929	22,214	29,175	626
Lancaster	8,896	30,587	70,662	1,327
Lee	30,419	54,558	147,416	3,670
Loudoun	19,852	39,206	44,576	647
Louisa	14,309	48,672	42,613	951
Lunenburg	14,058	35,933	49,990	874
Madison	8,952	32,613	62,372	1,006
Mathews	7,884	60,993	80,851	667
Mecklenburg	32,622	65,357	70,272	1,428
Middlesex	7,273	27,847	28,037	474
Montgomery	19,605	72,109	158,721	2,071
Nansemond	32,801	119,197	50,193	995
Nelson	16,345	46,206	78,857	1,920
New Kent	4,300	16,061	6,189	64
Norfolk	30,082	117,231	96,091	1,631
Northampton	18,565	55,881	81,045	944
Northumberland	11,081	39,613	52,858	691
Nottoway	14,866	38,751	71,986	1,146
Orange	12,070	31,832	38,754	776
Page	14,852	42,308	80,847	1,479
Patrick	15,787	39,404	51,932	1,515
Pittsylvania	61,424	116,220	154,645	2,566
Powhatan	6,143	22,486	74,136	1,436
Prince Edward	14,520	67,191	96,766	1,829
Prince George	10,311	37,674	85,178	1,307
Prince William	13,951	150,967	56,143	790
Princess Anne	16,282	142,531	39,355	801
Pulaski	20,566	52,313	192,922	2,511
Rappahannock	7,717	25,425	28,834	451
Richmond	6,878	23,249	27,141	597
Roanoke	35,289	112,617	190,204	2,305
Rockbridge	20,902	53,232	75,596	1,231
Rockingham	29,709	80,032	92,723	1,739
Russell	25,957	46,805	90,781	1,676
Scott	24,181	79,071	99,159	1,911
Shenandoah	20,655	56,631	66,025	862
Smyth	25,125	114,458	130,475	2,607

Appendix J (*continued*)

	Population (1930)	A ($)	B ($)	C
Southampton	26,870	82,859	49,951	1,025
Spotsylvania	10,056	54,968	44,530	761
Stafford	8,050	36,481	85,890	1,082
Surry	7,096	25,306	22,736	420
Sussex	12,100	47,049	17,655	237
Tazewell	32,477	99,906	152,654	2,504
Warren	8,340	56,077	68,201	878
Warwick	43,246	106,438	25,649	431
Washington	33,850	106,314	143,937	3,217
Westmoreland	8,497	38,241	41,678	901
Wise	51,157	274,756	587,406	9,780
Wythe	20,704	61,801	93,872	1,487
York	7,693	120,719	37,224	443
Total	2,421,851	9,402,652	23,859,895	208,385

Sources: Column A: *A Review of CWA Activities in Virginia*. Column B: *Final FERA Report*, pp. 291–93. Column C: *Final FERA Report*, pp. 248–49.

Appendix K. Index of Gross Farm Income in Selected States, 1929-39 (1929=100)

	U.S.	Va.	N.Y.	Ill.	Kan.	Ga.	N.C.	Ala.	Tex.	Cal.	N.D.
1930	79	71	92	86	75	78	81	74	72	80	70
1931	58	60	69	60	55	49	57	53	56	62	34
1932	45	46	53	47	36	39	48	43	45	50	37
1933	51	54	59	51	37	53	73	53	56	56	43
1934	56	61	64	55	44	63	90	64	55	64	32
1935	67	73	72	76	53	70	94	68	62	71	46
1936	76	80	78	86	59	81	96	82	66	80	48
1937	81	84	83	95	70	78	109	78	81	86	51
1938	75	79	79	92	56	74	94	69	68	73	48
1939	75	76	82	92	57	71	93	62	67	76	55

Source: *Statistical Abstracts*, 1931–41.
Note: Figures do not include rental and benefit payments.

Appendixes

Appendix L. Percentage of Commercial Firm Failures, 1929–40

	United States	Virginia		United States	Virginia
1929	1.04	.76	1935	.58	.30
1930	1.21	1.09	1936	.46	.45
1931	1.33	1.31	1937	.46	.55
1932	1.53	1.57	1938	.61	.67
1933	1.03	.81	1939	.70	.63
1934	.62	.52	1940	.63	.64

Source: *Statistical Abstracts*, 1931–41.

Notes

Chapter 1

1. Arnold Toynbee, *A Study of History* (New York, 1946), abridgment of vols. 1–4, p. 315; Virginia Moore, *Virginia Is a State of Mind* (New York, 1942), p. 184.

2. Jean Gottmann, *Virginia at Mid-Century* (New York, 1955), p. 555.

3. *Thirty-second Annual Report of the Department of Labor and Industry of the State of Virginia, 1929* (Richmond, 1930), pp. 4–6 (hereafter cited as *Department of Labor*); *University of Virginia Newsletter*, June 1, 1928, Jan. 15, March 15, Oct. 15, 1932 (one-page bimonthly publication then issued by the Department of Rural Social Economics; hereafter cited as *Newsletter*); Norfolk *Virginian-Pilot*, Jan. 1, 1929.

4. Alvin L. Hall, "Virginia Back in the Fold—The Gubernatorial Campaign and Election of 1929," *Virginia Magazine of History and Biography* 73 (1965): 280–302.

5. See John Kenneth Galbraith, *The Great Crash* (Cambridge, Mass., 1955); and Peter Temin, *Did Monetary Forces Cause the Great Depression?* (New York, 1976).

6. *Virginian-Pilot*, Oct. 25, Nov. 16, 1929; *Times-Herald* quoted in the Farmville *Herald*, Dec. 5, 1930.

7. John Slaughter, *Income Received in the Various States, 1929–1935* (New York, 1937), p. 33.

8. *Virginian-Pilot*, Jan. 1, 1930; James E. Ward, Jr., "A Billion Dollar Manufacturing State by 1930," *Newsletter*, Jan. 1, 1930; *Inaugural Address of John Garland Pollard*, Jan. 15, 1930, Senate Doc. no. 5 (Richmond, 1930), pp. 6–7; New York *Times*, Sept. 12, 1930.

9. *Newsletter*, March 1, 1931; New York *Times*, Jan. 11, 1931; *Virginian-Pilot*, July 22, Aug. 13, 1930; Byrd to Reed, July 26, 1930, Reed Family Papers, Virginia Historical Society (hereafter VHS).

10. *Virginian-Pilot*, Aug. 16, 17, Oct. 18, 1930; Pollard to President Hoover, Aug. 26, 1931, Frank Bane Papers, box 3, University of Virginia Library (hereafter U.Va. Lib.); Lynchburg *News*, Oct. 23, 1930.

11. Lynchburg *News*, Jan. 9, 1931; Arthur James, *The State Becomes a Social Worker* (Richmond, 1942), pp. 240–42.

Notes

12. Roanoke *World-News*, April 20, 1931; *Virginian-Pilot*, Aug. 17, 1930; letter to Governor Pollard, Nov. 19, 1930, Executive Papers of the Governor, Virginia State Library (hereafter VSL).

13. Robert Sidney Smith, *Mill on the Dan* (Durham, N.C., 1960), pp. 177, 290–322; *Virginian-Pilot*, Sept. 29, Oct. 3, Nov. 26, 27, Dec. 16, 1930, Jan. 30, 31, 1931; Richmond *Times-Dispatch*, Feb. 8, 1931; Danville *Register*, Aug. 20, Oct. 15, Dec. 6, 1930.

14. *Newsletter*, Dec. 1, 1931; *Department of Labor*, 1930, pp. 7–9; ibid., 1931, p. 17; see also Appendixes A and B.

15. Danville *Register*, March 7, 1931; Reed to Byrd, Dec. 2, 1930, Reed Family Papers, VHS; Lynchburg *News,* Jan. 4, 1931. Farm prices and income are taken from *Virginia Farm Statistics,* bulletin 15 (Richmond, 1949), pp. 9–20, 150, and *Virginia Farm Economics,* no. 42 (Blacksburg, 1942), p. 688; see also Appendixes C, D, and E.

16. *Virginian-Pilot,* Jan. 1, 2, 1931; *Times-Dispatch,* Jan. 1, 1931.

17. Charles Schwartz and Robert Graham, "Personal Income by States, 1929–54," *Survey of Current Business* 35 (Sept. 1955): 12–22; response to questionnaire distributed by author.

18. *Report of the Commission to Study the Condition of the Farmers of Virginia* (Richmond, 1930), pp. 9–11; Treadwell Davison, "Self-Sufficiency Farms in Virginia," *Newsletter,* Feb. 15, 1935; W. E. Garnett, *Does Virginia Care?* (Blacksburg, 1936), p. 3; Wilson Gee, "Some of Our Forgotten Men," *Newsletter,* Feb. 1, 1927. More than one-fourth of Virginia's farm operators were tenants (47, 970). Counties in which more than 50 percent of the farmers were tenants were Southampton, Accomack, Pittsylvania, Halifax, and Mecklenburg. Roy Wood, "Farm Tenancy in Virginia" (M.A. Thesis, University of Virginia, 1948), pp. 34–36, 88.

19. Wilson Gee, "Farm Mortgage Debt," *Newsletter,* Nov. 15, 1927; James E. Ward, Jr., "Farm Mortgage Debt," ibid., March 1, 1932; D. C. Hudgens, "Diversified Agriculture in Virginia," ibid., Jan. 15, 1933; *Virginia Farm Statistics,* bulletin 15 (1949), pp. 150–52.

20. Slaughter, *Income,* p. 42. Of Virginia's total production income in 1929 of $928 million, $172 million was in agriculture, $149 million in manufacturing, $116 million in transportation, $127 million in trade, and $120 million in services.

21. *Virginian-Pilot,* March 29, May 12, July 11, 1931.

22. *Times-Dispatch,* Feb. 8, 13, March 12, 1931; Farmville *Herald,* Feb. 20, 27, March 13, 1931.

23. *Times-Dispatch,* July 31, 1931; Pollard to Hoover, Aug. 26, 1931, Frank Bane Papers, box 3, U.Va. Lib.

24. Va. Department of Public Welfare, *Public Welfare,* Nov. 1931, p. 1.

25. Ibid., July 1931, p. 4.

26. James, *The State Becomes a Social Worker,* pp. 242–44; Reed to Byrd, Sept. 5, 1931, Reed Family Papers, VHS.

27. *Virginian-Pilot,* Sept. 6, 20, 25, Dec. 20, 1931, Jan. 13, 1932; R. Cosby Moore, *Ah Youth—and Experience! A Brief History of Virginia National*

Bank, an address to the Newcomen Society, Norfolk, 1964 (New York, 1964); *Times-Dispatch*, Jan. 1, 1932, Lynchburg *News*, Jan. 3, 1932.

28. Federal Reserve Bank of Richmond, Fifth Federal Reserve District, *Monthly Review*, May 31, 1932, p. 5; *Virginia Farm Economics*, no. 2 (Aug. 1931), p. 12; response to questionnaire.

29. Danville *Register*, Oct. 17, 1931; Bryant to T. G. Burch (with copy to Carter Glass), Oct. 27, 1931, Carter Glass Papers, box 280, U.Va. Lib.

30. *Department of Labor*, 1931, pp. 7, 17; *Statistical Abstract of the United States*, 1937 (Washington, D.C., 1937), p. 765.

31. *Address of John Garland Pollard*, Jan. 13, 1932, Senate Doc. no. 1 (Richmond, 1932).

32. John Hopewell, "An Outsider Looking In: John Garland Pollard and Machine Politics in Twentieth Century Virginia" (Ph.D. diss., University of Virginia, 1976), pp. 284–310; *Virginian-Pilot*, Jan. 14, Feb. 3, 7, 1932; Lynchburg *News*, Feb. 5, 1932; *Times-Dispatch*, Feb. 7, 10, 1932.

33. *Virginian-Pilot*, Feb. 11, 12, 13, 1932; Lynchburg *News*, Feb . 24, 1932; *Times-Dispatch*, March 13, 1932.

34. Virginia's state tax load was 48 percent of the national per capita rate and its land taxes in 1930 were the lowest of twenty-eight states investigated. For 1930 and 1935 the Old Dominion had the lowest farm real estate tax in the country. In the latter year, Senator Byrd boasted that Virginia had been the only state in the Union not to raise taxes during the depression. *Times-Dispatch*, Jan. 13, Sept. 9, 12, 1932, Oct. 31, 1935; WPA Writers Program, *Virginia: A Guide to the Old Dominion* (New York, 1940), p. 104.

35. *Times-Dispatch*, Jan. 15, 1932.

36. John Denson, "Unrest in Virginia," a series of articles in the *Times-Dispatch*, Jan. 12–22, 1932; Roanoke *World-News*, March 29, 1932. See also *Times-Dispatch*, Jan. and Feb. 1932, for accounts of general dissatisfaction.

37. *Virginian-Pilot*, March 20, April 17, 1932; Harrisonburg *Daily News-Record*, Aug. 30, 1932; Charlottesville *Daily Progress*, June 28, 1932; *Times-Dispatch*, March 9, 13, 19, 27,April 7, May 1, June 6, 21, Sept. 11, 1932; Lynchburg *News*, Jan. 1, 1933; *Stabilization of Employment in Virginia and Building Up of Unemployment Reserves*, report of Governor's Commission, Feb. 1934 (Richmond, 1934), p. 38.

38. *Times-Dispatch*, June 11, 12, 13, 1932; Department of Labor and Industry Survey of Unemployment in Virginia, Aug. 16, 1932, Executive Papers, VSL; letter to Governor Pollard, Aug. 12, 1932, ibid.

39. Congress had created the RFC in January 1932 to loan money initially to banks and other businesses to stimulate the economy.

40. *Virginian-Pilot*, July 17, Aug. 12, 13, Sept. 20, 21, 1932; B. L. Hummel and C. G. Bennett, *Magnitude of the Emergency Relief Program in Rural Virginia, 1933–1935* (Blacksburg, 1937), pp. 74–75; *Times-Dispatch*, Nov. 18, 1933. Given new life by the New Deal, the RFC disbursed $40.5 million to Virginia over an eight-year period, most of it in loans ($16.9 million) and stock subscriptions ($10.7 million) to banks and trust companies. Loans were given to 116 Virginia banks and trust companies; 163 had their stock subscribed to.

Notes

The RFC also granted loans of $1.2 million to 90 business enterprises and $2 million for self-liquidating community projects such as toll bridges. Other recipients were mortgage loan companies, building and loan associations, and Emergency Relief Administration projects in Virginia. The Old Dominion ranked twenty-third in the amount disbursed; California led with $621 million. *Quarterly Report of the Reconstruction Finance Corporation,* 2d quarter, 1940 (Washington, D.C., 1940).

41. *Stabilization of Employment,* p. 9; Harrisonburg *Daily News-Record,* Nov. 26, 1932; Charlottesville *Daily Progress,* Nov. 25, 1932; *The First Fifty Years,* commemorative pamphlet of the Richmond Chapter of the American Red Cross (1967), p. 15; Robert D. Lynn, "The Social Functions of the Salvation Army in Richmond, Virginia" (M.A. Thesis, College of William and Mary, 1935), pp. 41, 132; Roanoke *World-News,* Jan. 22, Nov. 19, Dec. 8, 1932; *Virginian-Pilot,* Oct. 23, Nov. 2, 20, 23, 1932.

42. *Virginian-Pilot,* Nov. 30, 1932; *Times-Dispatch,* Nov. 23, 1932, Feb. 5, 1933.

43. *Virginian-Pilot,* Dec. 11, 1932; *Times-Dispatch,* Jan. 11, 1933.

44. William E. Leuchtenburg, *Franklin D. Roosevelt and the New Deal, 1932–1940* (New York, 1963), pp. 1–40.

45. *Monthly Review,* Jan. 31, 1933, pp. 1, 6; ibid., April 30, 1933, p. 4; *Virginia Farm Economics,* no. 14 (Oct. 1932), p. 190; *Times-Dispatch,* Oct. 2, 1932, Jan. 1, 1933; *Department of Labor,* 1932, p. 12; ibid., 1933, pp. 10, 19; Charlottesville *Daily Progress,* May 23, 1933; *Stabilization of Employment,* p. 27; Robert H. Barker, "Employment and Unemployment in Virginia, 1929 to 1932," *Newsletter,* March 15, 1933. The number employed in Virginia manufacturing dropped 22 percent from 1929 figures; in the nation the decline was over 35 percent. Income received in Virginia was down 34 percent from 1929, but in the nation it was down 42 percent. Old Dominion farm prices declined 20 percent from 1931 to 1932, but national prices dropped 25 percent. Robert H. Barker, "Recent Trends in Employment and Payrolls in Virginia Industry," ibid., June 1, 1937; Schwartz and Graham, "Personal Income," pp. 12–22; *Virginia Farm Economics,* no. 42 (July 1942), p. 688; see also Appendixes F and G for comparisons with other states.

Chapter 2

1. See Studs Terkel, *Hard Times* (New York, 1970), and Caroline Bird, *The Invisible Scar* (New York, 1966).

2. Much of the quoted but unannotated material in this chapter is taken from two questionnaires distributed in Virginia from 1970 to 1975 and now in my possession. A questionnaire for agricultural extension agents was mailed to them; one for the general population was distributed by my students to residents of nursing homes and retired ministers' homes and to older individuals living in their areas. Nearly 200 questionnaires were returned; the respondents resided in all parts of the state; they worked as lawyers, ministers, farmers, salesmen, housewives, domestics, etc.; one-third were women; one-sixth were black. Reliance on the memory of living persons poses special problems for the historian, but the general unanimity among all of the respondents about

conditions in Virginia and the coincidence of memory, newspaper accounts, and statistical data encouraged me to use this material.

3. The number of Virginia farmers increased 16 percent from 1930 to 1935, while the average size of a farm declined by 9 percent. The national increase in the number of farmers was 8.3 percent. Lewis M. Walker, Jr., "Increase in Farms 1930–1935", *Newsletter*, Feb. 1, 1936; *Statistical Abstract of Virginia* (Charlottesville, 1970), 2:372.

4. Interview with J. Barrye Wall, 1970.

5. The annual average number of distress transfers (bankruptcies, foreclosures, and assignments to creditors) from 1925 to 1939 in Virginia was 15.6/1,000 farms, eighteenth lowest in the country; the national rate was 19.8/1,000. The state's transfer rate on mortgaged farms was much higher—72.2/1,000, forty-second in the country. Lawrence Jones and David Durand, *Mortgage Lending Experience in Agriculture* (Princeton, N.J., 1954), pp. 28–29.

6. Smithfield *Times*, Nov. 13, 1930; interview with P. H. DeHart, Aug. 17, 1970; DeHart to author, Aug. 21, 1970.

7. Martine W. McNeill, "The Family Agency in an Unemployment Crisis" (M.A. Thesis, College of William and Mary, 1932), pp. 37–53; Martha Claire Mathes, "A Follow-up Study of the Family Agency in an Unemployment Crisis" (M.A. Thesis, College of William and Mary, 1933), pp. 40–41.

8. Anne Ossman, "The History of the Family Service Society: Policy and Function" (M.A. Thesis, College of William and Mary, 1950), pp. 13–35, 118.

9. Roanoke *World-News*, Nov. 26, 1934.

10. Entry of March 11, 1933, Henry Morrow Hyde Diary, Hyde Papers, U.Va. Lib.

11. Charles Calrow, "Retail Trade in Virginia," *The Commonwealth* 5 (March 1938): 13–14. See also Appendix H for a comparison of Virginia retail sales with those of other states.

12. An attempt to survey representative businesses across Virginia to determine their depression experiences was of limited success due to the loss of old records, the merger or closing of firms, and the failure of firms to keep more specific accounts.

13. Richard Tennant, *The American Cigarette Industry* (New Haven, 1950), pp. 88–89, 146–47; *Times-Dispatch*, Feb. 7, 1933.

14. Arthur Whitehall, Jr., *Textile and Apparel Industries in Virginia* (Charlottesville, 1948), pp. 1–2; Smith, *Mill on the Dan*, pp. 554–57; James Reynolds (E. I. DuPont) to author, Oct. 21, 1970; Dan Friedman (Friedman-Marks) to author, Aug. 10, 1970.

15. *Statistical Abstract of Virginia* (1970), 2:434; William A. Gwaltney to author, Aug. 19, 1970.

16. Dorothy Cleal and Hiram Herbert, *Foresight, Founders, and Fortitude: The Growth of Industry in Martinsville and Henry County, Virginia* (Bassett, Va., 1970), pp. 18, 74, 101.

17. Robert Huddleston (Westvaco) to author, Sept. 9, 1970; John Pugh (Newport News Shipbuilding) to author, Aug. 18, 1970.

Notes

18. A. M. Clement (Vepco) to author, Aug. 19, 1970; Vepco Annual Reports, 1925–40.

19. *Annual Reports on the Statistics of Railways in the United States* (Washington, D.C., 1925–39); Annual Reports of the Seaboard Air Line Railway, 1929, 1932, 1933, 1945; Roanoke *World-News*, Feb. 4, April 30, 1932, Dec. 6, 1934; H. Reid, *The Virginian Railway* (Milwaukee, 1961), pp. 86, 197–98; John Mordecai, *A Brief History of the Richmond, Fredericksburg and Potomac Railroad* (Richmond, 1941), pp. 72–80.

20. *Report of the Virginia State Planning Board* (Richmond, 1936), III-A:12–13, 21, 98–99; *Statistical Abstract* (1937), pp. 765–69; James E. Ward, Jr., "Recent Industrial Trends in Virginia," *Newsletter*, June 15, 1935. Virginia industrial wages declined 41 percent; national wages, 55 percent; see Appendix G for comparisons with other states.

21. Howard O. Sullins, "A History of the Public School Superintendency in Virginia" (D.Ed. diss., University of Virginia, 1970), pp. 372–76.

22. George E. Dutton, "The Cost of Public Education in Virginia from 1870 to 1939" (M.A. Thesis, University of Virginia, 1941), pp. 13, 30, 46; Norfolk *Journal and Guide*, Jan. 16, 1932; H. M. Henry, "The Effect of the Depression on Education in Virginia," *Virginia Journal of Education* 27 (Sept. 1933): 16–18, 20, 29; Sullins, "Public School Superintendency," pp. 396–97; Danville *Register*, May 8, 1931.

23. *The World Almanac*, 1930–40; Henry Lewis Suggs, "P. B. Young and the Norfolk *Journal and Guide*, 1910–1954" (Ph.D diss., University of Virginia, 1976), p. 186.

24. *Hampden-Sydney Alumni Record*, 1929–39; interview with Elizabeth Eggleston, 1970.

25. J. L. Blair Buck, *The Development of Public Schools in Virginia, 1607–1952* (Richmond, 1952), pp. 348–52; Richard A. Meade, "Rank of Virginia in Education," *The Virginia Public School System* (Richmond, 1944), pp. 43–45; Reid H. Duncan, "How Virginia Ranks with the 48 States," *Virginia Journal of Education* 31 (Feb. 1938): 196; ibid., 31 (Nov. 1937): 51–54.

26. WPA Writers Project, *The Negro in Virginia* (New York, 1940), pp. 336–40; Sara Gilliam, *Virginia's People* (Richmond, 1944), pp. 62, 107; Jane Purcell Guild, "Black Richmond," *Survey Graphic* 23 (1934): 276–78; *Journal and Guide*, May 30, Nov. 21, Dec. 5, 1931; Lyman Drewry, "Recent Changes in the Economic Position of the Negro in Virginia" (M.A. Thesis, University of Virginia, 1956), pp. 51–98, 156–60, 191–205. Further testimony about the discrimination that black Virginians experienced is found in the pages of the Norfolk *Journal and Guide*, Virginia's leading black newspaper.

27. Danville *Register*, Jan. 18, 1933.

28. *Journal and Guide*, Jan. 17, Feb. 21, 1931, Feb. 20, 1932; *Virginian-Pilot*, April 19, 1935; Danville *Register*, March 29, 1933; WPA Writers, *Negro in Virginia*, pp. 299–327. The number of black-owned banks in Virginia declined from six to three during the decade.

29. William E. Garnett and John Ellison, *Negro Life in Rural Virginia, 1865–1934*, bulletin 295 (Blacksburg, 1934), p. 13.

30. *Journal and Guide*, Dec. 17, 1932, Feb. 25, 1933, July 21, 1934; Raymond Wolters, *Negroes and the Great Depression* (Westport, Conn., 1970), p. 115; Guild, "Black Richmond," pp. 276–78; Garnett and Ellison, *Negro Life*, p. 14.

31. Ronald Cutler, "A History and Analysis of Negro Newspapers in Virginia" (M.A. Thesis, University of Richmond, 1965), pp. 32–35.

32. Interview with Marguerite Farmer, June 24, 1971; Mary C. Hankins, "The Growth of Public Outdoor Relief in Richmond, Virginia" (M.A. Thesis, College of William and Mary, 1935), pp. 10–22; Aaron Paul, "The Rural Almshouse of Virginia" (M.A. thesis, College of William and Mary, 1936), pp. 54–59, 72.

33. Interview with Farmer.

34. Ibid.; Hankins, "Public Outdoor Relief," pp. 22–27, 50–57, 131; Ossman, "Family Service Society," pp. 34, 103–4.

35. Roanoke *World-News*, Nov. 26, 1934.

36. *World Almanac*, 1933, p. 905.

37. For accounts of national indifference, see the introductory essay by Bernard Sternsher in Sternsher, ed., *Hitting Home: The Great Depression in Town and Country* (Chicago, 1970), and Sidney Verba and Kay Lehman Schlozman, "Unemployment, Class Consciousness, and Radical Politics: What Didn't Happen in the Thirties," *Journal of Politics* 39 (1977): 291–323.

Chapter 3

1. For a more complete account of Byrd's presidential candidacy, see Ronald L. Heinemann, "Harry Byrd for President: The 1932 Campaign," *Virginia Cavalcade* 25 (Summer 1975): 28–37; and Brent Tarter, "A Flier on the National Scene: Harry Byrd's Favorite Son Presidential Candidacy of 1932," *Virginia Magazine of History and Biography* 82 (1974): 282–305.

2. *Times-Dispatch*, Oct. 26, 1932; Lynchburg *News*, July 3, 1932.

3. Glass to Roosevelt, Feb. 7, 1933, Glass Papers, box 6, U.Va. Lib.

4. Entry of Feb. 5, 1933, Hyde Diary, Hyde Papers, U.Va. Lib.; Rixey Smith and Norman Beasley, *Carter Glass* (New York, 1939), pp. 326–38.

5. Portsmouth *Star*, March 5, 1933; *Times-Dispatch*, March 8, 10, 1933.

6. *Virginian-Pilot*, March 5, 6, 14, 1933; Charlottesville *Daily Progress*, Jan 16, 1933.

7. Portsmouth *Star*, April 3, 1933; *Times-Dispatch*, March 22, 1933.

8. Entry of April 24, 1933, Hyde Diary, Hyde Papers, U.Va. Lib.

9. *Times-Dispatch*, June 10, July 17, 1933; Lynchburg *News*, June 17, 1933; Portsmouth *Star*, June 17, 1933.

10. *Times-Dispatch*, April 29, May 15, 17, 19, June 1, 10, 13, 17, 1933; Roanoke *World-News*, June 5, 1933; Charlottesville *Daily Progress*, March 29, April 19, 25, May 1, 31, Aug. 15, 1933.

Notes

11. New York *Times,* June 25, 1933; *Times-Dispatch,* Aug. 3, 1933; Charlottesville *Daily Progress,* March 23, 1933.

12. Joseph Fry, "The Organization in Control: George Campbell Peery, Governor of Virginia, 1934–1938," *Virginia Magazine of History and Biography* 82 (1974): 314; *Virginian-Pilot,* June 28, 29, 30, 1933.

13. *Virginian-Pilot,* Aug. 30, Sept. 3, 1933; *Journal of the Virginia Senate,* Extra Session, 1933 (Richmond, 1933), p. 81.

14. *Virginia Farm Economics,* no. 22 (July 1933), p. 304; ibid., no. 23 (Aug. 1933), p. 319; *Virginian-Pilot,* Aug. 28, 1933; *Handbook of Labor Statistics* (Washington, D.C., 1936), p. 173; *Department of Labor,* 1933, p. 5.

15. Ellis Hawley, *The New Deal and the Problem of Monopoly* (Princeton, N.J., 1966), pp. 61–66; Louis Galambos, *Competition and Cooperation: The Emergence of a National Trade Association* (Baltimore, 1966), pp. 196–226; Leuchtenburg, *FDR and the New Deal,* pp. 56–58; *Report on the Operation of the National Industrial Recovery Act* (Washington, D.C., 1935), p. 1; John J. Corson, "The Work of the NRA in Virginia," *Newsletter,* April 15, 1934.

16. Leuchtenburg, *FDR and the New Deal,* pp. 64–66; *Times-Dispatch,* July 16, 1933.

17. *Times-Dispatch,* Aug. 24, 27, Oct. 8, 1933; *Virginian-Pilot,* Aug. 21, Sept. 5, 1933; Roanoke *World-News,* Oct. 12, 1933; Corson, "NRA in Virginia"; state report of July 22, 1935, and letter from J. J. Skorup, District Compliance Director, to Donald Renshaw, NRA Field Director, Jan. 13, 1934, National Recovery Administration Records, box 4955, Record Group (RG) 9, National Archives (hereafter NA).

18. State NRA report, Aug. 31, 1935, box 4955, and cataloged inventory of NRA records, p. 140, RG 9, NA; Corson, "NRA in Virginia"; H. M. Henry, "National Recovery and Virginia," *Newsletter,* May 15, 1934; *Times-Dispatch,* Feb. 12, Dec. 26, 1934.

19. Hawley, *New Deal and the Problem of Monopoly,* pp. 79–107; Leuchtenburg, *FDR and the New Deal,* pp. 67–68; *Times-Dispatch,* May 21, Aug. 25, Sept. 26, 1934.

20. Farmville *Herald,* Feb. 9, 1934; state NRA report, Nov. 15, 1935, box 4955, RG 9, NA.

21. Corson, "NRA in Virginia"; Thomas J. Wertenbaker, *Norfolk: Historic Southern Port* (Durham, N.C., 1962), p. 336; state NRA reports, May 25, 1935, and July 20, 1935, boxes 5065, 4955, and April 1935 records, box 5065, RG 9, NA; *Times-Dispatch,* March 23, April 8, May 22, 1934, April 12, 1935.

22. Hawley, *New Deal and the Problem of Monopoly,* pp. 79–80; James L. B. Williams, *An Economic and Social Survey of Westmoreland County* (Charlottesville, 1936), p. 66; *Times-Dispatch,* April 7, 1934; William Palmer to Carter Glass, April 12, 1934, and Ryland to Glass, Aug. 25, 1933, Glass Papers, boxes 147, 309, U.Va. Lib.

23. State NRA report, July 20, 1935, box 4955, RG 9, NA; WPA Writers, *Negro in Virginia,* p. 319; *Virginian-Pilot,* Aug. 10, 1933; *Journal and Guide* Aug. 12, 1933.

24. Hawley, *New Deal and the Problem of Monopoly,* pp. 58–66, 122; Leuchtenburg, *FDR and the New Deal,* p. 68; state NRA report, April 1935,

box 5065, RG 9, NA; Smith, *Mill on the Dan,* pp. 393–95; *Times-Dispatch,* Oct. 24, 25, 1933.

25. Corson to NRA Regional Director, Feb. 21, 1935, box 5065 RG 9, NA; Charlottesville *Daily Progress,* July 11, 1934; *Times-Dispatch,* July 20, 26, Aug. 21, Sept. 7, 1934.

26. P. H. Drewry to Jack Drewry, May 27, 1933, Patrick Henry Drewry Papers, box 17, U.Va. Lib.

27. Glass to Beck, Oct. 20, 1933, Glass to Ralph Dorsey, Dec. 3, 1934, Glass to Lippmann, Aug. 10, 1933, Glass Papers, boxes 309, 320, 4, ibid.; Smith and Beasley, *Glass,* pp. 361–62. See also A. Cash Koeniger, "Carter Glass and the National Recovery Administration," *South Atlantic Quarterly* 74 (1975): 349–64.

28. Virginia Manufacturers Association, *The Virginia Manufacturer,* Aug. 1934, p. 1; Cabell Phillips, "NRA—Help or Hindrance?", *Times-Dispatch,* Oct. 11–17, 1934; Vepco Annual Reports, 1933–34.

29. Lynchburg *News,* Sept. 3, 1933, Jan. 6, 1934; Richmond *Planet,* April 21, Nov. 3, 1934; *Journal and Guide,* March 2, 1935; *Times-Dispatch,* May 19, 1933, May 16, 1935; Portsmouth *Star,* May 27, 1933, June 7, Nov. 3, 1934. See also Richmond *News-Leader,* May 16, 1935.

30. *Times-Dispatch,* May 28, 1935; Leuchtenburg, *FDR and the New Deal,* pp. 69–70, 145; Hawley, *New Deal and the Problem of Monopoly,* p. 132; state NRA report, Nov. 15, 1935, box 4955, RG 9, NA.

31. *Times-Dispatch,* May 28, 1935.

32. Roanoke *World-News,* May 29, 1935.

33. *Times-Dispatch,* May 28, 1935; Portsmouth *Star,* May 28, 1935; Petersburg *Progress-Index,* reprinted in Portsmouth *Star,* June 14, 1935; Lynchburg *News,* May 29, 1935; Roanoke *World-News,* reprinted in Lynchburg *News,* May 30, 1935; *News-Leader,* May 29, 1935.

34. *Department of Labor,* 1934, pp. 5–6; ibid., 1935, p. 20; *Times-Dispatch,* May 28, 1935.

35. *Times-Dispatch,* May 28, 29, 30, June 8, 1935; state NRA reports, Aug., Sept., and Oct. 24, 1935, box 4955, RG 9, NA.

36. State NRA reports, July 22 and Aug. 1, 1935, and other records, boxes 4955, 5065, RG 9, NA.

37. *Times-Dispatch,* Aug. 12, 1935; Harold Ickes, *Back to Work: The Story of PWA* (New York, 1935), pp. 48–49; Leuchtenburg, *FDR and the New Deal,* pp. 70–71.

38. *Times-Dispatch,* June 17, 24, Sept. 15, 21, Dec. 15, 1933; Charlottesville *Daily Progress,* Nov. 25, Dec. 21, 1933; New York *Times,* Nov. 12, 1933; Harrisonburg *Daily News-Record,* Oct. 12, 1933.

39. *America Builds: The Record of PWA* (Washington, D.C., 1939), p. 121; *Times-Dispatch,* Feb. 27, 1934, Oct. 2, 1935, Dec. 23, 1936, Jan. 4, June 5, 1938; Sheridan Gorman, "Raising Pinnacles of Power at Danville," ibid., Aug. 8, 1937.

40. *Times-Dispatch,* Aug. 20, 23, 1935, Sept. 13, Oct. 18, Nov. 1, 1936, June 13, 1937; Ickes, *Back to Work,* pp. 92–93; copy of *Acts of the General*

Notes

Assembly, special session, 1933, found in NRA records, RG 9, NA; Roanoke *World-News*, June 27, 1935; *America Builds*, p. 135.

41. *PWA Provides Modern Hospitals* (Washington, D.C., 1937), pp. 7, 14; *Urban Housing: The Story of the PWA Housing Division, 1933–1936* (Washington, D.C., 1936), p. 33; Edward Stanford, *Library Extension under the WPA* (Chicago, 1944), pp. 89–91; *Times-Dispatch*, Oct. 29, 1933, July 29, 1934, March 10, 1936, March 8, 1937, Sept. 21, 23, 1938.

42. Glass to Ickes, April 26, 1935, Glass Papers, box 4, U.Va. Lib.

43. *Times-Dispatch*, March 5, 13, 1935, Aug. 28, 1938; Lynchburg *News*, March 22, 1935.

44. *Times-Dispatch*, March 10, 1936, Sept. 23, 1937, June 23, 25, 26, 1938.

45. *Annual Report of the Federal Works Agency*, 1941 (Washington, D.C., 1941), pp. 96, 308–12; *America Builds*, pp. 264, 284; E. W. Clark, Acting Commissioner of PWA, to Hunter Haines of Grolier Information, June 24, 1940, box 46, Public Works Administration Records, RG 135, NA. Letters to Virginia congressmen and public officials along with listings of PWA projects in Virginia are in this collection, as are the records of the individual projects, but much of the PWA collection has been destroyed. Virginia ranked eighteenth in the number of nonfederal projects, twenty-second in the amount allotted, and twenty-first in total cost of projects. Ten states had over 500 nonfederal projects, led by Ohio with 1,059. Virginia ranked fourth in the number of federal projects and third in their cost.

46. *Times-Dispatch*, March 25, 30, 1933, Nov. 4, 1935; Herbert Western, "America's Shock Troops," ibid., March 14, 1937.

47. Ibid.; James E. Ward, Jr., and Treadwell Davison, "The C.C.C. Camps in Virginia," *Newsletter*, Dec. 15, 1934; "The CCC in Virginia," *Public Welfare*, April 1938, p. 1.

48. Final CCC report, Civilian Conservation Corps Records, RG 35, NA; *Times-Dispatch*, March 20, 1936; John Guthrie, "The CCC and American Conservation," *Scientific Monthly* 57 (1943): 401–12.

49. Wilbur C. Hall, "Virginia's State Parks," *Newsletter*, April 15, 1937; *Times-Dispatch*, Sept. 15, 1934, March 28, 1936; A. V. Shea, Jr., "Shenandoah National Park and Skyline Drive," *Newsletter*, Jan. 1, 1935. The Shenandoah National Park had been authorized in 1926, and Virginians had contributed funds with which to purchase the land. Skyline Drive was begun in 1930 with funds approved by President Hoover. See also Dennis Elwood Simmons, "The Creation of Shenandoah National Park and the Skyline Drive, 1924–1936" (Ph.D. diss., University of Virginia, 1978).

50. *Annual Reports of the Tennessee Valley Authority* (Washington, D.C., 1934–39, 1945, 1954).

51. Leuchtenburg, *FDR and the New Deal*, p. 53; *Times-Dispatch*, July 2, 1933, Oct. 20, 1934; C. Lowell Harriss, *History and Policy of the Home Owners' Loan Corporation* (New York, 1951), pp. 1–3, 20–22, 32–33, 75.

52. *Times-Dispatch*, Sept. 9, Dec. 14, 1934, Jan. 4, 1935, April 5, 1936, April 17, 1938; *Annual Report of the Federal Works Agency*, 1941, pp. 118–19, 342.

Notes

53. Martin Hutchinson to Curry Hutchinson, Nov. 20, 1933; Martin A. Hutchinson Papers, box 1, U.Va. Lib.; Roanoke *World-News*, Dec. 29, 1933; Danville *Register*, Jan. 4, 5, 1934; *Department of Labor*, 1934, p. 14. Between March 1933 and January 1934 the index of Virginia industrial employment rose from 68 to 85 (1929 = 100). In the nation it rose from 56 to 71; in North Carolina, from 79 to 106; in New York, from 54 to 67. Robert H. Barker, "Industrial and Commercial Recovery," *The Commonwealth* 1 (May 1934): 15–16.

54. P. H. Drewry to Jack Drewry, Oct. 27, 1933, F. W. Jones to P. H. Drewry, Nov. 22, 1933, Drewry Papers, box 17, U.Va. Lib; Curry Hutchinson to Martin Hutchinson, Nov. 14, 1933, Hutchinson Papers, box 1, ibid.

Chapter 4

1. Searle F. Charles, *Minister of Relief: Harry Hopkins and the Depression* (Syracuse, N.Y., 1963), pp. 19–43; Arthur E. Burns and Edward A. Williams, *A Survey of Relief and Security Programs* (Washington, D.C., 1938), pp. 12–18.

2. James, *The State Becomes a Social Worker*, pp. 252–61; *Final Statistical Report of the FERA* (Washington, D.C., 1942), p. 133; *Times-Dispatch*, Dec. 19, 1936; Mary Roberts (a FERA case worker and an assistant district director for WPA during the thirties) to author, Aug. 26, 1971.

3. Charles, *Minister of Relief*, pp. 50–64. Complaints were numerous from business that wages were too high and from labor that the scales were being violated. Approximating PWA scales, wages for workers ranged from forty cents to $1.00 an hour. White-collar workers received $60 to $100 per month, with top administrators getting up to $150. Civil Works Administration Records, box 48, RG 69, NA; Pamela Brown, *Analysis of Civil Works Program Statistics* (Washington, D.C., 1939), p. 6.

4. Brown, *Civil Works Program*, pp. 6, 30–31; *A Review of CWA Activities in Virginia* (Richmond, 1934), pt. 1, pp. 4, 17–26, pt. 2, pp. 2–6; *Times-Dispatch*, Nov. 15, 1933.

5. *Times-Dispatch*, April 2, 1934.

6. Ibid., April 1, 1934.

7. Charles, *Minister of Relief*, pp. 61–69.

8. June 1935 VERA report to FERA, box 298, Federal Emergency Relief Administration Records, RG 69, NA; *Times-Dispatch*, March 24, April 3, 8, 1934. From May 1934 through Dec. 1935, 51 percent of the relief money spent in Virginia went to work relief and 11 percent to direct relief; in the nation the percentages were 42 percent and 39 percent respectively. Hummel and Bennett, *Magnitude of the Emergency Relief Program*, p. 65.

9. John N. Webb, *The Transient Unemployed* (Washington, D.C., 1935), pp. 1, 58–64, 76–83; Hopkins to Arthur James, state Welfare Commissioner, Oct. 9, 1933, and memos of Sept. 9, 1933, and Aug. 7, 1934, box 391, and June 1935 VERA report to FERA, box 298, RG 69, NA; M. S. Burchard, "How Virginia Solved Transient Relief," *Times-Dispatch*, Aug. 23, 1936.

Notes

10. Burchard, "Transient Relief"; Roanoke *World-News*, March 28, 1935; E. Elizabeth Glover, "The Transient Situation in Richmond" (M.A. Thesis, College of William and Mary, 1934), pp. 25, 36, 42; memo of Aug. 7, 1934, box 301, RG 69, NA; Fredericksburg *Free Lance-Star*, April 7, 1934.

11. Letters to FERA and VERA, box 300, and memo of Aug. 7, 1934, and Representative Otis Bland to FERA, Feb. 2, 1935, box 301, RG 69, NA; Danville *Register*, Feb. 21, 25, 1934; *Times-Dispatch*, March 25, 28, 1934.

12. Burns and Williams, *Survey of Relief*, p. 32; *Times-Dispatch*, Feb. 11, Aug. 5, 10, 1934.

13. Burns and Williams, *Survey of Relief*, p. 31; *Times-Dispatch*, Sept. 14, 1934; Hummel and Bennett, *Magnitude of the Emergency Relief Program*, pp. 24–25; Audrey MacArthur, "The Emergency Educational Program in Virginia in 1933 and 1934" (M.A. Thesis, College of William and Mary, 1935), pp. 154–61; *Final Report of FERA*, pp. 112, 229, 297.

14. Allen Moger, *Virginia: Bourbonism to Byrd, 1870–1925* (Charlottesville, 1968), p. 253; Roberts to author, Aug. 26, 1971.

15. Memos and letters, boxes 302 and 303, and June 1935 VERA report to FERA, box 298, RG 69, NA; *Times-Dispatch*, July 12, 1934; *The Commonwealth* 2 (1935): 20; Thomas C. Walker, *The Honey-Pod Tree* (New York, 1958), pp. 238–40.

16. Hummel and Bennett, *Magnitude of the Emergency Relief Program*, pp. 20–23, 81–88; B. L. Hummel and C. G. Bennett, *Relief History of Emergency Relief Cases in Rural Virginia, 1935* (Blacksburg, 1937), p. 31; B. L. Hummel, C. G. Bennett, and W. W. Eure, *Youth on Relief in Virginia, 1935* (Blacksburg, 1936), p. 38; *First Annual Report of the Resettlement Administration* (Washington, D.C., 1936), p. 159.

17. *Times-Dispatch*, July 24, Aug. 16, 1934, March 10, 1935; *The Commonwealth* 2 (1935): 20.

18. Report of Citizens Service Exchange of Richmond, Dec. 31, 1933, box 298, RG 69 NA; Richard Lowitt and Maurine Beasley, eds., *One Third of a Nation: Lorena Hickok Reports on the Great Depression (Urbana, Ill., 1981), pp. 258–64.

19. *Final Report of FERA*, pp. 103–4.

20. *Times-Dispatch*, July 12, 1933; *News-Leader*, April 11, 1935.

21. *Times-Dispatch*, Nov. 27, 1934; Roanoke *World-News*, April 20, 1934.

22. Hopkins to Pollard, Aug. 16, 1933, box 298, RG 69, NA.

23. Memo from Hopkins to Williams, Feb. 10, 1934, and telegram from Hopkins to Peery, March 6, 1934, ibid.

24. *Times-Dispatch*, March 7, 1934; Harrisonburg *Daily News-Record*, March 8, 10, 1934; memo from L. L. Ecker-R, research statistician, to Hopkins, April 12, 1934, box 298, and Johnstone to Aubrey Williams, March 7, 1934, box 300, RG 69 NA.

25. Charles, *Minister of Relief*, pp. 31, 68–69.

26. J. M. Grayson to Peery, April 19, 1935, Executive Papers, VSL.

27. *Times-Dispatch*, Oct. 25, Nov. 27, Dec. 13, 1934.

28. *Final Report of FERA*, pp. 169–72; C. P. Spaeth to Hopkins, April 10, 1934, box 298, RG 69, NA; *Times-Dispatch*, Nov. 1, 1934.

29. *Times-Dispatch*, Nov. 1, 1934.

30. Ibid., Sept. 29, 1934; Byrd to William Reed, Oct. 6, 1934, Reed Family Papers, VHS.

31. Harrisonburg Daily *News-Record*, Oct. 30, Dec. 15, 1934; correspondence between Peery and Hopkins, Oct. 1934, box 298, RG 69, NA; *Times-Dispatch*, Dec. 16, 1934. Peery claimed that $3 million of the $14 million being spent on roads was going to relief.

32. Hummel and Bennett, *Magnitude of the Emergency Relief Program*, pp. 15–17; see also Appendix I.

33. Virginia League of Municipalities report to Governor Peery, Oct. 30, 1934, Executive Papers, VSL; *Times-Dispatch*, Nov. 25–29, 1934.

34. *Times-Dispatch*, Oct. 29, Nov. 14, 16, Dec. 13, 1934, July 7, 1935; Howard Smith to FERA, Aug. 28, 1934, Hopkins to Smith, Sept. 4, 1934, box 298, RG 69, NA.

35. Letters, boxes 298, 299, and 303, RG 69, NA; *Virginian-Pilot*, May 16, 1935.

36. *Journal and Guide*, Jan. 6, 13, 27, 1934; Richmond *Planet*, March 24, April 7, May 26, Aug. 4, 1934.

37. Hopkins to William Smith, Oct. 10, 1934, Smith to Hopkins, Oct. 16, 1934, box 298, RG 69, NA; Roosevelt quoted in Rexford Tugwell, *The Democratic Roosevelt* (New York, 1957), p. 444.

38. Cabell Phillips, "Relief and the Farmer," *Times-Dispatch*, May 5–9, 1935; ibid., May 10, 1935.

39. Ibid., Dec. 13, 1934, July 7, 1935.

40. Report by Gertrude Gates, Oct. 1934, and report from Johnstone to Hopkins, Jan. 26, 1935, box 300, RG 69, NA.

41. April 1935 report, box 298, ibid.

42. *Times-Dispatch*, April 11, 12, 1935; *News-Leader*, April 11, 12, 1935; Clifton Forge *Review*, reprinted in Portsmouth *Star*, April 30, 1935; Roanoke *World-News*, April 18, 1935.

43. *Times-Dispatch*, April 30, 1935.

44. Ibid., April 29, 30, May 1, May 4, 1935.

45. *Virginian-Pilot*, April 14, 1935; Joseph Fry "George C. Peery: Byrd Regular and Depression Governor," in Edward Younger and James T. Moore, eds., *The Governors of Virginia, 1860–1978* (Charlottesville, 1982), pp. 261–76; Robert F. Hunter, "Virginia and the New Deal," in John Braeman, Robert Bremner, and David Brody, eds., *The New Deal* (Columbus, Ohio, 1975), 2:111.

46. Letters from William Smith to area administrators, Nov. 1935, box 298, RG 69, NA; *Final Report of FERA*, pp. 103, 133, 169–172, 291–93, 298.

47. *Final Report of FERA*, pp. 248–49, 291–93; Hummel and Bennett, *Magnitude of the Emergency Relief Program*, pp. 2–3; Hummel, Bennett, and

Notes

Eure, *Youth on Relief*, p. 38; James E. Ward, Jr., "Virginia's Relief Situation," *Newsletter*, Feb. 1, 1935; Philip Hauser, *Workers on Relief in the United States in March, 1935* (Washington, D.C., 1937), abridged edition of second volume, pp. 120–21. About 20 percent of the populations of Hopewell and Bristol and Wise, Giles, Powhatan, and Cumberland counties were on relief. In June 1935 there were 211,100 Virginians on relief; 126,866 were rural and 84,234, urban; of the rural persons, 95,218 were white and 31,648 were black; of the urban persons on relief, 38,481 were white and 45,753 were black. See also Appendix J for a breakdown of FERA funding by counties and cities.

Chapter 5

1. Charles, *Minister of Relief*, pp. 66–69, 94–98; Burns and Williams, *Survey of Relief*, pp. 36–38.

2. Donald Howard, *The WPA and Federal Relief Policy* (New York, 1943), pp. 140–42, 160, 165–67, 178; Charles, *Minister of Relief*, pp. 119, 141–45, 150–51; Burns and Williams, *Survey of Relief*, pp. 43–48.

3. *Times-Dispatch*, Jan. 25, 29, Feb. 7, 21, 28, March 19, 20, 24, April 6, 9, 1935.

4. *The W.P.A. Record in Virginia* 1 (Oct. 1936): 16. This was a magazine published by the WPA of Vriginia in 1936–37.

5. *Times-Dispatch*, Jan. 5, May 15, 25, 1935; Charles, *Minister of Relief*, p. 129; memo of VERA to area administrators, July 16, 1935, box 300, FERA Records, RG 69, NA; Smith to Byrd, Aug. 10, 1935, box 2680, Works Progress Administration Records, RG 69, NA.

6. *Times-Dispatch*, March 25, 1936, Nov. 11, 1938; records in boxes 2673 and 2683, WPA Records, RG 69, NA.

7. M.S. Burchard To WPA, Oct. 22, 1935, box 300, FERA Records, RG 69, NA; *WPA Record in Virginia* 1 (March 1937): 2–3. From 1933 to 1938 Virginians received 40 million pounds of food and 787,000 pounds of clothing through the commodities program. *Times-Dispatch*, April 8, 1938.

8. Feb. 1, 1936, and May 1939 reports, box 2687, WPA Records, RG 69, NA; response to questionnaire.

9. Virginia WPA, *Around the Health and Sanitation Circle with WPA in Virginia*, (c. 1937), pp. 1–2, 6; *WPA Record in Virginia* 1 (Oct. 1936): 7; ibid., 1 (Dec. 1936): 7; *Times-Dispatch*, Nov. 3, 1935, May 23, 1938; G. Watson James, Jr., "WPA Goes to School," *Virginia Journal of Education* 33 (1940): 196–98.

10. Glen Taylor and Donald Gillies, *Assigned Occupations of Persons Employed on WPA Projects, November 1937* (Washington, D.C., 1939), pp. 66–67; Hauser, *Workers on Relief*, pp. 120–21.

11. Writers Project, Final WPA Report, and WPA Records, box 2694, RG 69, NA; William F. McDonald, *Federal Relief Administration and the Arts* (Columbus, Ohio, 1969), p. 739; Daniels quoted in Jerre Mangione, *The Dream and the Deal: The Federal Writers Project, 1935–1943* (Boston, 1972), pp. 259–60.

Notes

12. Among these were *A Guide to Prince George and Hopewell, Churches of Roanoke, Government of Roanoke, Jefferson's Albemarle, Sussex County, Prince William,* and "The White Man Comes to Stay" and "War Whoops in the Wilderness," two studies of colonial Virginia. Several plays were also written, among which were "James Monroe of Virginia" and "Let Freedom Ring." The best collection of works of the Writers Project is found in the Virginia State library.

13. Mangione, *The Dream and the Deal,* p. 269; Charles Perdue, Jr., Thomas Barden, and Robert Phillips, eds., *Weevils in the Wheat: Interviews with Virginia Ex-Slaves* (Charlottesville, 1976), pp. xv-xxii; May 1939 report, box 2687, WPA Records, RG 69, NA.

14. Library Project, Final report, and Feb. 10, 1939, report, box 2701, WPA Records, RG 69, NA; Final Report of the National Youth Administration for Virginia, p. 3, National Youth Administration Records, RG 119, NA; Edward Stanford, *Library Extension,* pp. 53, 89.

15. Virginia Art Project, Final Report, and May 1939 report, box 2687, WPA Records, RG 69, NA; *WPA Record in Virginia* 1 (Oct. 1936): 11; Handicraft Project, Final Report, WPA Records, RG 69, NA.

16. *WPA Record in Virginia* 1 (Oct. 1936): 5–7; *Times-Dispatch,* Nov. 21, 1935, March 10, Nov. 18, 1937.

17. WPA Records, box 2690, RG 69, NA; Jane DeHart Mathews, *The Federal Theatre, 1935–1939* (Princeton, N.J., 1967), pp. 277, 295.

18. John Ardinger, "The Barter Theatre of Virginia," *Newsletter,* April 15, 1955; Porterfield to Mrs. Roosevelt, Feb. 25, 1935, box 302, FERA Records, RG 69, NA.

19. *WPA Record in Virginia* 1 (Oct. 1936): 13; ibid., 1 (Dec. 1936): 5; ibid., 1 (Jan. 1937): i, 1–14.

20. Betty and Ernest K. Lindley, *A New Deal for Youth: The Story of the NYA* (New York, 1938); *18 Months with the Virginia Youth Administration* (May 1937), a pictorial study published by Virginia NYA.

21. Interview with Walter Newman, Aug. 18, 1970.

22. Virginia NYA, *The Young Virginian* 1 (April, June, and Aug. 1936); Final NYA Report for Virginia, pp. 13–14, 59–71, 141–43, RG 119, NA; interview with Newman.

23. Final NYA Report for Virginia, pp. 1, 100, 105, 121, RG 119, NA; Newman to Williams, Feb. 19, 1942, Aubrey Williams Papers, box 12, Franklin D. Roosevelt Library, Hyde Park, New York (hereafter FDR Lib.).

24. A survey of WPA projects in 1936 indicated widespread approval of them by Virginia sponsors; 98.5 percent of the projects were considered desirable and useful. Survey record, box 2673, WPA Records, RG 69, NA; *Times-Dispatch,* Nov. 3, 1936.

25. *Times-Dispatch,* Dec. 1, 1935, May 15, 1936, July 3, 1938; Charles, *Minister of Relief,* p. 146; interview with Robert H. Hubard, Aug. 3, 1970; responses to questionnaires; letters, box 2694, WPA Records, RG 69, NA; Howard, *WPA and Federal Relief Policy,* p. 259.

26. *Times-Dispatch,* March 24, 1938, June 23, 1937, Nov. 7, 1936.

Notes

27. Final Report of Virginia WPA, p. 1, WPA Records, RG 69, NA; Executive Papers of Governor Peery, VSL.

28. *Times-Dispatch*, June 28, 29, July 3, Oct. 21, Nov. 5, 1938; Lynchburg *News*, July 6, 23, 1938, Jan. 1, 1939; Charles, *Minister of Relief*, pp. 203–4.

29. *Times-Dispatch*, Dec. 20, 1935, Jan. 1, April 5, 1936, Aug. 26, 1938; Final Report of Virginia WPA, p. 5, and letters, boxes 2680 and 2681, WPA Records, RG 69, NA.

30. Letters, boxes 2678, 2679, 2680, 2703, WPA Records, RG 69, NA; *WPA Record in Virginia*, 1 (Feb. 1937): 5, 12–13; Howard, *WPA and Federal Relief Policy*, pp. 285–89; Walker, *The Honey-Pod Tree*, pp. 224–56; Perdue et al., *Weevils in the Wheat*, p. xvii.

31. Richmond letter of May 15, 1936, and Clinchport letter of Jan. 19, 1939, boxes 2685, 2701, WPA Records, RG 69, NA.

32. Robertson to Farley, Oct. 9, 1935, box 2685, Byrd to Aubrey Williams, April 21, 1936, and telephone conversation between Williams and Smith, April 22, 1936, box 2678, Williams to Smith, Jan. 3, 1938, box 2679, and records, box 2678, WPA Records, RG 69, NA; Charles, *Minister of Relief*, p. 205. Such exemptions were not unusual and were granted in areas where relief loads were low or on jobs that required a high degree of craftsmanship. Flexibility was also granted Smith in reducing wage scales to allow more people to work.

33. Petersburg worker's file, box 2682, and Merryman to FDR, Nov. 11, 1937, and to Virginia WPA, Oct. 4, 1938, Merryman File, box 2681, WPA Records, RG 69, NA.

34. Letter to WPA, May 15, 1937, box 2703, ibid.

35. *Report of the Work Program of the Works Progress Administration by the National Appraisal Committee on Community Improvements* (Washington, D.C., 1939), pp. 13, 22–25, 27, 31, 61; *Times-Dispatch*, June 19, 1938.

36. *Final Report on the WPA Program, 1935-1943*, (Washington, D.C., 1946), p. 124; Howard, *WPA and Federal Relief Policy*, pp. 542, 597–98, 673, 858; "National Unemployment Census, 1937," *Monthly Labor Review* 46 (Feb. 1938): 355-62; Hunter, "Virginia and the New Deal," p. 114.

37. *Final Report on the WPA Program*, pp. 30, 36, 110-12, 115, 124, 134–36; Final Report of Virginia WPA, pp. 1, 5-6, WPA Records, RG 69, NA.

38. Responses to questionnaire; Final Report of Training and Reemployment Division, WPA Records, RG 69, NA.

39. *Congressional Record*, May 16, 1940, vol. 86, pt. 6, pp. 6250–51.

40. Charles, *Minister of Relief*, p. 2.

41. See William Bremer, " 'Along the American Way': The New Deal's Work Relief Programs for the Unemployed," *Journal of American History* 62 (1975): 636–52.

Chapter 6

1. Murray Benedict, *Farm Policies of the United States, 1790-1950* (New York, 1953), pp. 277, 283–84; Leuchtenburg, *FDR and the New Deal*, pp. 23-24, 48-50; Broadus Mitchell, *Depression Decade* (New York, 1947), pp.

179–88; *Agricultural Adjustment, 1933-1935* (Washington, D.C., 1936) p. 1 (first annual report of the Agricultural Adjustment Administration).

2. Benedict, *Farm Policies*, pp. 303–4; Leuchtenburg, *FDR and the New Deal*, pp. 51-52, 72–74; Harold Rowe, *Tobacco under the AAA* (Washington, D.C., 1935), pp. 133–39; John C. deWilde, "The AAA and Exports of the South," *Foreign Policy Reports*, 11 (March 13, 1935): 45.

3. *Times-Dispatch*, July 26, Sept. 11, 16, Dec. 24, 1933, April 22, 1934; *Agricultural Adjustment, 1933-1935*, p. 128; Robert Hunter, "The AAA between Neighbors: Virginia, North Carolina, and the New Deal Farm Program," *Journal of Southern History* 44 (1978): 546-48; Rowe, *Tobacco under the AAA*, pp. 103, 109-14, 133-39, 154. Production control was not new to the Virginia farmer; numerous voluntary tobacco associations had been formed in the twenties. However, without strong government support and the compulsory features of the AAA, they failed to cut back the crop appreciably. Joseph Robert, *The Story of Tobacco in America* (Chapel Hill, N.C., 1949), p. 204; Danville *Register*, Feb. 8, 1930.

4. These included 50 percent of the cotton producers (6,000) and 80 percent of the tobacco growers (31,000); 10,500 corn-hog contracts, representing 15 percent of the corn acreage were signed; and one-eighth of the wheat farmers (7,636), representing 35 percent of the wheat acreage, had signed. The number of contracts totaled more than the number of participating farmers since some farmers planted more than one crop for marketing. Participation was greater among the larger farms. AAA to William Daughtrey, state AAA Executive Officer, June 24, 1938, Agricultural Adjustment Administration Records, RG 145, NA; Dennis Fitzgerald, *Livestock under the AAA* (Washington, D.C., 1935), pp. 448–51.

5. *Times-Dispatch*, Dec. 4, 14, 1934; Annual Narrative and Statistical Reports from State Offices and County Agents, Alleghany County, 1934, on microfilm at Virginia Polytechnic Institute and State University Library; interview with P. H. DeHart.

6. In 1934 the peanut crop was handled through a marketing agreement, but in 1935 it came into the basic commodity plan. *Agricultural Adjustment, 1933-1935*, pp. 244-45.

7. *Times-Dispatch*, March 21, May 23, 29, June 7, 9, 14, 15, 17, 1934.

8. Ibid., June 13, 1934.

9. Robert Hopper to Tugwell, June 15, 1934, Department of Agriculture Records, RG 16, NA.

10. *Southside Virginia News* (Petersburg), June 14, 1934.

11. See letters in Byrd Papers, box 1, U.Va. Lib.

12. W. Holmes Robertson to Moore (who was a Virginian), June 11, 1934, RG 16, NA; Holsinger to Wallace, June 21, 1933, July 30, 1934, May 17, 1935, RG 145, NA; *Times-Dispatch*, Aug. 15, 1934, Oct. 27, 1935. The Virginia Grange also voted support of the AAA program.

13. *Times-Dispatch*, Oct. 1, 1934, March 24, 1936.

14. Edward Brunner and E. Hsin Pao Yang, *Rural America and the Extension Service* (Menasha, Wis., 1949), pp. 81–82; statistical reports from county agents, Amelia County, 1934; Anthony J. Badger, *Prosperity Road: The New Deal, Tobacco, and North Carolina* (Chapel Hill, N.C., 1980), pp. 92–94.

Notes

15. *Times-Dispatch*, Dec. 15, 16, 17, 22, 1934, May 29, July 2, 1935; *Agricultural Adjustment, 1933–1935*, pp. 191, 206–7; B. L. Hummel, "Federal Crop Control in Virginia," *The Commonwealth* 1 (Sept. 1934): 5–6, 21–22.

16. *Times-Dispatch*, April 17, 23, May 28, July 11, 13, 16, 21, 24, Aug. 25, 1935. Although Byrd qualified to receive AAA payments, he never applied for them. Alden Hatch, *The Byrds of Virginia* (New York, 1969), p. 450.

17. *Times-Dispatch*, July 1, 11, 17, Oct. 3, 5, Nov. 3, 1935; *Agricultural Adjustment, 1933–35,*, p. 250; Hunter, "The AAA between Neighbors," pp. 549–53, 563–66.

18. *Agricultural Adjustment, 1933–1935*, pp. 45–47, 292, 295; Leland Tate, "The Agricultural Adjustment Program in Virginia," *Newsletter*, March 15, 1936; Henry Richards, *Cotton and the AAA* (Washington, D.C., 1936), p. 120; see also Appendix D on crop prices and Appendix K for a comparison of Virginia farm income with that of other states.

19. *Agricultural Adjustment, 1933–35*, pp. 1–11; Benedict, *Farm Policies*, pp. 311–15; Edwin Nourse, Joseph Davis, and John Black, *Three Years of the Agricultural Adjustment Administration*, (Washington, D.C., 1937), p. 150; Richards, *Cotton and the AAA*, pp. 290, 418.

20. Benedict, *Farm Policies*, p. 313; Rowe, *Tobacco under the AAA*, pp. 207, 213, 245; Hunter, "The AAA between Neighbors," p. 548; John Hutcheson, *The Why and the Whither of the AAA*, Virginia Agricultural Extension Division, bulletin 135 (Blacksburg, Dec. 1934); *Virginia Farm Economics*, no. 29 (April 1934), pp. 387–91; Tate, "Agricultural Adjustment in Virginia."

21. William Garnett and Allen D. Edwards, *Virginia's Marginal Population: A Study in Rural Poverty*, Virginia Agricultural Experiment Station, bulletin 335 (Blacksburg, 1941), pp. 46, 65–66; *Statistical Abstract* (1934), p. 547; David Conrad, *The Forgotten Farmers: The Story of Sharecroppers in the New Deal* (Urbana, Ill., 1965), pp. 59, 205–9; letter from AAA to William Daughtrey; interview with P. H. DeHart; responses of Virginia agricultural agents to questionnaire; Badger, *Prosperity Road*, pp. 200–235.

22. Responses to questionnaire; interview with William Daughtrey, Aug. 17, 1970; Danville *Register*, March 21, 1933, Nov. 1, 1934, Nov. 1, 1935.

23. *Times-Dispatch*, April 14, July 12, 17, 1935, Jan. 5, 7, 1936; Benedict, *Farm Policies*, p. 348.

24. Curry Hutchinson to Martin Hutchinson, May 30, 1935, Hutchinson Papers, box 2, U.Va. Lib.; *Times-Dispatch*, Jan. 7, 8, 1936.

25. *Annual Report of AAA*, 1936, pp. 1, 2, 10, 196; Benedict, *Farm Policies*, pp. 350–51; *Times-Dispatch*, Feb. 16, May 6, 1936.

26. *Times-Dispatch*, Jan. 13, Feb. 26, March 1, 3, 8, April 9, 22, 1936, June 20, 1937.

27. Ibid., April 2, 1936; Homer Bast, "The Conservation of Southern Soil," *Newsletter*, Jan. 15, 1939; Benedict, *Farm Policies*, pp. 318–19; Soil Conservation Service Records, boxes 139 and 140, RG 114, NA.

28. *Annual Report of AAA*, 1936, pp. 194–96; *Times-Dispatch*, July 9, 1936; *The Commonwealth* 3 (Oct. 1936): 15.

29. *Times-Dispatch*, Dec. 18, 1937, Feb. 10, 15, 1938; Benedict, *Farm Policies*, pp. 332–33, 375–82, 388–90.

30. *Times-Dispatch*, Feb. 17, March 15, April 24, 1938; Hunter, "The AAA between Neighbors," p. 559; A. B. Evans to Harry Byrd, May 16, 1938, RG 145, NA.

31. *Times-Dispatch*, May 1, 4, 5, 6, 1938; Lynchburg *News*, May 4, 1938; Hutson to G. L. Corbin, May 5, 1938, RG 145, NA.

32. *Times-Dispatch*, July 23, 1938.

33. Ibid., Dec. 11, 1938; Badger, *Prosperity Road*, pp. 169–74; interview with Daughtrey. Unlike tobacco farmers, cotton growers approved continuation of the quota system in 1939.

34. *Annual Report of the Secretary of Agriculture*, 1940 (Washington, D.C., 1940), pp. 119–21.

35. *Annual Report of AAA*, 1938–39, pp. 91, 123–26; ibid., 1939–40, pp. 72, 132; Murray Benedict, *Can We Solve the Farm Problem?* (New York, 1955), pp. 441–46; Van Perkins, *Crisis in Agriculture* (Berkeley, Calif., 1969), pp. 6–7, 35: letter from DeHart to author.

36. Benedict, *Farm Policies*, pp. 280–83; *Times-Dispatch*, Sept. 11, 1936; *Annual Report of the Farm Credit Administration*, 1938 (Washington, D.C., 1938), p. 120. The loss rate on Federal Land Bank and Land Bank Commissioner loans in Virginia was about half the national average. Jones and Durand, *Mortgage Lending Experience*, pp. 36–38.

37. W. Forbes Morgan, "Financing the Farmer," *The Commonwealth* 1 (Oct. 1934): 8–9; Harry Love, "Development of Production Credit and Its Operation in Virginia, 1934–1943," *Newsletter*, Dec. 15, 1944; Benedict, *Farm Policies*, pp. 280–83; *Times-Dispatch*, Sept. 11, 1936; response to questionnaire.

38. *Annual Report of the Resettlement Administration*, 1936, p. 159; ibid., 1937, pp. 1–2; *Times-Dispatch*, June 18, 1935.

39. William Garnett, *Does Virginia Care?*, pp. 1, 10; Garnett, "What Will Virginia Do About It?", *Virginia Journal of Education* 28 (1935): 282–84; Garnett and Edwards, *Virginia's Marginal Population*. Thirty-seven percent of Virginia farmers were also forced to obtain off-the-farm employment to maintain themselves. B. L. Hummel and R. B. Hummel, *Part-time Farming in Virginia* (Blacksburg, 1938), p. 2.

40. Treadwell Davison, "Self-Sufficiency Farms in Virginia." The percentage of self-sufficiency farms in the United States was 8 percent; Virginia's percentage was the third highest in the nation.

41. Farm Security Administration, *Rural Rehabilitation in Region IV* (Raleigh, N.C., 1938), pp. 11–13; records of the Farm Security Administration, boxes 70 and 72, RG 96, NA; David George, "The Virginia Farmer Approaches Cooperation," *Times-Dispatch*, Oct. 10, 1937; *Annual Report of RA*, 1936, p. 163.

42. Final Report on the combined Appomattox-Buckingham Project, box 479, RG 114, NA. The Soil Conservation Service worked with the RA on these land utilization projects.

43. Report on Prince Edward Project, box 481, and other reports, boxes 477–86, ibid.; *Times-Dispatch*, April 13, 14, 1936, Oct. 2, 1938; Farmville *Herald*, Aug. 6, 1971.

44. Benedict, *Farm Policies*, p. 326; Paul Conkin, *Tomorrow a New World: The New Deal Community Program* (Ithaca, N.Y., 1959), pp. 1, 6, 93, 113, 167, 201, 220; Donald Holley, "The Negro in the New Deal Resettlement Program," *New South* 27 (Winter 1972): 56.

45. Conkin, *Tomorrow a New World*, pp. 113, 163–67, 224, 333; Sidney Baldwin, *Poverty and Politics: The Rise and Decline of the Farm Security Administration* (Chapel Hill, N.C., 1968), pp. 111, 319, 356; *Times-Dispatch*, May 24, 27, Sept. 3, 1937. Byrd charged that the cost of each home would range from $6,000 to $10,000, while Wallace estimated $3,800 per home. The actual cost was $6,357 for each unit, which included the cost of the land, roads, and management. Byrd would eventually become a critic of FSA as well, believing it wasteful and socialistic in orientation.

46. Benedict, *Farm Policies*, pp. 362–63; *Annual Report of the Farm Security Administration*, 1938 (Washington, D.C., 1938), pp. 1–2; *Times-Dispatch*, July 3, 1937, May 8, Nov. 13, 1938. Tenancy was high in Virginia and rising (29.5 percent of the farm operators in 1935 were tenants), but it was nowhere near the national rate (over 40 percent) or the southern state average (53 percent). Lewis Walker, Jr., "Increase in Farm Tenants in Virginia, 1930–1935," *Newsletter*, April 15, 1936; W. G. Poindexter, Jr., "Share Croppers in the South," ibid., Dec. 1, 1936; Roy Wood, "Farm Tenancy in Virginia," pp. 34, 88.

47. B. L. Hummel and R. B. Hummel, *The Rehabilitation of Virginia Farm Families* (Blacksburg, 1939), pp. i, 1, 12, 17, 28–31; *Annual Report of FSA*, 1941, pp. 28–32, 42, 44, 49–51.

48. Interview with Daughtrey; Donald Holley, "Aspects of Southern Farm Life; Comment," *Agricultural History* 53 (1979): 203–5; Edward L. Schapsmeier and Frederick H. Schapsmeier, "Farm Policy from FDR to Eisenhower: Southern Democrats and the Politics of Agriculture," ibid., pp. 352–71.

49. Allen Berry, "Rural Electric Cooperatives in Virginia" (M.A. Thesis, University of Virginia, 1951), pp. 1–68, 102; response to questionnaire.

50. Berry, "Rural Electric Cooperatives," pp. 131–36; *Times-Dispatch*, Dec. 6, 1935, April 18, May 2, 15, 19, 27, 1936.

51. *Times-Dispatch*, Oct. 30, 1938; responses to questionnaire; *Annual Report of the Rural Electrification Administration*, 1939 (Washington, D.C., 1940), pp. 5, 47, 158 (opposite) 324–25, 351–54; W. Hubert Baughn, "Electricity in Rural Virginia," *Newsletter*, Nov. 1, 1942; Berry, "Rural Electric Cooperatives," p. 1.

52. See Theodore Saloutos, "New Deal Agricultural Policy: An Evaluation," *Journal of American History*, 61 (1974): 394–416.

53. Hunter, "The AAA between Neighbors," pp. 566–69. See Badger, *Prosperity Road*, pp. 207–8, and Richard Kirkendall, "The New Deal and Agriculture," in Braeman et. al., *The New Deal*, 1: 83–109, for conservative assessments of the New Deal agricultural programs.

Chapter 7

1. Joseph A. Fry, "George Cambell Peery: Conservative Son of Old Virginia" (M.A. Thesis, University of Virginia, 1970), pp. 40–51.

2. *Address by John Garland Pollard*, Jan. 10, 1934 (Richmond, 1934); *Times-Dispatch*, Jan. 17, 1934; Lynchburg *News*, Jan. 18, 1934; Hopewell, "Pollard," p. 427.

3. *Address of George Campbell Peery*, Jan. 17, 1934 (Richmond, 1934); Fry, "Peery: Conservative Son of Old Virginia," pp. 55–59; *Times-Dispatch*, March 10, 11, 1934.

4. *Report of the Virginia State Planning Board*, 1:162; Charlottesville *Daily Progress*, March 8, June 21, 1934; *Times-Dispatch*, June 2, July 21, 1934; Curry Hutchinson to Martin Hutchinson, March 27, 1934, Hutchinson Papers, box 2, U.Va. Lib.

5. *Times-Dispatch*, July 4, 1934.

6. *The Commonwealth* 1 (Oct. 1934):16; ibid., 2 (Jan. 1935): 3, 8; ibid., 2 (Feb. 1935): 3; *Report of the Virginia State Planning Board*, 1:164; *Department of Labor*, 1935, pp. 5, 10; A. V. Shea, Jr., "The Financial Strength of Virginia," *Newsletter*, Nov. 1, 1934; W. Parker Mauldin, "Bank Suspensions in the U.S. and Virginia, 1921–1934," ibid., Dec. 1, 1935.

7. Schwartz and Graham, "Personal Income," pp. 12–22; *Statistical Abstract*, 1937, pp. 765–67; Douglas Freeman, *Review of Reviews* 93 (Jan. 1936): 37; *Times-Dispatch*, Oct. 29, Nov. 5, 10, 21, Dec. 8, 1935.

8. *Times-Dispatch*, Oct. 30, 1935.

9. V. O. Key, Jr., *Southern Politics in State and Nation*, (New York, 1949), pp. 19, 26.

10. In 1940 Virginia ranked seventh in the nation in the number of state employees with 16,883. *Statistical Abstract*, 1941, p. 223.

11. Raymond Pulley, *Old Virginia Restored: An Interpretation of the Progressive Impulse* (Charlottesville, 1968), p. 183. This discussion of organization politics is taken largely from Pulley, pp. 171–88; Key, *Southern Politics*, pp. 19–33; Herman Horn, "The Growth and Development of the Democratic Party in Virginia since 1890" (Ph.D. diss. Duke University, 1949), pp. 124, 137–45, 295–313, 424–28; Allen W. Moger, "Virginia's Conservative Political Heritage," *South Atlantic Quarterly* 50 (1951); 318–29; William Crawley, "The Governorship of William M. Tuck, 1946–1950: Virginia Politics in the 'Golden Age' of the Byrd Organization" (Ph.D. diss., University of Virginia, 1974), pp. 29–38; William Crawley, *Bill Tuck: A Political Life in Harry Byrd's Virginia* (Charlottesville, 1978), chap. 1: and J. Harvie Wilkinson III, *Harry Byrd and the Changing Face of Virginia Politics, 1945–1966*, (Charlottesville, 1968), pp. 1–61.

12. Letters in Byrd Papers, boxes 113 and 148, U.Va. Lib.; letters to Charles Harkrader, editor of the Bristol *Herald-Courier*, Charles Harkrader Papers, ibid.; Hopewell, "Pollard," pp. 284, 365. On Byrd's maneuvering to remove Swanson from the Senate, see Byrd to William Reed, Dec. 10, 12, 16, 1932, box 57, Byrd to Richard E. Byrd, Dec. 13, 31, 1932, Jan. 26, 1933, and R. E.

Notes

Byrd to H. F. Byrd, Jan. 28, 1933, Byrd Papers, boxes 425 and 426, U. Va. Lib.

13. Byrd to Reed, Feb. 4, 1932, Reed Family Papers, VHS.

14. Hopewell, "Pollard," p. 286.

15. Hatch, *The Byrds of Virginia*, p. 402.

16. Byrd to Reed, July 9, 1931, Byrd Papers, box 108, U.Va. Lib. For Byrd's concern over deficits, see Byrd to Combs, Oct. 5, 1931, July 28, 1932, ibid., boxes 103, 113; Byrd to Reed, May 26, 1931, Sept. 11, 14, 1931, Reed Family Papers, VHS; and Byrd to Governor Pollard, Dec. 30, 1931, John Garland Pollard Papers, College of William and Mary Library.

17. Byrd to Harkrader, Harkrader Papers, U.Va. Lib.; Crawley, "Governorship of William Tuck," p. 29; Hopewell, "Pollard," pp. 240, 276, 284, 310, 320.

18. Fry, "Organization in Control," pp. 309, 314; Hopewell, "Pollard," pp. 217, 238–39, 272, 289, 297–99; Benjamin Muse, *The Reporter*, 17 (Oct. 3, 1957): 26. Hopewell concludes that Pollard accepted a "secondary role" to Byrd during his governorship. Regarding action to prevent a potential deficit, Byrd once wrote to Reed, "Of course do not mention this as I do not want the Governor to think I am taking any part in his duties." Byrd to Reed, May 26, 1931, Reed Family Papers, VHS.

19. Byrd to Reed, June 16, 1933, Reed Family Papers, VHS. That Byrd realized how popular Roosevelt was is indicated by his release at the end of the 1933 and 1934 congressional sessions of letters from National Democratic Party Chairman Jim Farley thanking him for supporting the administration. Roanoke *World-News*, June 21, 1933; Byrd to Charles Harkrader, July 20, 1934, Harkrader Papers, U.Va. Lib. See also Joe B. Tarter, "Freshman Senator Harry F. Byrd, 1933–1934" (M.A. Thesis, University of Virginia, 1972), pp. 28–32.

20. Lynchburg *News*, May 29, 1934; *Times-Dispatch*, March 15, 1935, May 29, 1937, Dec. 6, 1938; Robert T. Cochran, Jr., "Virginia's Opposition to the New Deal, 1933–1940" (M.A. thesis, Georgetown University, 1950), p. 8; Tarter, "Freshman Senator," pp. 37, 63–65; Hatch, *The Byrds of Virginia*, p. 448.

21. Koeniger, "Carter Glass," p. 351; Glass to Harkrader, Aug. 4, 1934, Glass Papers, box 320, U.Va. Lib.; Daniels quoted in E. David Cronon, "A Southern Progressive Looks at the New Deal," *Journal of Southern History* 24 (1958):151–76. See also Otis Graham, *An Encore for Reform: The Old Progressives and the New Deal* (New York, 1967).

22. Glass to Leffingwell, July 12, 1933, Glass Papers, box 4, U.Va. Lib.; Smith and Beasley, *Carter Glass*, pp. 354, 358–59; *Times-Dispatch*, Jan. 28, 1934; Charlottesville *Daily Progress*, June 21, 1934.

23. James T. Patterson, *Congressional Conservatism and the New Deal*, (Lexington, Ky., 1967), p. 358.

24. Frank Louthan, secretary of VMA, to Glass, Nov. 21, 1934, Glass Papers, box 320, U.Va. Lib.; *Times-Dispatch*, May 4, 1934.

25. *Times-Dispatch*, Aug. 21, 23, 1934.

26. *News-Leader*, Feb. 21, Oct. 30, 1935. On one occasion in New York City when Freeman used these terms to defend Virginia's position on relief, Mayor Fiorello LaGuardia responded, "It is difficult for any one to talk political liberalism with a man who is hungry." New York *Times*, July 21, 1935.

27. *Times-Dispatch*, May 29, July 10, 1934; Lynchburg *News*, Jan. 5, 1935.

28. Hutchinson to Woodrum, Aug. 28, 1934, Hutchinson Papers, box 2, U.Va. Lib.

29. William Larsen, *Montague of Virginia* (Baton Rouge, La., 1965), pp. 275–81; *Times-Dispatch*, Aug. 2, 1934; Byrd to Glass, July 11, 14, 1934, Glass Papers, box 320, U.Va. Lib.

30. Patterson, *Congressional Conservatism*, pp. 172, 237, 294, 303, 327, 339–43; James E. Sargent, "Clifton A. Woodrum of Virginia: A Southern Progressive in Congress, 1923–1945," *Virginia Magazine of History and Biography*, 89 (1981): 356; *Times-Dispatch*, April 6, 1938.

31. *News-Leader* April 17, 1935; Portsmouth *Star*, June 13, 1934; Bristol *Herald-Courier*, July 8, 1934, reprinted in the Portsmouth *Star*, July 10, 1934; Danville *Register*, Nov. 8, 1934.

32. *Times-Dispatch*, May 21, 22, 1935; Jack Kirby, *Westmoreland Davis: Virginia Planter-Politician, 1859–1942* (Charlottesville, 1968), pp. 185–190.

33. Alvin Hall, "James H. Price and Virginia Politics, 1878–1943" (Ph.D. diss., University of Virginia, 1970), pp. 44–45, 115; Kirby, *Davis*, pp. 188–90.

34. Woodrum to Hutchinson, Aug. 30, 1934, Hutchinson Papers, box 2, U.Va. Lib.

35. *Times-Dispatch*, Jan. 29, Aug. 13, Sept. 14, 1935, Sept. 20, Oct. 4, 9, 14, 1936; Lynchburg *News*, June 18, 1936; Roanoke *World-News*, Oct. 24, 1936; Andrew Buni, *The Negro in Virginia Politics, 1902–1965* (Charlottesville, 1967), pp. 104, 116–17; Glass to Byrd, Oct. 5, 1936, Byrd Papers, box 139, U.Va. Lib.

36. *Times-Dispatch*, Aug. 2, 5, 6, 1936.

37. Ibid., Dec. 8, 1935, Nov. 1, 1936; Drewry to Farley, Sept. 15, 1936, Roosevelt Official File 300, Roosevelt Papers, box 91, FDR Lib.

38. *Times-Dispatch*, Aug. 22, Sept. 8, Oct. 21, 1936, Jan. 1, 1937; Roanoke *World-News*, Sept. 23, 1936. The Hunter articles are in the WPA Records, box 2673, RG 69, NA.

39. *Times-Dispatch*, Oct. 28, Nov. 1, 1936. The final Gallup Poll gave FDR 53.8 percent of the vote nationwide and 68 percent of the vote in Virginia.

40. Ralph Eisenberg, *Virginia Votes, 1924–1968* (Charlottesville, 1971), pp. 101–4; *Virginian-Pilot*, Nov. 4, 1936; Danville *Register*, Nov. 4, 1936; *Times-Dispatch*, Nov. 1, 4, 5, 1936; Lynchburg *News*, Nov. 5, 1936.

41. Lynchburg *News*, Feb. 7, March 10, 1937; *Times-Dispatch*, Feb. 6, 9, 12, 14, 15, 21, 1937.

42. *Times-Dispatch*, Feb. 22, 28, March 4, 7, 24, 1937.

43. Ibid., March 30, April 13, May 19, 25, July 23, 1937.

Notes

44. Leuchtenburg, *FDR and the New Deal*, pp. 232–239; James T. Patterson, "A Conservative Coalition Forms in Congress, 1933–1939," *Journal of American History* 52 (1966): 757–72.

45. *Times-Dispatch*, Jan. 12, 1936, Jan. 13, June 2, 1937, April 9, 1938; Richard Polenberg, *Reorganizing Roosevelt's Government* (Cambridge, Mass., 1966), pp. 31–35; Hatch, *The Byrds of Virginia*, p. 454. A watered-down version of the bill passed a year later.

46. Byrd to Glass, April 29, 1937, Glass Papers, box 383, U.Va. Lib.

47. *Times-Dispatch*, July 19, 29, 30, Aug. 3, Nov. 10, 1938; Leuchtenburg, *FDR and the New Deal*, pp. 266–68, 271–74; Lynchburg *News*, July 2, 1938; Buni, *The Negro in Virginia Politics*, p. 143.

48. Alvin Hall, "Price and Virginia Politics," pp. 11–21, 62–63, 75–128; Carl Vipperman, "The Coattail Campaign: James H. Price and the Election of 1937 in Virginia," *Essays in History*, History Club, University of Virginia, 8, (1962–63): 47–61; New York *Times*, July 28, 1935; *Times-Dispatch*, Dec. 24, 1936.

49. *Times-Dispatch*, April 25, Aug. 4, 5, Nov. 4, 1937.

50. Ibid., Jan. 20, 1938.

51. Ibid., Feb. 1, 17, 25, March 8, 12, 13, 20, May 29, 1938.

52. Moore to Price, Nov. 28, 1938, Price to Moore, Nov. 30, 1938 (with enclosed memo), R. Walton Moore Papers, box 16, FDR Lib.; James Farley, *Jim Farley's Story*, (New York, 1948), p. 161.

53. Alvin Hall, "Politics and Patronage: Virginia's Senators and the Roosevelt Purges of 1938," *Virginia Magazine of History and Biography* 82 (1974): 331–50; Hall, "Price and Virginia Politics," pp. 148–50, 221–23, 237; Crawley, "Governorship of William Tuck," pp. 80–82; Combs to Byrd, Feb. 7, 1939, Byrd Papers, box 158, U.Va. Lib.

54. Hall, "Price and Virginia Politics," pp. vii, 211–20, 354–55; *Times-Dispatch*, Feb. 2, March 16, 18, 1938.

55. Hall, "Price and Virginia Politics," pp. 215–31, 245, 327–50; Hall, "Politics and Patronage," pp. 338–40; Horn, "Democratic Party in Virginia," pp. 438–43; Glass to Byrd, July 5, 1938, Glass Papers, box 383, U.Va. Lib. For a suggestion that the Byrd machine might have been vulnerable to outside pressure, see A. Cash Koeniger, "The New Deal and the States: Roosevelt versus the Byrd Organization in Virginia," *Journal of American History*, 68 (1982): 876–96.

56. Responses to questionnaire.

Chapter 8

1. James, *Social Worker*, pp. 80, 244–61; Joseph Cepuran, *Public Assistance and Child Welfare: The Virginia Pattern, 1646 to 1964* (Charlottesville, 1968), pp. 14–25; Department of Public Welfare of Virginia, *Twenty-second Annual Report*, (Richmond, 1931), p. 6.

Notes

2. Anne Geddes, *Trends in Relief Expenditures*, (Washington, D.C., 1937), pp. 91–92; James, *Social Worker*, pp. 68, 74; *Times-Dispatch*, Jan. 5, 1936; Danville *Register*, reprinted in Portsmouth *Star*, Jan. 30, 1935.

3. *The Virginia Manufacturer*, March 1935; ibid., June 1935; *News-Leader*, Jan. 25, 29, 1935; *Times-Dispatch*, Jan. 24, 25, 1935.

4. *Times-Dispatch*, Jan. 27, 29, 30, 31, March 31, April 11, 1935; *Virginian-Pilot*, April 21, 1935. Letters to the editor from Virginians generally were critical of Byrd and Peery on this issue.

5. *Times-Dispatch*, April 20, June 20, 1935; Broadus Mitchell, *Depression Decade*, pp. 308–13; *News-Leader*, Jan. 25, 1935; Leuchtenburg, *FDR and the New Deal*, pp. 132–33.

6. *Times-Dispatch*, June 21, Aug. 10, 16, Nov. 24, 1935, Jan. 9, 1936.

7. Ibid., Jan. 30, Feb. 15, 22, 27, March 3, 6, 7, 1936.

8. Fry, "George C. Peery: Byrd Regular and Depression Governor," p. 271; *Times-Dispatch*, March 9, 1936; Petersburg *Progress-Index* and Roanoke *World-News*, both reprinted in *Times-Dispatch*, March 12, 1936.

9. James, *Social Worker*, pp. 78–80, 277, 282–86; Howard, *WPA and Federal Relief Policy*, pp. 68, 858; Burns and Williams, *Survey of Relief*, pp. 83–84.

10. *Times-Dispatch*, Sept. 20, Nov. 7, Dec. 3, 5. 12, 18, 1936; *Report of the Unemployment Compensation Commission of Virginia*, 1938 (Richmond, 1939), p. 13. The cost of the extra session was estimated to be $70,000.

11. James, *Social Worker*, pp. 295–96; William Stauffer, "Old Age Assistance," *The Commonwealth* 5 (Jan. 1938); 13; *Southern Planter*, Oct. 1937. Ironically, three Virginians held top positions in the national administration of the security plan. Frank Bane, former head of the Virginia Public Welfare Department, was the executive director of the Social Security Board; John J. Corson, former head of Virginia NRA, was Bane's executive assistant; and Colonel Le Roy Hodges was chief of the Bureau of Old Age Benefits. Charles McKinley and Robert W. Trase, *Launching Social Security*, (Madison, Wis., 1970), pp. 401–2, 497.

12. *Report of the Commission on Old Age Assistance in Virginia*, Senate Doc. no. 3 (Richmond, 1937), pp. 19, 30–33, 36; *Times-Dispatch*, Dec. 16, 1937.

13. *Times-Dispatch*, Feb. 26, March 24, Aug. 19, 1938; *Public Welfare*, March 1938, pp. 1, 3; Arthur Burns and Edward Williams, *Federal Work, Security, and Relief Programs* (Washington, D.C., 1941), p. 146; Department of Public Welfare, *Twenty-ninth and Thirtieth Annual Reports*, 1938–39, pp. 4, 12.

14. *Times-Dispatch*, May 30, Aug. 14, 1938; Farmer to author, July 4, 1971.

15. *Address of George C. Peery*, Jan. 12, 1938, Senate Docs. no. 1 and no. 1-A (Richmond, 1938); *Times-Dispatch*, Jan. 13, 19, 1938; Fry, "Peery: Byrd Regular and Depression Governor," pp. 273–74.

16. *Times-Dispatch*, Jan. 20, 25, Feb. 19, 27, March 4, 9, 11, 12, 13, 18, 23, 1938.

Notes

17. Ibid., Feb. 8, 26, March 13, April 25, 1938; annual reports of the Virginia Department of Labor, 1930–42; Lynchburg *News*, Feb. 2, 1938. An improved mine safety law was passed by the 1940 Assembly.

18. Raymond Nelson, "Labor Unionization in the South" (M.A. Thesis, University of Virginia, 1940), pp. 147–63; F. Ray Marshall, *Labor in the South* (Cambridge, Mass., 1967), pp. 4–5, 133, 332–43.

19. *The Virginia Manufacturer*, July 1935; *News-Leader*, June 20, 1935.

20. *Times-Dispatch*, May 17, 1935, April 13, 14, 1937; *Decisions and Orders of the National Labor Relations Board* (Washington, D.C., 1936), 1:411, 429, 431; *Court Decisions Relating to the National Labor Relations Act* (Washington, D.C., 1944), 1:350; Marshall, *Labor in the South*, pp. 176–78.

21. Walter Galenson, *The CIO Challenge to the AFL* (Cambridge, Mass., 1960), pp. 3, 13–14, 20, 194, 326; Lynchburg *News*, Jan. 30, 1937. Surprisingly, the VFL initially supported Lewis's efforts at industrial unionism, a position that was reversed when the mineworkers lost their power in the VFL councils. *Times-Dispatch*, May 20, 1936, April 4, 1937.

22. Joseph A. Fry, "Rayon, Riot, and Repression: The Covington Sit-Down Strike of 1937," *Virginia Magazine of History and Biography* 84 (1976): 3–18; *Times-Dispatch*, March 11, 20, 23, 31, April 1, 8, July 8, 9, 10, 18, 1937.

23. Christopher L. Tomlins, "AFL Unions in the 1930s: Their Performance in Historical Perspective," *Journal of American History* 65 (1979): 1121–42; *Times-Dispatch*, March 18, 19, 20, 25, 30, April 3, 16, 20, May 7, 11, 14, 1937; Herbert R. Northrup, "The Tobacco Workers International Union," *Quarterly Journal of Economics* 56 (1942): 606–26.

24. *Department of Labor*, 1942, p. 36; George Starnes, John McCutcheon, and James Stepp, *A Survey of the Methods for the Promotion of Industrial Peace* (Charlottesville, 1939), pp. 129–30.

25. *Times-Dispatch*, March 3, Aug. 1, Oct. 24, 1937, May 25, June 12, 15, Oct. 23, 25, 27, 1938; John Moloney, "Some Effects of the Federal Fair Labor Standards Act upon Southern Industry," *Southern Economic Journal* 11 (July 1942): 15–23. The introduction of the minimum wage along with the increases imposed earlier by NRA codes forced many tobacco companies to introduce more machinery into the stemming operation, and this cost many black workers their jobs. Herbert Northrup, *The Negro in the Tobacco Industry* (Philadelphia, 1970), pp. 26–29.

26. *Times-Dispatch*, Jan. 27, 1935, Jan. 1, June 27, 1937, April 15, Oct. 21, 1938; Raymond Bottom, *Virginia's Record of Economic Progress*, Virginia Chamber of Commerce (Richmond, 1940), p. 1; Starnes et al., *Industrial Peace*, pp. 120–22; Calvin Hoover and B. U. Ratchford, *Economic Resources and Policies of the South* (New York, 1951), p. 193; Homer Bast and Charles Schwartz, "Manufacturing Development in Virginia," *Newsletter*, Dec. 1, 1939.

27. See annual reports of the Virginia Department of Labor, 1929–37; Schwartz and Graham, "Personal Income," pp. 12–22; Bast and Schwartz, "Manufacturing Development"; W. A. Cox, "The Port of Hampton Roads, Virginia, USA," *Newsletter*, May 1, 1938; *Final Report on the WPA Program*, pp. 110–12; *Times-Dispatch*, April 21, 1937, Jan. 14, Dec. 27, 1938. For this

period (1929–37), the value of industrial production in the United States declined 13.8 percent; only eight other states had increases. Virginia was also one of only five states to have exceeded 1929 income in 1937.

28. Leuchtenburg, *FDR and the New Deal*, pp. 243–44; Kenneth Roose, *The Economics of Recession and Revival* (New Haven, 1954), pp. 238–39; *Times-Dispatch*, June 19, Sept. 19, 1937.

29. "National Unemployment Census, 1937" pp. 355–62; *Times-Dispatch*, Jan. 1, 3, May 17, Oct. 28, 1938, Jan. 1, 1939; *The Commonwealth* 5 (April 1938): 3; ibid., 5 (July 1938): 3; *Final Report on the WPA Program*, pp. 110–12.

30. WPA Writers, *Guide to Virginia*, p. 115; Marshall, *Labor in the South*, p. 299. In 1939, 12.8 percent of the nonagricultural labor force in Virginia was in a union.

Chapter 9

1. David A. Shannon, ed., *The Great Depression* (Englewood Cliffs, N.J., 1960), p. x.

2. For comparisons with selected other states, see Appendixes F–L.

3. Response to questionnaire; Davison, "Self-Sufficiency Farms."

4. Robert H. Barker, "Manufacturing and the Depression in Virginia," *Newsletter*, Feb. 15, 1934; *Statistical Abstract*, 1937, p. 765; Raymond Bottom, *Virginia's Record of Economic Progress*, p. 3.

5. Shea, "Financial Strength of Virginia"; Eric W. Lawson, "Analysis of National Banking in Virginia, 1922–1935" (Ph.D. diss., University of Virginia, 1938), pp. 13, 19–21; Mauldin, "Bank Suspensions"; *Statistical Abstract*, 1933, p. 277; see also Appendix L. In 1933, 7.2 percent of the national banks in Virginia and 6.9 percent of the state banks were suspended; for the nation the figures were 11.1 percent and 10.5 percent, respectively. The number of commercial failures in Virginia in 1932 was 487, 1.5 percent of the business concerns in the state, a percentage slightly above the national average.

6. Allan G. Gruchy, *Supervision and Control of Virginia State Banks* (New York, 1937), pp. 76–79, 208; Lewis M. Walker, Jr., "Bank Savings in the United States, 1930–1935," *Newsletter*, Oct. 15, 1936; M. E. Bristow, "Recent Banking Trends in Virginia," ibid., Feb. 1, 1938. Only five states had a smaller percentage of decrease in savings deposits than Virginia.

7. State Board of Health, *Thirty-first Annual Report*, 1939 (Richmond, 1939), p. 103; Gilliam, *Virginia's People*, p. 82.

8. Tate, "Emergency Relief in Virginia"; Hummel and Bennett, *Magnitude of the Emergency Relief Program*, pp. 3, 16, 64. Georgia, Florida, North and South Carolina, and Louisiana contributed less state money than Virginia but received more FERA money.

9. Don Reading, "New Deal Activity and the States, 1933 to 1939," *Journal of Economic History* 33 (Dec. 1973): 792–810. Reading and Gavin Wright, in "The Political Economy of New Deal Spending: An Econometric Analysis," *Review of Economics and Statistics* 56 (1974): 30–38, suggest that political

considerations may have strongly influenced New Deal spending. This does not appear to have been the case in Virginia.

10. New York *Times,* March 15, 1931.

11. Harrisonburg *Daily News-Record,* Dec. 13, 1932; Freeman, *Review of Reviews* 93 (1936): 37.

12. Virginius Shackelford to Randolph Scott, June 29, 1933, Virginius R. Shackelford Papers, U.Va. Lib.

13. Wood, "Farm Tenancy in Virginia," p. 88; Thomas Hurlburt, "Significant Trends in Virginia Agriculture between Two World Wars" (M.A. thesis, University of Virginia, 1952), pp. 9–12, 73–74; *Virginia Farm Statistics,* bulletin 15 (1949), pp. 151–52; Edwin Holm, Jr., "Virginia's Indebtedness," *Newsletter,* March 1, 1940; Edna Trull, *Resources and Debts of the Forty-Eight States* (New York, 1937), p. 6; Schwartz and Graham, "Personal Income," pp. 12–22.

14. Garrett to John P. McConnell, April 30, 1935, William A. Garrett Papers, box 2, U.Va. Lib.

15. Key, *Southern Politics,* p. 27.

16. W. E. Garnett and Charles Burr, "Virginia's Place in the President's Challenge to the South," *The Commonwealth* 5 (Oct. 1938): 7–11.

17. Meade, "Rank of Virginia in Education," p. 44; *Times-Dispatch,* Sept. 30, 1937; B. F. Walton, "An Analysis of Expenditures for Public Schools in Virginia from 1909 to 1939" (M.A. Thesis, University of Virginia, 1942), p. 135.

18. *The Commonwealth* 3 (Jan. 1936): 5–7; Walton, "Public School Expenditures," p. 101; Rudyard Goode, "The Distribution and Disposition of Highway Funds in Virginia" (Ph.D. diss., University of Virginia, 1953), p. 350. For the decade, expenditures for public education increased $2.4 million, while highway revenue receipts jumped $11.4 million.

19. Annual reports of the State Highway Commission, 1929–39; *Times-Dispatch,* Aug. 7, 1933; Portsmouth *Star,* Dec. 7, 1934; Manassas *Journal,* Aug. 24, 1933; *The Commonwealth* 5 (Jan. 1938): 5–12. On one occasion Governor Peery authorized the highway department to incur a debt in order to match federal funds for roads. No such exception was ever granted to apply funds to relief or schools. *Times-Dispatch,* Feb. 28, 1935.

20. Guy Friddell, *Colgate Darden: Conversations with Guy Friddell* (Charlottesville, 1978), pp. 47, 69.

21. *Times-Dispatch,* Jan. 26, Oct. 31, 1935.

22. Danville *Register,* Nov. 12, Dec. 20, 1935; *Virginian-Pilot,* Jan. 5, 6, 1938; *Times-Dispatch,* March 2, 1937; *The Virginia Parole System: An Appraisal of Its First Twelve Years* (Charlottesville, 1955), pp. 2–5; Roanoke *World-News,* Oct. 30, 1936; Newport News *Daily Press,* Nov. 17, 1941.

23. *Virginia Parole System,* p. 1.

24. Reed to Byrd, Aug. 8, 1931, Byrd Papers, box 108, U.Va. Lib.

25. See Allen Kifer, "The Negro under the New Deal" (Ph.D. diss., University of Wisconsin, 1961); Raymond Wolters, *Negroes and the Great Depression;* and George Tindall, *The Emergence of the New South, 1913–1945* (Baton Rouge, La., 1967), p. 543.

Notes

26. Harvard Sitkoff, *A New Deal for Blacks* (New York, 1978), pp. 43–46, 58–59, 82–83, 331; Tindall, *Emergence of the New South*, pp. 543–49; Buni, *The Negro in Virginia Politics*, pp. 112–17; Hunter, "Virginia and the New Deal," pp. 126, 133.

27. Hutcheson, *Why and Whither of AAA;* Tindall, *Emergence of the New South*, p. 523; Nelson, "Labor Unionization in the South," pp. 147–63.

28. Alonzo Hamby, ed., *The New Deal*, 2d ed. (New York, 1981), p. 5. For a "New Left" critique of New Deal failures, see Barton Bernstein, "The New Deal: The Conservative Achievements of Liberal Reform," in Bernstein, ed., *Towards a New Past* (New York, 1968), and Howard Zinn, ed., *New Deal Thought* (Indianapolis, 1966).

29. See Kirkendall, "The New Deal and Agriculture"; Badger, *Prosperity Road;* James T. Patterson, *The New Deal and the States* (Princeton, N.J., 1969); and Bremer, "Along the American Way."

30. See Badger, *Prosperity Road*, pp. xvi, 233; Patterson, *New Deal and the States;* Braeman et al., *The New Deal*, vol. 2; and Robert Ingalls, *Herbert H. Lehman and New York's Little New Deal* (New York, 1975). For a perceptive analysis of the criticism of the "New Left" historians, see Jerold S. Auerbach, "New Deal, Old Deal, Raw Deal: Some Thoughts on New Left Historiography," *Journal of Southern History* 35 (1969): 18–30.

31. Farmville *Herald*, April 17, 1935.

32. Response to questionnaire.

33. *Address of John Garland Pollard*, Jan. 10, 1934; *Address of George Peery*, Jan. 12, 1938; *Times-Dispatch*, Dec. 14, 25, 1935.

34. James T. Patterson, "The New Deal and the States," *American Historical Review* 73 (1967): 72–73, 84; Braeman et al., *The New Deal*, vol. 2.

35. See William Nichols, *Southern Traditions and Regional Progress* (Chapel Hill, N.C., 1960).

36. Tindall, *Emergence of the New South*, pp. 390, 400–549; see also Dewey Grantham, *The Democratic South* (Athens, Ga., 1963), pp. 69–72; and Frank Freidel, *FDR and the South* (Baton Rouge, La., 1965). Despite the progress, however, there was no major closing of the per capita income gap by the South; education was not upgraded; and the union movement remained weak. See Carole Scott, "The Economic Impact of the New Deal on the South" (Ph.D. diss., Georgia State College, 1969), pp. 171, 199, 211.

37. *Times-Dispatch*, Dec. 26, 1938.

Bibliography

Manuscript Collections

Franklin D. Roosevelt Library, Hyde Park, New York
Harry Hopkins Papers
R. Walton Moore Papers
Franklin D. Roosevelt Papers
Aubrey Williams Papers

Swem Library, College of William and Mary
John Garland Pollard Papers
A. Willis Robertson Papers

University of Virginia Library
Frank Bane Papers
Harry F. Byrd Papers
Everett R. Combs Papers
Westmoreland Davis Papers
Patrick Henry Drewry Papers
William A. Garrett Papers
Carter Glass Papers
John D. Guthrie Papers
Charles J. Harkrader Papers
Thomas Lomax Hunter Papers
Martin A. Hutchinson Papers
Henry Morrow Hyde Papers
Virginius R. Shackelford Papers
C. Bascom Slemp Papers
Robert Whitehead Papers

Virginia Historical Society Library
William T. Reed Family Papers

Virginia Polytechnic Institute and State University Library
Annual Narrative and Statistical Reports from State Offices and County
Agents, Department of Agricultural Extension Service (on microfilm)

Virginia State Library
Executive Papers of John Garland Pollard
of George C. Peery
of James Price

Bibliography

National Archives
National Recovery Administration Records. Records Group 9
United States Department of Agriculture Records. RG 16
Civilian Conservation Corps Records. RG 35
Civil Works Administration Records. RG 69
Federal Emergency Relief Administration Records. RG 69
Works Progress Administration Records. RG 69
Farm Security Administration Records. RG 96
Soil Conservation Service Records. RG 114
National Youth Administration Records. RG 119
Public Works Administration Records. RG 135
Agricultural Adjustment Administration Records. RG 145

Interviews

William Daughtrey, P. H. DeHart, Elizabeth Eggleston, Marguerite Farmer, Robert Hubard, Walter Newman, J. Barrye Wall.

United States Government Publications

(All published in Washington, D.C., by the Government Printing Office unless otherwise noted.)
Activities of the Works Progress Administration, testimony of Harry Hopkins before the Subcommittee of the House Committee on Appropriations, April 8, 1936. Senate Document no. 226.
America Builds: The Record of PWA, 1939.
Annual Reports of the Agricultural Adjustment Administration, 1933–40.
of the Farm Credit Administration, 1933–38.
of the Farm Security Administration, 1937–41.
of the Federal Security Agency, 1941.
of the Federal Works Agency, 1941.
of the Resettlement Administration, 1936–37.
of the Rural Electrification Administration, 1939.
of the Secretary of Agriculture, 1940.
of the Secretary of Labor, 1931, 1938–39.
of the Tennessee Valley Authority, 1934–39, 1945, 1954.
Annual Reports on the Statistics of Railways in the United States, 1925–39.
Court Decisions Relating to the National Labor Relations Act, 1944.
Decisions and Orders of the National Labor Relations Board, 12 vols., 1936–39.
Fifteenth Census of the United States (1930), 1932–1933.
Final Report on the WPA Program, 1935–1943, 1946.
Handbook of Labor Statistics, 1936, 1941.
Monthly Report of the Federal Emergency Relief Administration, 1933–36.
Public Buildings: Survey of Architecture in PWA Funded Buildings, 1933–1939, 1939.
PWA Provides Modern Hospitals, 1937.

Bibliography

Quarterly Report of the Reconstruction Finance Corporation, 2d quarter, 1940.
Report on the Operation of the National Industrial Recovery Act, 1935.
Sixteenth Census of the United States (1940), 1942.
Statistical Abstract of the United States, 1930–42.
Urban Housing: The Story of the PWA Housing Division, 1933–1936, 1936.
What the Resettlement Administration Has Done, 1936.
WPA studies:
  Brown, Pamela. *Analysis of Civil Works Program Statistics*, 1939.
  Burns, Arthur E., and Edward A. Williams. *Federal Work, Security and Relief Programs*, 1941.
  ———. *A Survey of Relief and Security Programs*, 1938.
  Catlin, Malcolm. *WPA Projects: Analysis of Projects Placed in Operation through June 30, 1937*, 1937.
  Geddes, Anne. *Trends in Relief Expenditures*, 1937.
  Hauser, Philip. *Workers on Relief in the United States in March 1935* (abridged edition of 2-volume edition), 1937.
  Report on the Progress of the WPA Program, June 30, 1938.
  Report on the Work Program of the Works Progress Administration by the National Appraisal Committee on Community Improvements, 1939.
  Taylor, Glen S., and Donald Gillies. *Assigned Occupations of Persons Employed on WPA Projects, November, 1937*, 1939.
  Webb, John. *The Transient Unemployed*, 1935.
  Whiting, Theodore. *Final Statistical Report of the Federal Emergency Relief Administration*, 1942.
  Wood, Katherine. *Urban Workers on Relief*, pt. 2, 1937.

Virginia State Documents

(All published in Richmond by the Division of Purchase and Printing or the Superintendent of Public Printing unless otherwise noted.)
Address of Harry Flood Byrd, January 8, 1930. Senate Document no. 1, 1930.
Address of John Garland Pollard, January 15, 1930. Senate Document no. 5, 1930.
Address of John Garland Pollard, January 13, 1932. Senate Document no. 1, 1932.
Address of John Garland Pollard with Addenda, January 10, 1934. Senate Document no. 1, 1934.
Address of George C. Peery, January 17, 1934, House Document no. 6, 1934.
Address of George C. Peery with Addenda, January 12, 1938. Senate Document nos. 1 and 1-A, 1938.
Annual Reports of the Department of Labor and Industry, 1918–44.
  of the Department of Public Welfare, 1925–39.
  of the State Board of Health, 1926–39.
  of the State Corporation Commission, 1939.
  of the State Highway Commission, 1929–39.
  of the Unemployment Compensation Commission, 1937–38, 1954.

241

Bibliography

Journal of the House of Delegates of Virginia, 1932–38.
Journal of the Senate of the Commonwealth of Virginia, 1932–38.
Meade, Richard A. "Rank of Virginia in Education," in *The Virginia Public School System.* Virginia Education Commission Report, 1944.
Report of the Commission on Old Age Assistance in Virginia. Senate Document no. 3, 1937.
Report of the Commission on Stabilization of Employment in Virginia and Building Up of Unemployment Reserves, 1934.
Report of the Commission to Study the Condition of the Farmers of Virginia, 1930.
Report of the Labor Relations Commission. Senate Document no. 3, 1940.
Report of the Virginia State Planning Board. Vols. I and III-A, 1935–36.
Statement of the Vote. Compiled by the Secretary of the Commonwealth for State and National Elections, 1932–42.
Stauffer, William H. "School Finances in Virginia." Senate Document no. 4, 1934.
Virginia Farm Statistics. Virginia Department of Agriculture, 1923–49.

Annual Reports of Virginia Industries

Reynolds Metals. Louisville: 1928–40.
Richmond, Fredericksburg and Potomac Railroad Co. Richmond: 1929, 1932, 1933.
Seaboard Airline Railway Co. Norfolk: 1929, 1932, 1933, 1945.
Virginia Electric and Power Co. Richmond: 1925–40.

Newspapers

Bristol *Herald-Courier*
Charlottesville *Daily Progress*
Danville *Register*
Farmville *Herald*
Fredericksburg *Free Lance-Star*
Harrisonburg *Daily News-Record*
Lynchburg *News*
Manassas *Journal*
Newport News *Daily Press*
New York *Times*
Norfolk *Journal and Guide*
Norfolk *Virginian-Pilot*
Portsmouth *Star*
Richmond *News-Leader*
Richmond *Planet*
Richmond *Times-Dispatch.* See especially:
    Brill, Edmund. "Modernizing Hospitals in Virginia," March 21, 1937.
    Burchard, M. S. "How Virginia Solved Transient Relief," Aug. 23, 1936.
    Denson, John. "Unrest in Virginia," Jan. 12–22, 1932.

Bibliography

George, David. "The Virginia Farmer Approaches Cooperation," Oct. 10, 1937.
Gorman, Sheridan. "Raising Pinnacles of Power at Danville," Aug. 8, 1937.
Phillips, Cabell. "NRA—Help or Hindrance," Oct. 11–17, 1934.
_____. "Relief and the Farmer," May 5–8, 1935.
_____. "Virginia's Relief Dilemma" Nov. 25–29, 1934.
Western, Herbert. "America's Shock Troops," March 14, 1937.
Roanoke *World-News*
Smithfield *Times*
Southside Virginia *News* (Petersburg)
Winchester *Evening Star*

Periodicals

The Commonwealth, 1934–39. See especially:
Barker, Robert H. "Industrial and Commercial Recovery," 1 (May 1934): 15–16.
_____. "Seven Years of Virginia Industry," 3 (June 1936): 7.
Calrow, Charles. "Retail Trade in Virginia." 5 (March 1938): 13–14.
Corson, John J. "The Good Things of NRA," 2 (July 1935): 12.
Drinker, Gertrude. "Virginia Dairying Progresses," 4 (Nov. 1937): 7–9.
Garnett, W. E., and Charles Burr. "Virginia's Place in the President's Challenge to the South," 5 (Oct. 1938): 7–11.
Hummel, B. L. "Federal Crop Control in Virginia," 1 (Sept. 1934): 5–6, 21–22.
Morgan, W. Forbes. "Financing the Farmer," 1 (Oct. 1934): 8–9.
Newman, Clarence. "Wages and Hours," 5 (Aug. 1938): 9.
Stauffer, William. "Old Age Assistance," 5 (Jan. 1938): 13.
_____. "Unemployment Compensation." 4 (Jan. 1937): 7.
Manufacturer's Record, 1934–35.
Monthly Review (Federal Reserve), 1929–39.
Public Welfare (Department of Public Welfare), 1931–39.
Record of the Hampden-Sydney Alumni Association, 1929–39.
The Southern Planter, 1932–38.
University of Virginia Newsletter, 1925–55. See especially:
Ardinger, John. "The Barter Theatre of Virginia," April 15, 1955.
Barker, Robert H. "Employment and Unemployment in Virginia," March 15, 1933.
_____. "Manufacturing and the Depression in Virginia," Feb. 15, 1934.
_____. "Recent Trends in Employment and Payrolls in Virginia Industry," June 1, 1937.
_____. "The Industrial Development of Virginia," Jan. 15, 1938.
Bast, Homer. "The Conservation of Southern Soil," Jan. 15, 1939.
_____, and Charles Schwartz. "Manufacturing Development in Virginia," Dec. 1, 1939.
Baughn, W. Hubert. "Electricity in Rural Virginia," Nov. 1, 1942.
Bristow, M. E. "Recent Banking Trends in Virginia," Feb. 1, 1938.
Byrd, William E. Jr. "Farm Tenancy in Virginia: 1880–1930," Nov. 1, 1931.

Bibliography

Corson, John J. "The Work of the NRA in Virginia," April 15, 1934.
_____. "Production Values per Farm Worker: 1926," Dec. 15, 1927.
Cox, W. A. "The Port of Hampton Roads, Virginia, USA," May 1, 1938.
Davison, Treadwell. "Self-Sufficiency Farms in Virginia," Feb. 15, 1935.
Eller, C. Howe. "Rural Health Service in Virginia," May 1, 1937.
Gee, Wilson, "Farm Mortgage Debt," Nov. 15, 1927.
_____. "Some of Our Forgotten Men," Feb. 1, 1927.
Hall, Wilbur C. "Virginia's State Parks," April 15, 1937.
Henry, H. M. "National Recovery and Virginia," May 15, 1934.
Holm, Edwin, Jr. "Virginia's Indebtedness," March 1, 1940.
Hudgens, D.C. "Diversified Agriculture in Virginia," Jan. 15, 1933.
Leap, W. L. "Public Welfare in Virginia," June 15, 1931.
_____. "The 1930 Drought," March 1, 1931.
Love, Harry M. "Development of Production Credit and Its Operation in Virginia, 1934–1943," Dec. 15, 1944.
Mauldin, W. Parker. "Bank Suspensions in the U.S. and Virginia, 1921–34," Dec. 1, 1935.
Meacham, William Shands. "Probation and Parole in Virginia," June 15, 1943.
Poindexter, W. G., Jr. "Share Croppers in the South," Dec. 1, 1936.
Shea, A. V., Jr. "Shenandoah National Park and Skyline Drive," Jan. 1, 1935.
_____. "The Financial Strength of Virginia," Nov. 1, 1934.
Schwartz, Charles F. "Income Payments in Virginia, 1929–1941," Oct. 15, 1942.
Tate, Leland B. "Emergency Relief in Virginia," Nov. 15, 1935.
_____. "The Agricultural Adjustment Program in Virginia," March 15, 1936.
Walker, Lewis M., Jr. "Bank Savings in the United States, 1930–1935," Oct. 15, 1936.
_____. "Increase in Farms, 1930–1935," Feb. 1, 1936.
_____. "Increase in Farm Tenants in Virginia 1930–1935," April 15, 1936.
Ward, James, E., Jr. "A Billion Dollar Manufacturing State by 1930," Jan. 1, 1930.
_____. "Farm Mortgage Debt," March 1, 1932.
_____. "Recent Industrial Trends in Virginia," June 15, 1935.
_____. "Rural Rehabilitation in Virginia," April 1, 1935.
_____. "State and Municipal Defaults," Nov. 1, 1933.
_____. "Virginia's Federal Tax Load," Dec. 1, 1934.
_____. "Virginia's Relief Situation," Feb. 1, 1935.
_____, and Treadwell Davison. "The CCC Camps in Virginia," Dec. 15, 1934.

Virginia Farm Economics (Department of Agricultural Economics and Rural Sociology, Virginia Polytechnic Institute and State University), 1931–42.
Virginia Journal of Education, 1933–40.
The Virginia Manufacturer, 1934–38.
The World Almanac, 1929–40.

Unpublished Studies

Bartle, Barbara. "Virginius Dabney: Southern Liberal in the Era of Roosevelt." M.A. Thesis, University of Virginia, 1968.

Berry, Allen J. "Rural Electric Cooperatives in Virginia." M.A. Thesis, University of Virginia, 1951.

Blanton, S. Walker. "Virginia in the 1920s: An Economic and Social Profile." Ph.D. diss., University of Virginia, 1969.

Cochran, Robert T., Jr. "Virginia's Opposition to the New Deal, 1933–1940." M.A. Thesis, Georgetown University, 1950.

Crawley, William B., Jr. "The Governorship of William Munford Tuck, 1946–1950: Virginia Politics in the 'Golden Age' of the Byrd Organization." Ph.D. diss., University of Virginia, 1974.

Cutler, Ronald. "A History and Analysis of Negro Newspapers in Virginia." M.A. Thesis, University of Richmond, 1965.

Drewry, Lyman, Jr. "Recent Changes in the Economic Position of the Negro in Virginia." M.A. Thesis, University of Virginia, 1956.

DuBose, John Pendleton. "The Federal Emergency Relief Administration: Its Organization and Relationship with the States." M.A. Thesis, University of Virginia, 1935.

Dutton, George E. "The Cost of Public Education in Virginia from 1870 to 1939." M.A. Thesis, University of Virginia, 1941.

Eckenrode, Hamilton J. "Virginia since 1865: 1865–1945, A Political History." Manuscript in the University of Virginia Library.

Ferrell, Henry C., Jr. "Claude A. Swanson of Virginia." Ph.D. diss., University of Virginia, 1964.

Fry, Joseph Andrew. "George Campbell Peery: Conservative Son of Old Virginia." M.A. Thesis, University of Virginia, 1970.

Glover, E. Elizabeth. "The Transient Situation in Richmond." M.A. thesis, College of William and Mary (RPI Branch), 1934.

Goode, Rudyard B. "The Distribution and Disposition of Highway Funds in Virginia." Ph.D. diss., University of Virginia, 1953.

Hall, Alvin L. "James H. Price and Virginia Politics, 1878 to 1943." Ph.D. diss., University of Virginia, 1970.

Hankins, Mary Coleman. "The Growth of Public Outdoor Relief in Richmond, Virginia." M.A. Thesis, College of William and Mary (RPI Branch), 1935.

Hawkes, Robert T., Jr. "The Political Apprenticeship and Gubernatorial Term of Harry Flood Byrd." M.A. Thesis, University of Virginia, 1967.

———. "The Career of Harry Flood Byrd, Sr., to 1933." Ph.D. diss., University of Virginia, 1975.

Heinemann, Ronald L. "Depression and New Deal in Virginia." Ph.D. diss., University of Virginia, 1968.

Hopewell, John. "An Outsider Looking In: John Garland Pollard and Machine Politics in Twentieth Century Virginia." Ph.D. diss., University of Virginia, 1976.

Horn, Herman L. "The Growth and Development of the Democratic Party in Virginia since 1890." Ph.D. diss., Duke University, 1949.

Bibliography

Hurlburt, Thomas, W. "Significant Trends in Virginia Agriculture between Two World Wars." M.A. Thesis, University of Virginia, 1952.

Kifer, Allen. "The Negro under the New Deal." Ph.D. diss., University of Wisconsin, 1961.

Kirby, Jack T. "Westmoreland Davis, a Virginia Planter, 1859–1942." Ph.D. diss., University of Virginia, 1965.

Lawson, Eric Wilfred. "Analysis of National Banking in Virginia, 1922–1935." Ph.D. diss., University of Virginia, 1938.

Lynn, Robert D. "The Social Function of the Salvation Army in Richmond, Virginia." M.A. Thesis, College of William and Mary (RPI Branch), 1935.

MacArthur, Audrey. "The Emergency Educational Program in Virginia in 1933 and 1934." M.A. Thesis, College of William and Mary (RPI Branch), 1935.

McNeil, Martine. "The Family Agency in an Unemployment Crisis." M.A. Thesis, College of William and Mary (RPI Branch), 1932.

Marcello, Ronald. "The North Carolina Works Progress Administration and the Politics of Relief." Ph.D. diss., Duke University, 1968.

Mathes, Martha Claire. "A Follow-up Study of the Family Agency in an Unemployment Crisis." M.A. Thesis, College of William and Mary (RPI Branch), 1933.

Mathews, Charles A. "An Analysis of Financial Progress and Trends in the Counties of Virginia, 1927–1937." M.A. Thesis, University of Virginia, 1938.

Minton, John Dean. "The New Deal in Tennessee, 1932–1938." Ph.D. diss., Vanderbilt University, 1959.

Nelson, Raymond. "Labor Unionization in the South." M.A. Thesis, University of Virginia, 1940.

Olinger, James. "The Congressional Career of John W. Flannagan." M.A. Thesis, East Tennessee State, 1954.

Ossman, Anne. "The History of the Family Service Society (Richmond, Virginia)." M.A. Thesis, College of William and Mary (RPI Branch), 1950.

Paul, Aaron. "The Rural Almshouse of Virginia." M.A. Thesis, College of William and Mary (RPI Branch), 1936.

Pulley, Raymond H. "Old Virginia Restored: An Interpretation of the Progressive Impulse." Ph.D. diss., University of Virginia, 1966.

Scott, Carole E. "The Economic Impact of the New Deal on the South." Ph.D. diss., Georgia State College, 1969.

Semes, Robert L. "The Virginia Press Looks at the New Deal, 1933–1937." M.A. Thesis, University of Virginia, 1968.

Simmons, Dennis Elwood. "The Creation of Shenandoah National Park and the Skyline Drive, 1924–1936." Ph.D. diss., University of Virginia, 1978.

Suggs, Henry Lewis. "P. B. Young and the Norfolk *Journal and Guide*, 1910–1954." Ph.D. diss., University of Virginia, 1976.

Sullins, Howard O. "A History of the Public School Superintendency in Virginia." D.Ed. diss., University of Virginia, 1970.

Tarter, Joe B. "Freshman Senator Harry F. Byrd: 1933–1934." M.A. thesis, University of Virginia, 1972.

Vogt, George L. "The Development of Virginia's Republican Party." Ph.D. diss., University of Virginia, 1978.

Walton, B.F. "An Analysis of Expenditures for Public Schools in Virginia from 1909 to 1939." M.A. Thesis, University of Virginia, 1942.

Bibliography

Willis, Leo Stanley. "E. Lee Trinkle and the Virginia Democracy, 1876–1939." Ph.D. diss., University of Virginia, 1972.
Wolfe, Jonathan J. "Virginia in World War II." Ph.D. diss., University of Virginia, 1971.
Wood, Roy. "Farm Tenancy in Virginia." M.A. Thesis, University of Virginia, 1948.

Books and Pamphlets

Abbott, Edith. *Public Assistance*. Chicago, 1940.
Advisory Council on the Virginia Economy. *Improving the Economic Conditions of Farmers in Virginia*. Richmond, 1951.
_____. *Report on the Economic Position of Virginia and Virginia Revenues and Expenditures*. 1957.
Allen, Frederick Lewis. *Only Yesterday*. New York, 1931.
Allswang, John M. *The New Deal and American Politics*. New York, 1978.
Andrews, James N., Jr. *An Economic and Social Survey of Orange County*. Charlottesville, 1939.
Arnold, Joseph L. *The New Deal in the Suburbs: A History of the Greenbelt Town Program 1935–1954*. Columbus, Ohio, 1971.
Badger, Anthony J. *Prosperity Road: The New Deal, Tobacco, and North Carolina*. Chapel Hill, N.C., 1980.
Baldwin, Sidney. *Poverty and Politics: The Rise and Decline of the Farm Security Administration*. Chapel Hill, N.C., 1968.
Benedict, Murray R. *Can We Solve the Farm Problem?* New York, 1955.
_____. *Farm Policies of the United States, 1790–1950*. New York, 1953.
Bird, Caroline. *The Invisible Scar*. New York, 1966.
Bottom, Raymond B. *Virginia's Record of Economic Progress*. Richmond, 1940.
Bradshaw, Herbert C. *History of Prince Edward County, Virginia*. Richmond, 1955.
Braeman, John, Robert Bremner, and David Brody, eds. *The New Deal*. 2 vols. Columbus, Ohio, 1975.
Browder, Walter G., and Linwood E. Lunsford. *An Economic and Social Survey of Dinwiddie County*. Charlottesville, 1937.
Brunner, Edmund, and E. Hsin Pao Yang. *Rural America and the Extension Service*. Menasha, Wisc., 1949.
Buck, J. Blair. *The Development of Public Schools in Virginia, 1607–1952*. Richmond, 1952.
Buni, Andrew. *The Negro in Virginia Politics, 1902–1965*. Charlottesville, 1967.
Bureau of Public Administration. *The Virginia Parole System: An Appraisal of Its First Twelve Years*. Charlottesville, 1955.
Campbell, Christiana M. *The Farm Bureau and the New Deal*. Urbana, Ill., 1962.
Cepuran, Joseph. *Public Assistance and Child Welfare: The Virginia Pattern, 1646 to 1964*. Charlottesville, 1968.
Charles, Searle F. *Minister of Relief: Harry Hopkins and the Depression*. Syracuse, N.Y., 1963.
Chestnutt, Samuel. *The Rural South*. Montgomery, Ala., 1939.

Bibliography

Cleal, Dorothy, and Hiram Herbert. *Foresight, Founders, and Fortitude: The Growth of Industry in Martinsville and Henry County, Virginia*. Bassett, Va., 1970.

Cohen, Irwin B., et al. *An Economic and Social Survey of Botetourt County*. Charlottesville, 1942.

Cole, Taylor, and John Hallowell, eds. *The Southern Political Scene, 1938–1948*. Gainesville, Fla., 1948.

Conkin, Paul. *The New Deal*. New York, 1967.

———. *Tomorrow a New World: The New Deal Community Program*. Ithaca, N.Y., 1959.

Connor, Maynard, and William K. Bing. *An Economic Study of Patrick County*. Charlottesville, 1937.

Conrad, David. *The Forgotten Farmers: The Story of Sharecroppers in the New Deal*. Urbana, Ill., 1965.

Crawley, William B., Jr. *Bill Tuck: A Political Life in Harry Byrd's Virginia*. Charlottesville, 1978.

Dabney, Virginius. *Virginia: The New Dominion*. New York, 1971.

Davis, Joseph S. *Wheat and the AAA*. Washington, D.C., 1935.

Eisenberg, Ralph. *Virginia Votes, 1924–1968*. Charlottesville, 1971.

Ekirch, Arthur A., Jr. *Ideologies and Utopias*. Chicago, 1969.

Farley, James. *Behind the Ballots*. New York, 1938.

———. *Jim Farley's Story*. New York, 1948.

Farm Security Administration. *Rural Rehabilitation in Region IV*. Raleigh, N.C., 1938.

Federal Civil Works Administration. *A Review of CWA Activities in Virginia*. 2 pts. Richmond, 1934.

Fitzgerald, Dennis A. *Livestock under the AAA*. Washington, D.C., 1935.

Freidel, Frank. *Franklin D. Roosevelt*. 4 vols. Boston, 1952–73.

———. *FDR and the South*. Baton Rouge, La., 1955.

———. *The New Deal in Historical Perspective*. 2d ed. Washington, D.C., 1959.

Friddell, Guy. *Colgate Darden: Conversations with Guy Friddell*. Charlottesville, 1978.

———. *What Is It about Virginia?* Richmond, 1966.

Galambos, Louis. *Competition and Cooperation: The Emergence of a National Trade Association*. Baltimore, 1966.

Galbraith, John Kenneth. *The Great Crash, 1929*. Cambridge, Mass., 1955.

Galenson, Walter. *The CIO Challenge to the AFL*. Cambridge, Mass., 1960.

Garnett, W. E. *Does Virginia Care?* Blacksburg, 1936.

———, and Allen Edwards. *Rural Poverty*. Blacksburg, 1938.

———. *Virginia's Marginal Population: A Study in Rural Poverty*. Blacksburg, 1941.

———, and John Ellison. *Negro Life in Rural Virginia, 1865–1934*. Blacksburg, 1934.

Gilliam, Sara. *Virginia's People*. Richmond, 1944.

Gittler, Joseph. *Virginia's People*. Richmond, 1944.

Glass, Robert C., and Carter Glass, Jr. *Virginia Democracy*. 3 vols. Springfield, Ill., 1937.

Golub, Eugene, O. *The "Isms": A History and Evaluation*. New York, 1954.

Gottmann, Jean. *Virginia at Mid-Century*. New York, 1955.

Bibliography

Graham, Otis, Jr. *An Encore for Reform: The Old Progressives and the New Deal*. New York, 1967.

———, ed. *The New Deal: The Critical Issues*. Boston, 1971.

Greenhut, Melvin L., and W. Tate Whitman, eds. *Essays in Southern Economic Development*. Chapel Hill, N.C., 1964.

Gruchy, Allan G. *Supervision and Control of Virginia State Banks*. New York, 1937.

Haley, Elliot Clarke, et al. *An Economic and Social Survey of Warren County*. Charlottesville, 1943.

Hamby, Alonzo L., ed. *The New Deal*. 2d ed. New York, 1981.

Hanna, Frank. *State Income Differentials, 1919–1954*. Durham, N.C., 1959.

Harriss, C. Lowell. *History and Policy of the Home Owners' Loan Corporation*. New York, 1951.

Hatch, Alden. *The Byrds of Virginia*. New York, 1969.

Hawley, Ellis. *The New Deal and the Problem of Monopoly*. Princeton, N.J., 1966.

Hemphill, William E., Marvin W. Schlegel, and Sadie E. Engelberg. *Cavalier Commonwealth*. 2d ed. New York, 1963.

Historical Records Survey. *Chesterfield County*. Richmond, 1938.

———. *Prince George County*. Richmond, 1941.

Hoover, Calvin B., and B. U. Ratchford. *Economic Resources and Politics of the South*. New York, 1951.

Howard, Donald S. *The WPA and Federal Relief Policy*. New York, 1943.

Hummel, B. L., and C. G. Bennett. *Education of Persons in Rural Relief Households of Virginia*. Blacksburg, 1937.

———. *Farm Rehabilitation Possibilities among Rural Households on Relief in Virginia*. Blacksburg, 1937.

———. *Industries and Occupations of the Rural Relief Population in Virginia, June, 1935*. Blacksburg, 1936.

———. *Magnitude of the Emergency Relief Program in Rural Virginia, 1933–1935*. Blacksburg, 1937.

———. *Relief History of Emergency Relief Cases in Rural Virginia, 1935*. Blacksburg, 1937.

———. *Rural Emergency Relief Cases in Virginia Accepted for Employment in the Works Program*. Blacksburg, 1936.

———, and Lois Adams. *Selected Case Studies of Rural Relief and Rehabilitation Cases in Virginia*. Blacksburg, 1937.

———, and W. W. Eure. *Youth on Relief in Virginia, 1935*. Blacksburg, 1936.

———, and R. B. Hummel. *Part-time Farming in Virginia*. Blacksburg, 1938.

———. *The Rehabilitation of Virginia Farm Families*. Blacksburg, 1939.

———. *Six Years of Relief in Rural Virginia, 1932–1937*. Blacksburg, 1939.

Hunter, Thomas Lomax. *Something Rotten in PWA*. Copy found in WPA Records, RG 69, National Archives.

Hutcheson, John R. *The Why and the Whither of the AAA*. Virginia Agricultural Extension Division, bulletin no. 135. Blacksburg, 1934.

Ickes, Harold. *Back to Work: The Story of PWA*. New York, 1935.

Ingalls, Robert. *Herbert H. Lehman and New York's Little New Deal*. New York, 1975.

James, Arthur. *The Public Welfare Function of Government in Virginia*. Richmond, 1934.

Bibliography

_____. *The State Becomes a Social Worker*. Richmond, 1942.

Jolley, Harley. *The Blue Ridge Parkway*. Knoxville, Tenn., 1969.

Jones, Lawrence A., and David Durand. *Mortgage Lending Experience in Agriculture*. Princeton, N.J., 1954.

Key, V.O., Jr. *Southern Politics in State and Nation*. New York, 1949.

Kimmel, Lewis. *Cost of Government, 1923–1934*. New York, 1934.

_____. *Cost of Government, 1934–1936*. New York, 1937.

Kirby, Jack T. *Westmoreland Davis: Virginia Planter-Politician, 1859–1942*. Charlottesville, 1968.

Lambie, Joseph T. *From Mine to Market: History of Coal Transportation on the Norfolk and Western*. New York, 1954.

Larsen, William. *Montague of Virginia*. Baton Rouge, La., 1965.

Lee, Susan P., and Peter Passell. *A New Economic View of American History*. New York, 1979.

Lekachman, Robert. *The Age of Keynes*. New York, 1966.

Leuchtenburg, William E. *Franklin D. Roosevelt and the New Deal*. New York, 1963.

Lindley, Betty, and Ernest K. Lindley. *A New Deal for Youth: The Story of the NYA*. New York, 1938.

Lowitt, Richard, and Maurine Beasley, eds. *One Third of a Nation: Lorena Hickok Reports on the Great Depression*. Urbana, Ill., 1981.

Lutz, Francis. E. *Chesterfield: An Old Virginia County*. Richmond, 1954.

McDonald, William F. *Federal Relief Administration and the Arts*. Columbus, Ohio, 1969.

McKinley, Charles, and Robert W. Trase. *Launching Social Security*. Madison, Wis., 1970.

McKinzie, Richard. *The New Deal for Artists*. Princeton, N.J. 1973.

Mangione, Jerre. *The Dream and the Deal: The Federal Writers Project, 1935–1943*. Boston, 1972.

Marshall, F. Ray. *Labor in the South*. Cambridge, Mass., 1967.

Mason, Lucy. *To Win These Rights*. New York, 1952.

Mathews, Jane DeHart. *The Federal Theatre, 1935–1939*. Princeton, N.J., 1967.

Meade, Julian R. *I Live in Virginia*. New York, 1935.

Mertz, Paul E. *New Deal Policy and Southern Rural Poverty*. Baton Rouge, La., 1978.

Michie, Allan, and Frank Ryhlick. *Dixie Demagogues*. New York, 1939.

Mitchell, Broadus. *Depression Decade*. New York, 1947.

Moger, Allen. *Virginia: Bourbonism to Byrd, 1870–1925*. Charlottesville, 1968.

Moley, Raymond. *The First New Deal*. New York, 1966.

Moore, R. Cosby. *Ah Youth-and Experience! A Brief History of Virginia National Bank*. An address to the Newcomen Society, Norfolk, 1964. New York, 1964.

Moore, Virginia. *Virginia Is a State of Mind*. New York, 1942.

Mordecai, John. *A Brief History of the Richmond, Fredericksburg and Potomac Railroad*. Richmond, 1941.

Nichols, William. *Southern Traditions and Regional Progress*. Chapel Hill, N.C., 1960.

Northrup, Herbert. *The Negro in the Tobacco Industry*. Philadelphia, 1970.
Nourse, Edwin, Joseph Davis, and John Black. *Three Years of the Agricultural Adjustment Administration*. Washington, D.C., 1937.
Odum, Howard W. *Southern Regions of the United States*. Chapel Hill, N.C., 1936.
Palmer, James E., Jr. *Carter Glass: Unreconstructed Rebel*. Roanoke, 1938.
Patterson, James T. *Congressional Conservatism and the New Deal*. Lexington, Ky., 1967.
_____. *The New Deal and the States*. Princeton, N.J., 1969.
Perdue, Charles, Jr., Thomas Barden, and Robert Phillips, eds. *Weevils in the Wheat: Interviews with Virginia Ex-Slaves*. Charlottesville, 1976.
Perkins, Van. *Crisis in Agriculture: The Agricultural Adjustment Administration and the New Deal*. Berkeley, Calif., 1969.
Polenberg, Richard. *Reorganizing Roosevelt's Government*. Cambridge, Mass., 1966.
Pulley, Raymond. *Old Virginia Restored*. Charlottesville, 1968.
Rauch, Basil. *The History of the New Deal, 1933–1938*. New York, 1944.
Reid, H. *The Virginian Railway*. Milwaukee, 1961.
Richards, Henry. *Cotton and the AAA*. Washington, D.C., 1936.
Richmond Chapter of the American Red Cross. *The First Fifty Years, 1917–1967*. 1967.
Robert, Joseph C. *The Story of Tobacco in America*. Chapel Hill, N.C., 1949.
Roose, Kenneth. *The Economics of Recession and Revival*. New Haven, 1954.
Roosevelt, Elliott, ed. *FDR: His Personal Letters, 1928–1945*. 2 vols. New York, 1950.
Rothbard, Murray N. *America's Great Depression*. Princeton, N.J., 1963.
Rothery, Agnes. *Virginia: The New Dominion*. New York, 1940.
Rowe, Harold B. *Tobacco under the AAA*. Washington, D.C., 1935.
Salmond, John A. *The Civilian Conservation Corps, 1933–1942*. Durham, N.C., 1967.
Schapsmeier, Edward L., and Frederick H. Schapsmeier. *Henry Wallace of Iowa: The Agrarian Years, 1910–1940*. Ames, Iowa, 1968.
Schlesinger, Arthur M., Jr. *The Coming of the New Deal*. Boston, 1959.
_____. *The Politics of Upheaval*. Boston, 1960.
Shannon, David A., ed. *The Great Depression*. Englewood Cliffs, N.J., 1960.
Sitkoff, Harvard. *A New Deal for Blacks*. New York, 1978.
Slaughter, John A. *Income Received in the Various States, 1929–1935*. New York, 1939.
Smith, Rixey, and Norman Beasley. *Carter Glass: A Biography*. New York, 1939.
Smith, Robert Sidney. *Mill on the Dan: A History of Dan River Mills, 1882–1950*. Durham, N.C., 1960.
Stanford, Edward B. *Library Extension under the WPA*. Chicago, 1944.
Starnes, George, and John Hamm. *Some Phases of Labor Relations in Virginia*. New York, 1934.
_____, John R. McCutcheon, and James M. Stepp. *A Survey of the Methods for the Promotion of Industrial Peace*. Charlottesville, 1939.
Sterner, Richard. *The Negro's Share*. New York, 1943.

Bibliography

Sternsher, Bernard, ed. *The New Deal—Doctrines and Democracy*. Boston, 1966.

———, ed. *Hitting Home: The Great Depression in Town and Country*. Chicago, 1970.

Temin, Peter. *Did Monetary Forces Cause the Great Depression?* New York, 1976.

Tennant, Richard. *The American Cigarette Industry*. New Haven, Conn., 1950.

Terkel, Studs. *Hard Times: An Oral History of the Great Depression*. New York, 1970.

Thomas Jefferson Center for Political Economy. *Statistical Abstract of Virginia*. 2 vols. Charlottesville, 1970.

Tindall, George B. *The Emergence of the New South, 1913–1945*. Baton Rouge, La., 1967.

Toynbee, Arnold. *A Study of History*. 2 vol. abridgment. New York, 1946.

Tugwell, Rexford. *The Democratic Roosevelt*. New York, 1957.

Virginia NYA. *18 Months with the Virginia Youth Administration*. 1937.

———. *The Young Virginian*. 1936–37.

Virginia WPA. *Around the Health and Sanitation Circle with WPA in Virginia*. 1937.

———. *The WPA Record in Virginia*. Richmond, 1936–37.

Walker, Thomas Calhoun. *The Honey-Pod Tree*. New York, 1958.

Wecter, Dixon. *The Age of the Great Depression, 1929–1941*. New York, 1948.

Wertenbaker, Thomas J. *Norfolk: Historic Southern Port*. 2d ed. Durham, N.C., 1962.

Whitehill, Arthur M., Jr. *Textile and Apparel Industries in Virginia*. Charlottesville, 1953.

Wilkinson, J. Harvey, III. *Harry Byrd and the Changing Face of Virginia Politics, 1945–1966*. Charlottesville, 1968.

Williams, James L. B. *An Economic and Social Survey of Westmoreland County*. Charlottesville, 1936.

Williams, J. Kerwin. *Grants-in-Aid under the Public Works Administration*. New York, 1939.

Wolfskill, George. *Happy Days Are Here Again!* Hinsdale, Ill, 1974.

———. *The Revolt of the Conservatives: A History of the American Liberty League*. Boston, 1962.

———, and John Hudson. *All But the People: Franklin D. Roosevelt and His Critics, 1933–1939*. London, 1969.

Wolters, Raymond. *Negroes and the Great Depression*. Westport, Conn., 1970.

Writers Program of WPA in Virginia. *The Negro in Virginia*. New York, 1940.

———. *Virginia: A Guide to the Old Dominion*. New York, 1940.

Younger, Edward, and James T. Moore, eds. *The Governors of Virginia, 1860–1978*. Charlottesville, 1982.

Zinn, Howard, ed. *New Deal Thought*. Indianapolis, 1966.

Bibliography

Articles

Arrington, Leonard. "The New Deal in the West: A Preliminary Statistical Inquiry," *Pacific Historical Review* 38 (1969): 311–16.

Auerbach, Jerold S. "New Deal, Old Deal, Raw Deal: Some Thoughts on New Left Historiography," *Journal of Southern History* 35 (1969): 18–30.

Bernstein, Barton. "The New Deal: The Conservative Achievements of Liberal Reform." Pp. 263–88 in *Towards a New Past*, ed. Barton Bernstein. New York, 1968.

Braeman, John. "The New Deal and the 'Broker State': A Review of the Recent Scholarly Literature," *Business History Review* 46 (1972): 409–29.

Bremer, William. "'Along the American Way': The New Deal's Work Relief Programs for the Unemployed," *Journal of American History* 62 (1975): 636–52.

Byrd, Harry Flood. "Better Government at Lower Cost," *Yale Review* 22 (Autumn 1932): 66–77.

Carlson, Avis. "Deflating the Schools," *Harper's* 167 (1933): 705–13.

Cronon, E. David. "A Southern Progressive Looks at the New Deal," *Journal of Southern History* 24 (1958): 151–76.

Curtis, William. "The Development of Unemployment Insurance in the South," *Southern Economic Journal* 15 (1948): 43–53.

Davenport, Walter. "The Virginia Reel," *Collier's* 84 (Nov. 2, 1929): 12ff.

De Vyver, Frank. "The Present Status of Labor Unions in the South," *Southern Economic Journal* 5 (1939): 485–98.

———. "The Present Status of Labor Unions in the South—1948," *Southern Economic Journal* 16 (1949): 1–22.

DeWilde, John C. "The AAA and Exports of the South," *Foreign Policy Reports* 11 (March 13, 1935): 38–48.

Duncan, Reid H. "How Virginia Ranks with the 48 States," *Virginia Journal of Education* 31 (Feb. 1938): 196.

Fishel, Leslie. "The Negro in the New Deal Era," *Wisconsin Magazine of History* 48 (Winter 1964–65): 111–26.

Fite, Gilbert. "Farmer Opinion and the Agricultural Adjustment Act, 1933," *Mississippi Valley Historical Review* 48 (March 1962): 656–73.

Freeman, Douglas Southall. *Review of Reviews* 93 (Jan. 1936): 37.

Fry, Joseph A. "George C. Peery: Byrd Regular and Depression Governor." Pp. 261–76 in *The Governors of Virginia, 1860–1978*, eds. Edward Younger and James T. Moore. Charlottesville, 1982.

———. "The Organization in Control: George Campbell Peery, Governor of Virginia, 1934–1938," *Virginia Magazine of History and Biography* 82 (1974): 306–30.

———. "Rayon, Riot, and Repression: The Covington Sit-Down Strike of 1937," *Virginia Magazine of History and Biography* 84 (1976): 3–18.

———. "Senior Adviser to the Democratic 'Organization': William Thomas Reed and Virginia Politics, 1925–35," *Virginia Magazine of History and Biography* 85 (1977): 443–69.

253

Bibliography

Garnett, William E. "What Will Virginia Do about It?" *Virginia Journal of Education* 28 (April 1935): 282–84.

Gavins, Raymond. "Hancock, Jackson, and Young: Virginia's Black Triumvirate, 1930–1945," *Virginia Magazine of History and Biography* 85 (1977): 470–86.

Gooch, Robert. "Reconciling Jeffersonian Principles with the New Deal," *Southwestern Social Science Quarterly* 16 (June 1935).

Guild, Jane Purcell. "Black Richmond," *Survey Graphic* 23 (June 1934): 276–78.

Guthrie, John. "The CCC and American Conservation," *Scientific Monthly* 57 (Nov. 1943): 401–12.

Hall, Alvin L. "Politics and Patronage: Virginia's Senators and the Roosevelt Purges of 1938," *Virginia Magazine of History and Biography* 82 (1974): 331–50.

———. "Virginia Back in the Fold—The Gubernatorial Campaign and Election of 1929," *Virginia Magazine of History and Biography* 73 (1965): 280–302.

Hanna, Frank A. "Income in the South since 1929." Pp. 239–92 in *Essays in Southern Economic Development*, ed. Melvin Greenhut and W. Tate Whitman. Chapel Hill, N.C., 1964.

Hawkes, Robert T., Jr. "The Emergence of a Leader: Harry Flood Byrd, Governor of Virginia, 1926–1930," *Virginia Magazine of History and Biography* 82 (1974): 259–81.

Heinemann, Ronald L. "Blue Eagle or Black Buzzard? The National Recovery Administration in Virginia," *Virginia Magazine of History and Biography* 89 (1981): 90–100.

———. "Harry Byrd for President: The 1932 Campaign," *Virginia Cavalcade* 25 (Summer 1975): 28–37.

———. "Workers on Welfare: The WPA in Virginia," *Virginia Social Science Journal* 8 (Nov. 1973): 62–67.

Henry, H. M. "The Effect of the Depression on Education in Virginia," *Virginia Journal of Education* 27 (Sept. 1933): 16–20.

Holley, Donald. "Aspects of Southern Farm Life: Comment," *Agricultural History* 53 (1979): 203–5.

———. "The Negro in the New Deal Resettlement Program," *New South* 27 (Winter 1972): 53–65.

Hunter, Robert F. "The AAA between Neighbors: Virginia, North Carolina, and the New Deal Farm Program," *Journal of Southern History* 44 (1978): 537–70.

———. "Carter Glass, Harry Byrd, and the New Deal, 1932–1936," *Virginia Social Science Journal* 4 (Nov. 1969): 91–103.

———. "Virginia and the New Deal." Pp. 103–36 in *The New Deal*, vol. 2, eds. John Braeman, Robert Bremner, and David Brody. Columbus, Ohio, 1975.

James, G. Watson, Jr. "WPA Goes to School," *Virginia Journal of Education* 33 (Jan. 1940): 196–98.

Kirkendall, Richard. "The New Deal and Agriculture." Pp. 83–109 in *The New Deal*, vol. 1, ed. John Braeman et al. Columbus, Ohio, 1975.

Koeniger, A. Cash. "Carter Glass and the National Recovery Administration," *South Atlantic Quarterly* 74 (1975): 349–64.

Bibliography

_____. "The New Deal and the States: Roosevelt versus the Byrd Organization in Virginia," *Journal of American History* 68 (1982): 876–96.

Moger, Allen W. "Virginia's Conservative Political Heritage," *South Atlantic Quarterly* 50 (1951): 318–29.

Moloney, John F. "Some Effects of the Federal Fair Labor Standards Act upon Southern Industry," *Southern Economic Journal* 11 (1942): 15–23.

Muse, Benjamin. *The Reporter* 17 (Oct. 3, 1957): 26.

"National Unemployment Census, 1937," *Monthly Labor Review* 46 (1938): 355–62.

Northrup, Herbert R. "The Tobacco Workers International Union," *Quarterly Journal of Economics* 56 (1942): 606–26.

Patterson, James T. "A Conservative Coalition Forms in Congress, 1933–1939," *Journal of American History* 52 (1966): 757–72.

_____. "The New Deal and the States," *American Historical Review* 73 (1967): 70–84.

Reading, Don. "New Deal Activity and the States, 1933 to 1939," *Journal of Economic History* 33 (1973): 792–810.

Saloutos, Theodore. "New Deal Agricultural Policy: An Evaluation," *Journal of American History* 61 (1974): 394–416.

Sargent, James E. "Clifton A. Woodrum of Virginia: A Southern Progressive in Congress, 1923–1945," *Virginia Magazine of History and Biography* 89 (1981): 341–64.

Schapsmeier, Edward L., and Frederick H. Schapsmeier. "Farm Policy from FDR to Eisenhower: Southern Democrats and the Politics of Agriculture," *Agricultural History* 53 (1979): 352–71.

Schwartz, Charles, and Robert Graham. "Personal Income by States, 1929–1954," *Survey of Current Business* 35 (Sept. 1955): 12–22.

Tarter, Brent. "A Flier on the National Scene: Byrd's Favorite-Son Presidential Candidacy of 1932," *Virginia Magazine of History and Biography* 82 (1974): 282–305.

Tomlins, Christopher L. "AFL Unions in the 1930s: Their Performance in Historical Perspective," *Journal of American History* 65 (1979): 1121–42.

Verba, Sidney, and Key Lehman Schlozman. "Unemployment, Class Consciousness, and Radical Politics: What Didn't Happen in the Thirties," *Journal of Politics* 39 (1977): 291–323.

Vipperman, Carl J. "The Coattail Campaign: James H. Price and the Election of 1937 in Virginia," *Essays in History* (History Club, University of Virginia) 8 (1962–63): 47–61.

White, William S. "Meet the Honorable Harry (the Rare) Byrd," *Reader's Digest* 82 (April 1963): 205–12.

Wright, Gavin. "The Political Economy of New Deal Spending: An Econometric Analysis," *Review of Economics and Statistics* 56 (Feb. 1974): 30–38.

Index

Index

Index

Index

Index

Tobacco industry (*cont.*)
impact of minimum wage on,
168; *see also* Appendix B
Tobacco Workers International
Union, 167
Toynbee, Arnold, 1
Transients, 28; FERA camps and
bureaus for, 72–74; 85, 90–91
Trinkle, E. Lee, 142–43, 149
Tugwell, Rexford, 108

Unemployment, 28, 30; (1930) 5,
7; (1931) 6, 13; (1932) 16, 19;
(1933) 49–50; (1934) 130–31;
(1937–38) 102, 170
Unemployment Compensation
Commission, 160
Unemployment insurance, 155,
158–62, 170, 181, 184
Unemployment Relief Committee,
11
Unions, *see* Labor in Virginia *and
specific unions*
United Mine Workers, 165
United States Housing Authority,
67
United States v. Butler, 114
United Textile Workers of
America, 6–7, 165–66
University of Virginia, 62
Unrest in Virginia, 15, 18, 25, 28,
38, 43, 68, 79, 111, 176
Urban conditions, 26–30, 79–80;
see also specific cities

Van Devanter, Willis, 146
Veterans Board of Appeals, 129
Virginia: apathy and deference in,
1, 43, 98, 133–34, 153, 164,
183, 187–88; class structure
of, 1, 133, 152–53, 172, 176;
conservatism in, 1–2, 4, 153,
177–78; race relations in, 2,
36–37, 99, 153, 164, 185, 189;
fiscal soundness of, 6, 10, 77,
81, 129, 131, 174; population
of, 8, 175; rural dominance in,
8, 14–15, 134, 153, 183;
stoicism in, 23, 42, 132, 177;

voluntarism in, 42, 81,
113–14, 187–88; number and
percentage of population on
relief in, 49, 80–81, 85–87,
102, 160, 175, 222n, Appendix
J; traditionalism of, 176, 179,
187–88, 190; vital statistics of,
175
Virginia—comparisons with nation
and other states, 21, 28; 1930
conditions, 7; tenancy, 9,
228n; 1931 conditions, 10,
12–13; 1932 conditions, 19;
industrial losses, 33–34, 212n,
214n; 1933 conditions, 49;
housing loans, 67; relief
populations, 80–81;
agricultural payments, 111,
119; farm credit, 120; 1935
conditions, 131; industrial
recovery, 169, 219n; 1937
recession, 170; impact of
depression, 172–76; banking,
235n; *see also* Appendixes F,
G, H, I, K, L
Virginia Appraisal Committee
(WPA), 101–2
Virginia Art Project, 93
Virginia Bar Association, 146
Virginia Conservation and
Development Commission,
116; state park system, 66,
123
Virginia Consumers League, 160
Virginia Department of
Corrections, 182
Virginia Department of Education,
95–96
Virginia Department of Labor, 16,
49, 168
Virginia Department of Public
Welfare, 40, 76, 155–56, 160,
162
Virginia economy: diversity of,
8–10, 30–34; and state
income, 4, 8–10, 131, 178,
210n, Appendix F; and impact
of depression, 19–20, 173–78;
see also Economic conditions;
Farming in Virginia; Industry
in Virginia

266